The Word of God is Not Bound:

The Encounter of Sikhs and Christians in India and the United Kingdom

John Parry

Centre for Contemporary Christianity
Bangalore
2009

The Word of God is Not Bound

First Indian Edition - 2009

Hardback **Rs. 400/-**, US $ 15, GBP 10
Paperback **Rs. 300/-**, US $ 12, GBP 8

Published by

Siga Arles
Centre for Contemporary Christianity
PO Box 4601,
Bangalore - 560 046, India
E-mail: <cfcc94@gmail.com> <arles@sify.com>

Printed at:
National Printing Press, Bangalore Ph: 25710658

Contents

Contents

Contents

Publisher's Note

Centre for Contemporary Christianity started in 1994 with a keen interest to hold seminars on topics of immediate relevance to the church in her mission. Renewal of ministry, mission and theological education was the goal of the seminars. Various groups of people involved in varieties of ministries in the society were invited to meet with likeminded and similar others in order to discover each other, to learn of the agendas of each other, to get informed of the problems and achievements and to network with as many as possible within the whole body of Christ. This journey had proved fruitful to all who participated in the seminars.

Later **Centre for Contemporary Christianity** began to publish books. First it was a report of a national forum *Pilgrimage 2100* which made a *Self Reflection on Indian Evangelicalism*. At a time when there were severe problems faced by the evangelicals in India, in 1995, a group of 32 Indian evangelical men met at the Union Biblical Seminary to reflect on the history, heritage and methods of the evangelical movement and to explore to understand what went wrong and discover how to bring healing and corrective. 2004 onwards the CFCC published books quite consistently. The first series were the **Studies in the Gospel Interface with Indian Contexts**, publishing mostly post graduate research documents dealing with Indian situations in mission history and methodology. The second series brought global wisdom to bear upon the increasing number of mission students in India, by either reprinting or freshly producing noteworthy books in the **Missiological Classics Series**. The third is the **Pastoral Concern Series**. Some books were released as **General Books** and now the Contemporary Issues Booklets, known as **CIB-lets**, are being initiated.

I am delighted that we could include Dr. John Parry's work in our CONTEXT series. The fact that he deals with the prospects of relationship between the people of Christian faith with those of the Sikh faith makes his work a rare material. Since we live in an age of ecumenism, wherein we attempt to understand and collaborate with people of all faiths, it becomes significant to produce literature that will help. We have certain amount of literature that deals with majoritarian faith communities and their views. But to pick up smaller groups and also to develop the necessary insights is one of the challenges that the church has faced down through the ages. The World Missionary Conference of 1910 onwards, the inter-religious relations became an area of importance. When the World Council of Churches opened its sub-unit on Dialogue with People of Other Faiths and Ideologies, Stanley Samartha, Wesley Ariarajah and successors have led the global interaction on dialogue as a mission method and its significance. Already we published Mathew Philip's work *The Unique Christ: Dialogue in Mission* which interpreted the significance of Eli Stanley Jones and his round table approach of dialogue in mission. We also released Geomon George's *Religious Pluralism: Challenges for Pentecostalism in India* and M.T. Cherian's *Hindutva Agenda and Minority Rights: A Christian Response*. Now, it is our joy to release an Indian edition of John Parry's *The Word of God is Not Bound*.

Friends of mine who work in Mongolia were visiting in Beijing and Xian where they saw the "Nestorian Monument," erected in the 8th century to commemorate Christianity in China from Syria. They found the inscription quite interesting as part of it read: "The true Lord is without origin, profound, invisible, and unchangeable; with power and capacity to perfect and transform. He raised up the earth and established the heavens." That God is sought after by people in varieties of ways. Instead of a competitive and disruptive relation, an evangelical spirit touched by an ecumenical attitude, attempts to create a cooperative and amicable relation of solidarity. In publishing this book, CFCC offers a tool for such perspectival growth which could lead to a future of solidarity between the Sikhs and the Christians in developing an attitude of love, acceptance, mutual goodwill, solidarity and co-operation.

CFCC is grateful to Dr John Parry for allowing us to publish his work. We pray that this book will strengthen the series with further scholarly input to those who are eager to learn of the context and to work positively with its transformation.

Publisher's Note

Centre for Contemporary Christianity started in 1994 with a keen interest to hold seminars on topics of immediate relevance to the church in her mission. Renewal of ministry, mission and theological education was the goal of the seminars. Various groups of people involved in varieties of ministries in the society were invited to meet with likeminded and similar others in order to discover each other, to learn of the agendas of each other, to get informed of the problems and achievements and to network with as many as possible within the whole body of Christ. This journey had proved fruitful to all who participated in the seminars.

Later **Centre for Contemporary Christianity** began to publish books. First it was a report of a national forum *Pilgrimage 2100* which made a *Self Reflection on Indian Evangelicalism*. At a time when there were severe problems faced by the evangelicals in India, in 1995, a group of 32 Indian evangelical men met at the Union Biblical Seminary to reflect on the history, heritage and methods of the evangelical movement and to explore to understand what went wrong and discover how to bring healing and corrective. 2004 onwards the CFCC published books quite consistently. The first series were the **Studies in the Gospel Interface with Indian Contexts**, publishing mostly post graduate research documents dealing with Indian situations in mission history and methodology. The second series brought global wisdom to bear upon the increasing number of mission students in India, by either reprinting or freshly producing noteworthy books in the **Missiological Classics Series**. The third is the **Pastoral Concern Series**. Some books were released as **General Books** and now the Contemporary Issues Booklets, known as **CIB-lets**, are being initiated.

I am delighted that we could include Dr. John Parry's work in our CONTEXT series. The fact that he deals with the prospects of relationship between the people of Christian faith with those of the Sikh faith makes his work a rare material. Since we live in an age of ecumenism, wherein we attempt to understand and collaborate with people of all faiths, it becomes significant to produce literature that will help. We have certain amount of literature that deals with majoritarian faith communities and their views. But to pick up smaller groups and also to develop the necessary insights is one of the challenges that the church has faced down through the ages. The World Missionary Conference of 1910 onwards, the inter-religious relations became an area of importance. When the World Council of Churches opened its sub-unit on Dialogue with People of Other Faiths and Ideologies, Stanley Samartha, Wesley Ariarajah and successors have led the global interaction on dialogue as a mission method and its significance. Already we published Mathew Philip's work *The Unique Christ: Dialogue in Mission* which interpreted the significance of Eli Stanley Jones and his round table approach of dialogue in mission. We also released Geomon George's *Religious Pluralism: Challenges for Pentecostalism in India* and M.T. Cherian's *Hindutva Agenda and Minority Rights: A Christian Response*. Now, it is our joy to release an Indian edition of John Parry's *The Word of God is Not Bound*.

Friends of mine who work in Mongolia were visiting in Beijing and Xian where they saw the "Nestorian Monument," erected in the 8th century to commemorate Christianity in China from Syria. They found the inscription quite interesting as part of it read: "The true Lord is without origin, profound, invisible, and unchangeable; with power and capacity to perfect and transform. He raised up the earth and established the heavens." That God is sought after by people in varieties of ways. Instead of a competitive and disruptive relation, an evangelical spirit touched by an ecumenical attitude, attempts to create a cooperative and amicable relation of solidarity. In publishing this book, CFCC offers a tool for such perspectival growth which could lead to a future of solidarity between the Sikhs and the Christians in developing an attitude of love, acceptance, mutual goodwill, solidarity and co-operation.

CFCC is grateful to Dr John Parry for allowing us to publish his work. We pray that this book will strengthen the series with further scholarly input to those who are eager to learn of the context and to work positively with its transformation.

Centre for Contemporary Christianity is turning into an academic Research Centre from 2009 to offer post graduate degrees in Missiology and Holistic Child Development. CFCC is open to mentor scholars who explore to tackle knowledge for the sake of faith and hope for people. New avenues will be opened as and when necessary. Laity, clergy, missionaries, evangelists and teachers are invited to benefit by extension and external study option and to qualify better for involvement.

CFCC commends this book to you with a great hope that you will promote solidarity with all peoples in constructing a better nation/world, especially along with the Sikhs.

CFCC is grateful to Mr. John and his staff team at National Printing Press for the efficient production of this volume.

Siga Arles
Director
Centre for Contemporary Christianity
Bangalore

9 March 2009

Preface

This book has been a long time in the making. It arose out of my doctoral thesis and it would be invidious of me not to acknowledge at the start the support and inspiration I was given to study Sikhism by Dr W. Owen Cole. I do remember, however, the indirect challenge Owen gave me when he suggested that there might not be enough material available for a Ph.D. thesis. It did not take me long to recognise that there was so little, but there was enough, and you now have it in your hands! Owen also introduced me to S. Piara Singh Sambhi. Those of us who knew him recognised in him one who did so much to open up the Sikh faith to British Christians. Together with Owen he produced one of the first of the recent introductions to Sikhism and later a book on Sikhism and Christianity. I warmly and unstintingly acknowledge their contribution. They were the inspiration to establish the consultations of Sikhs and Christians sponsored by the United Reformed Church about which you will read later.

I must pay tribute to many friends in Southall in West London who taught me the nature of Sikh hospitality. My regular visits to the Ramgharia Gurdwara, then under the leadership of Jaspal Bhambra, enabled me to gather together Sikhs and Christians for scripture study. With the help of Mrs Charanjit AjitSingh and Ajit Singh we explored our mutual scriptures in their original languages. The struggle to learn Fifteenth Century Panjabi really does pay off.

If it had not been a conversation with the Rev'd Dr Jack McKelvey, one-time Principal of Northern College, Manchester, I would not have been given the opportunity for full-time research. I acknowledge with deep gratitude the support given by the Staff and Governors of the college through the Mona Powell Fellowship. Thank you, and further thanks to the United Reformed Church which in various ways has contributed to the existence of this book. I am deeply grateful to Prof. Werner Ustorf of the University of Birmingham who guided me through my research.

And then comes India! Thank God for so many friends in the Panjab and in Delhi who gave me so much of their time, Rashid Chaudhary, James Massey, Darshan Singh, Anand Spencer and many others. I learnt so much from them. More recently, the Rt Rev'd Pradeep Samantaroy, Bishop of Amritsar, and his colleagues gave me so much warm support and hospitality as I updated the material for the book. I thank them for their warmth and their love.

That brings me to my family, our sons David and Gareth who put up with a crabby father whilst I was writing and Yvonne, my wife, who has given me so much support over nearly forty years. I am ever so grateful.

Foreword

It has been a really fascinating experience for me to read what seems to me to be a labour of love, the story of the encounter of the Sikhs and Christians in India and the United Kingdom.

It takes a person of faith to make a leap of faith to be able to say, 'The Word of God is Not Bound.' To my mind, it means recognising and accepting that God may be speaking not only within the 'bounds' but also across them. Being bound, chained or fettered are human conditions from which release is provided by the word of God. John Parry has adopted the title of his book from the Holy Bible and developed it to illustrate the Sikh Christian encounter over the last two centuries and the specific efforts made for conducting a dialogue during that period. It also makes me reflect on Guru Gobind Singh's two words 'Namastan Amajhbey;' (I bow in reverence to you, O God of no religion), in Jaap Sahib that the confines of religion apply only to those who confine themselves to a particular religion. God is above and beyond those confines and boundaries.

Dr John Parry has skilfully combined in this treatise, both his command of western theological scholarship and practice as an interfaith person, yet rooted in his own faith. He has successfully transcended the boundaries of Christianity and Sikhism to explore the history of Sikh and Christian encounter and dialogue the issues of values and spirituality. In this book I find that the academic theoretical aspects and life experiences are knitted well together, though an initial cursory glance might make one feel that there are different themes covered in different chapters.

I am highly impressed by the thoroughness with which Dr Parry has explored Sikh Christian relations and dialogue both in the Punjab and in the United Kingdom. He refers to the difficulties of accessing primary sources and the dearth of secondary sources but he has brought to light many original documents and journals which throw a good deal of light about the views of Christian missionaries and educational establishments for getting the Sikhs into the Christian fold in the early 19th century. Their early studies and the close proximity of different Christian Centres to the key historic and holy Sikh sites clearly supported that motive. New Sikh movements took shape to counter this and to engage in their own missionary activities amongst local people especially lower castes. Later attempts made by writers such as Keene, Guilford and Macauliffe to view the Sikh faith with respect by delving deeper into Sikh history and scriptures are well documented, as are the works of the Sikh writers in this text. The analysis of Gopal Singh's poem 'The man who never died' from the point of view of the Sikh reworking of Christian theology is superbly done. A 'turbaned Christ' is a possibility. The distinctive features of the Sikh faith and its similarity with Christianity in belief and practices are explored in a way which responds well to the concerns of the Sikhs about some western academics. This has enabled the writer to provide a more balanced and fair approach. No wonder that this systematic study has added tremendously to my learning.

As we note in Chapter Five of the text, the Sikh Christian Consultations in the 1980s in the United Kingdom took place with the sponsorship of the United Reformed Church and because of John's enterprising zeal and perseverance, yet he is too humble to take credit for those himself!

Any dialogue bilateral or multi-lateral, if it is not to be at a superficial level must challenge a person's own understanding and perceptions. It is not always cosy but invites one to question one's viewpoint. It can be quite uncomfortable because it may make the dialoguing individuals feel vulnerable but it can also be rewarding providing valuable insights in our quest for truth and may enable people to grow in their own faithfulness to their faith while being open to the other. My memory of the consultations in the United Kingdom is our grappling with the profound questions of human life and our common search for meaning.

I strongly hope that this book will go a long way towards improving our knowledge and understanding about Sikh Christian encounter during the last two centuries and for building better relationships by learning from that valuable experience.

Charanjit K. Ajit Singh
Chair of Trustees of the International Interfaith Centre, Oxford, U.K.

Introduction

During the last thirty years dialogue between people of differing faiths has become an increasingly important phenomenon in the Western world. It has been viewed with suspicion by some Christian bodies, but for many Christian individuals it has been of great significance not only in terms of their own spiritual growth, but as an inherent element in mutual understanding and the creation of better relationships in the plural communities of the world. Of course, this has been nothing new for the peoples of the Indian sub-continent where for centuries daily life has been lived in a plural environment.

A natural corollary of this has been the proliferation of studies of specific religious faiths and of dialogue itself. Yet there is an exception to this practice in terms, from a Western perspective, of the relatively neglected area of Sikh studies and specifically the encounter of Sikhs and Christians. That is not to say that nothing has been written. With the three hundredth anniversary of the founding of the Sikh *Khalsa* in 1999 there was a resurgence of material published on the Sikh faith in both the UK and India as Sikhs searched for an authentic expression of their faith and diaspora Sikhs renewed their interest in their roots.

This book attempts to outline the history of the encounter between Sikhs and Christians both in the Panjab and in the United Kingdom. It arises out of the daily contact I had with Sikhs in Southall in West London, the consequent establishment of a series of consultations of Sikhs and Christians sponsored by the United Reformed Church in the United Kingdom and a growing valued relationship with the Diocese of Amritsar in the Church of North India. My working hypothesis is that dialogue is not simply an exchange of information, but it prompts a new understanding of one's own faith and that of one's partner in dialogue. Further, those who participate in dialogue are ushered into new horizons of faith through the recognition that God is present.

Those Christians who were involved in the consultations were led to a deep respect for the Sikh faith, but were also struck by a shared ethos of protest and dissent. As discussions led to matters of deeper spirituality a recognition that both faiths shared reliance on the centrality of divine grace drew participants closer and the need for an exploration into the encounter grew in significance.

That I write from the perspective of a Christian I cannot hide, but I hope to be impartial and to do justice to both religious traditions. I do not attempt to establish the superiority of one system of faith over the other, but I recognise that the very nature of a study in mission history will certainly determine my areas of interest and research.

Studies in the field of mission history, nevertheless, provide the framework of the research for this book, but as such, it is also essentially multi-disciplinary drawing on various fields of study including that of the Sikh faith *per se*. Thus we will consider various issues associated with mission studies: the motivation for mission work among the Sikhs; the context of Protestant missions in India; the ethos and attitudes of missionaries from the 1830s onwards and the expectations of sending societies. Later we touch on Christology in the light of the encounter and the nature of an apologetic to Sikhs.

I shall also attempt to establish a sketch of Sikh critiques of Christianity, for Christians need to see themselves as others see us. Suffice it to point out here that Sikhs reject the exclusivity expressed by many Christians and do not see Christianity as the fulfilment of their faith.

All these issues contribute to our study. It is an overview of what has been written and discussed thus far. Most material dealing with the encounter has considered essentially doctrinal issues, such as Anand Spencer's work on the 'Word' / *shabad*[1] as a basis for dialogue or the theological overview provided by the partnership of Owen Cole and the late Piara Singh Sambhi.

There are a number of objectives to be considered. The first is essentially historical. We shall trace the unfolding pattern of the

---

1. See p. 76.

encounter and do so from the differing perspectives of the Christian missionaries and the Sikhs who were the 'targets' of mission. It is this section of the study that deals with the interaction of Panjabi church history and the revivalist Singh Sabha movement.

When faith meets faith, people of faith respond to each other in the light of their theological understanding of God (if one may not confine that term to a Christian meaning only) and God's dealings with humanity. Hence our theological objective is to consider the contribution made by one faith to the self-understanding of the other faith, for none may enter into dialogue without the risk of either change or the challenge to re-assess one's own faith. Furthermore, any encounter of two faiths may well contribute to humanity's treasury of the understanding of the divine purposes.

A third objective is to consider the methodology of approach made by the various mission bodies. Here we consider the impact made on the Sikh community by missionaries of the same race as the colonialist Raj.

A variety of resources have been used to fulfil these tasks. The first is an analysis of published material. Here access to the small, but growing, number of books on Sikhism is vital but difficult. The shelves of British university libraries are not overburdened, thus recourse must be made to collections of private individuals, *Gurdwaras* and the Sikh Missionary Society. The universities of the Panjab have done sterling work in producing material from their publications divisions both in terms of edited volumes and monographs. Sikh scholarship is also reflected in the production of a number of journals which are an invaluable aid in the understanding of Sikh perceptions of Christians and Christianity. Unpublished material comes in the form of dissertations and theses, notes from consultations and dialogue meetings and letters and reports, for instance, those found in the archives of the Church Missionary Society held in the University of Birmingham.

Discussions with people of faith have been an important resource, for this study requires not just objective historicity, as if that were actually possible, but the 'feel' of the spiritual interaction and quest. Little could have been done without the help of friends both Sikh and Christian be they at meetings specially organised for dialogue or in their homes or at casual visits to *Gurdwaras* or at interviews both formal and informal at Punjabi University Patiala, Guru Nanak Dev University in Amritsar or the 'Golden Temple.'

We start by a consideration of the high hopes and expectations with which Presbyterian missionaries from America entered the Panjab in the 1830s followed by members of the Church Missionary Society. The second chapter considers the consolidation of missionary work which involved studies of the Sikh faith and the publication of material written by Panjabi Christians. This latter aspect is a much needed acknowledge-ment of the role played by indigenous pastors and laypeople so often overlooked in reports to mission societies which concentrated on the work of expatriate missionaries, often with publicity to aid fund-raising in mind.

A third chapter deals with the increasing cooperation which was established marginally before and then after Independence, thanks mainly to the work of the Rev'd Dr Clinton Loehlin, particularly during the later part of his ministry in Batala. This town, some 25 miles north east of Amritsar was also the site for the Christian Institute of Sikh Studies, in the formation of which Loehlin played such an important part.

Our fourth chapter demonstrates the increasing understanding between the two faiths thanks to a variety of authors of the mid to late Twentieth Century whose works are assessed. By this time evangelical authors were seeking to establish a form of Christian apologetic to the Sikh community. Similarly the likes of the Rev'd Drs Anand Spencer and James Massey produced material which arose from their academic research.

We move away from the Indian sub-continent to the UK for the essence of the fifth chapter. Here we deal with the work of the 'Other Faiths' Committee of the United Reformed Church in the United Kingdom. The committee gave me considerable support to set up these consultations which were then the only examples of regular, formal bilateral dialogue in the world. This chapter is followed by a sixth, short chapter drawing some preliminary conclusions about the Christian faith and its presentation in the light of the encounter.

The seventh chapter takes us back, once again to the origins of the encounter, considering it this time from the perspective of the Sikh community. If the amount of material written by Christians about the encounter is relatively restricted, the material produced from a Sikh perspective is even more limited. Many of the critiques of Christianity are to be found *en passant* as one searches through books, periodicals and newspaper reports. Indeed, material from this last grouping is now extremely rare. What there is, as far as I am able to make out, will be considered as a contribution to the need to understand Sikh critiques of the Christian faith. This theme is taken further in the eighth chapter which deals with some of the theological issues that come to light.

The next two chapters deal with the one major presentation of the life of Jesus written by a Sikh. Elsewhere I have described this epic poem as being full of Christian theology, full of Sikh theology and full of neither! It is a remarkable re-presentation of the life and work of Jesus of Nazareth written in a style and using a conceptual framework that speaks to the Sikh mind. It, thus, represents a challenge to the Christian with regard to the question, 'Whose Christ is He? Is this figure, here freed from the dogma of Christianity, the liberated and liberating Christ? Is this figure so far removed as to be one who has little relationship to the Jesus Christ of the traditions in which we Christians were brought up? Or does one hear a very still, small voice from God?

It is forty years since Gopal Singh wrote his poem. Since then much has happened in the Panjab and within the Sikh nation that has made Sikhs reconsider the nature of what it is to be Sikh. This has been especially the case in the last two decades. Our penultimate chapter considers these developments particularly in terms of the encounter of the two faiths.

Finally, before attempting a conclusion, I have tried to write of my faith as a Christian in the light of the encounter. This is neither an apologetic to Sikhs, nor simply a credo, but an attempt to explain my faith in a way that Sikhs may understand. I have done this very much from a personal perspective since a fuller attempt at a Christian apologetic to Sikhs must be the subject of further research.

1

High Hopes

Calcutta, 1 November, 1833.

The Rev'd E.P. Swift

Dear Brother Swift:

You will learn some of the particulars concerning our voyage and our arrival, from other letters which we send. It is not necessary to refer to them now, unless to remind us, that goodness and mercy have still followed us; and that we have been brought under new obligations by the care and goodness of Providence, to devote our lives entirely to the service of God.

One of the first objects requiring attention, after our arrival, was to select a field of future labor. In making our selection, we have tried to secure divine direction, and have sought information and advice from all who were able to aid us in these matters. Our chief immediate difficulty has been, to decide where, out of so many places: for the whole land, almost, is before us, and millions are accessible in every direction. We feel grateful, that the path appears to be marked out so plainly, and that it leads us to the section of the country contemplated before we left the United States.

In view of the best light we can obtain, we feel clear in deciding on Umbala, Loodiana, or some other place in the Punjab, or territory between the Jumna and Sutledge rivers, as the place of our future labor, if the Lord please.

This territory is under the protection of the British government, though its chiefs enjoy a kind of independent authority. The people north of the Sutledge, in the territory of Lahore, are under the influence of Runjeet Singh, long the most formidable enemy of the British, but in friendship at present. They are all one people on both sides of the

Sutledge, called Seiks or Sikhs; speaking the same language, the Punjabee; having the same religion and the same customs; so that we may hope our influence will not be confined to this side of that river. Their number is between one and two millions, among whom no efforts have yet been made to introduce the gospel; while they are described as more free from prejudice, from the influence of Brahmins, and from caste, than any other people in India. Indeed the Seik religion is quite distinct, the founder of the sect having rejected many of the doctrines and practices both of the Hindoo and Mohammedan systems, and having endeavoured to form a more perfect system out of them. We are informed that they are in a good degree more teachable, and that there is, at present, among their chiefs and better classes, a great desire to become acquainted with English, in consequence of a recent order of the English authorities of this country abolishing Persian, and substituting English, as the Court language. The desire, it is believed, may be turned to good account, and become a passport to other kinds of instruction, and more direct efforts for their good.

This region of the country is connected by commercial business, with Afghanistan, Cashmere, and Tibet, in all of which countries, no efforts have been made to fulfil our Savior's last commandment.

As to health, this region is described to us in very favourable terms. Its vicinity to the Hinmeleh (sic) mountains, and its being so far north, make the information we have received very probable. Indeed Sinlah (sic), one of the principal sanitary refuges, is not very distant from Umbala; so that if health should become impaired, it would be quite convenient as a place of resort, and perhaps render it unnecessary to return to our own country....

In regard to our operations, the first thing will be to learn the language. We may also commence an English school immediately, with a view to ultimately forming an establishment, similar in many respects to the seminary at Batticola, in Ceylon, which is very generally approved. There is a Punjabee grammar, and a translation of the New Testament; but perhaps few other books to aid us in acquiring the language. If we form a high school among them, as from information received will probably appear expedient, we shall need apparatus....

And now, dear brother, you will bless the Lord with us, that he has made our path so plain, and that he appears to be directing us to so important a section of the country. May we have grace given to improve the opportunities of usefulness which Providence may open before us! We feel that we greatly need the prayers of the Lord's people, or rather, that we greatly need that guidance, wisdom and help which God usually is pleased to bestow in answer to prayer.

We wish also that there were many others to aid us. This field does seem to be very white unto harvest; and though the missionaries have not yet been permitted to see many conversions from heathenism, they are not discouraged. The brethren whom we have seen extend to us a cordial welcome, and express strong hopes that we may be followed by many others. A gentleman, high in political life, hopes that "India may have her share in the noble army of American missionaries." We are fully of the opinion that if you can send out one hundred missionaries, there is as much work as they all can accomplish, and far more which must be done very soon, or millions will die without hearing that there is a Savior....

We remain yours in the cause of the Savior,

John C. Lowrie, William Reed.[1]

Thus wrote Lowrie and Reed, the first Presbyterian missionaries in India in one of their early letters to their home mission board. As is often expressed in such letters, they had high hopes and aspirations for their future work and were the first to establish a mission station in the Panjab. Within their denomination there had been discussion as to whether they should be involved in inter-denominational mission work or through boards under Presbyterian control. Whilst the denomination had been involved in terms of money and personnel through the inter-denominational American Board of Commissioners for Foreign Missions, increasing pressure led to the Synod of Pittsburgh's first step in the formation of a denominational board in 1831 by the creation of the Western Foreign Missionary Society. North India was one of the fields of mission chosen.

1. See John C.B. Webster: *The Christian Community & Change in Nineteenth Century North India*, New Delhi, Macmillan, 1976, p. 13.
    The complete letter, of which a part is reproduced, is available in 'American Presbyterians in India/Pakistan - 150 years' *Journal of Presbyterian History*, Vol. 62, # 3, Fall 1984.

A letter sent to the theological seminary in Allegheny, Pennsylvania, seeking recruits for the mission field resulted in the appointment of two theological students in January 1832. These were John C. Lowrie and William Reed, who after a year of further study and seeking financial support left with their wives on the 'Star' for Calcutta on 30 May 1833. Their instructions had been to establish a mission station where no other missionaries were at work.

Upon arrival at Calcutta they were advised by both Alexander Duff of the Church of Scotland and Charles Trevelyan, the then Secretary to the Governor-General, to consider the Panjab as a suitable place in which to start their work. Captain Wade, the British Political Agent at Ludhiana, had issued an invitation to go there since the climate was good, it held out prospects for contact with Afghanistan, Kashmir and Tibet and, furthermore, 'no efforts had been made to introduce the Gospel' to the Sikhs who were described as being 'more free from prejudice, from the influence of Brahmins, and from caste, than any other people in India' and as 'in a good degree teachable.'[2] Lowrie alone established the mission station in Ludhiana having arrived there on 5 November 1834. His wife had died one year previously in Calcutta and Reed was taken so ill that he and his wife decided to return home but he died soon after setting sail from Calcutta. Lowrie's own health began to fail but shortly before he returned to America in 1836 a second group of missionaries had arrived. They were the Rev'ds James Wilson and John Newton and Miss Julia Davies who in their farewells had been addressed by Dr Elijah P. Swift, the Secretary of the American Missionary Society, on 29 October 1834. Notwithstanding its imperialist fashion Swift's description of the Sikh Gurus and their followers, although inaccurate, is not without prejudice, but not totally negative:

As a religious sect, this people took their rise in 1469, from Nanac Shah, who, after adopting the common method of pretended visions and miraculous endowments, and the practice of extraordinary austerities, travelled through the principal cities of India, preaching the peculiarities of this system and confirming its arguments by the power of his miracles. He appears to have been a man of genius and

2   See John C.B. Webster: *The Christian Community & Change in Nineteenth Century North India*, New Delhi, Macmillan, 1976, p. 13.

originality of character, and intent upon awakening a spirit of devotion among his countrymen... In process of time Gooroo Govind became the leader of the sect, and acquired greater fame and veneration than any of his predecessors... This people are distinguished for their excesses in the use of ardent spirits, opium, and other intoxicating drugs... As soldiers they are active, cheerful and brave, and in their general character they are more open and sincere than the Mahratas; less fierce and cruel than the Afghans, and more indulgent to the female sex than any other people in India.[3]

Swift also had indicated that Maharaja Ranjit Singh may have been unexpectedly willing to look favourably upon elements of the missionary enterprise. Few, if any, Europeans were normally allowed to enter his territory. However, he had come to know of Lowrie's school in Ludhiana and invited him in 1835 to Lahore, providing him with an escort and treating him with great honour. His intention was to have an English medium school founded at which Lowrie was to teach for six months each year. Lowrie was unable on health grounds to agree to this proposal and 'the missionary principle of teaching the Gospel in connection with literature and science was unacceptable to the Maharaja.' Later reflection indicated a belief that the visit to the Maharajah was not without results...

The missionary had made a good impression. The prejudice of the Sikhs against the Christian missionary was considerably modified, for during the long visit the missionary had many opportunities to tell the story of Jesus Christ and His salvation. The rajah accepted a present of an English Bible and a translation of the Old Testament in the Punjabi language and in the Gurmukhi character by the Serampore missionaries.[4]

3   See C.H.Loehlin: 'The History of Christianity in the Punjab' in *The Panjab Past and Present*, Vol. VII, Part 1, April 1973, p. 180 quoting the *United Church Review* of Nov. 1935, pp. 290f.

4   Wherry: *Our Missions in India, 1834-1924*, Stratford, Boston, 1926 p. 10; in turn quoting Lowrie: *Two Years in Upper India*, p. 144. The translation mentioned is that of Carey which was made in Bengal and printed under his direction between 1812 and 1818. It comprised just over half of the Old Testament and the whole of the New Testament. (The first full translation was published in 1959.) See C. H. Loehlin: 'The History of the Gurmukhi Panjabi Bible' in *Proceedings of Punjab History Conference* Vol. III, March 1968. Carey's recognition of the need for a Gurmukhi translation was due to the presence of Sikhs in Bengal thanks to the missionary journeys of Guru Tegh Bahadur. It would also explain the contact William Ward had with Sikhs which enabled him to write his account of Sikhism.

Whilst the missionary did talk about his faith, here was no early Sikh-Christian dialogue in terms of the mutual exploration of each other's faith. No doubt the Maharaja had a different purpose in mind, that is the educational development of his people. Hope existed for both parties. Lowrie's motivation and hope was unequivocally evangelistic, the Maharaja's educational.

The Presbyterians were among the pioneers in the Panjab of printed Panjabi literature, a type-script being developed in 1845. A Gurmukhi Panjabi Grammar was prepared by the Rev'd John Newton in 1851 and a later enlarged edition with exercises was brought out by the Rev'd C.B. Newton. John Newton and the Rev'd Levi Janvier published a Gurmukhi Panjabi Dictionary in 1854. Since Carey's translation of the New Testament of 1815 was considered of little practical value John Newton worked on a revision, publishing first Matthew's Gospel in 1840, John's Gospel in 1841 and the complete New Testament in 1868. The Ludhiana Mission Press published a number of books in Panjabi including *Enjilsar*, a summary of the Gospel in 1880, and a translation of *Pilgrim's Progress*. Of the contribution made by the missionaries Prof. Bhupinder Singh Dhillon writes:

> ... we can conclude that the prose produced by Christian missionaries during the 19th century is according to the rules of grammar. To make ideas more effective and clear, the right use of full-stops was made....None of these publications carry the name of either the author or the translator. From this we can guess that from the very beginning these works were produced by team work....In short, we can say that the prose of this period is the link between the old Punjabi prose and the modern Punjabi prose and it is indeed a valuable contribution.[5]

The Panjab Mission of the Presbyterian Church in the U.S.A. was one of the most active, yet for many years the number of conversions was

---

5.   C.H.Loehlin: 'Christianity and Sikhism' in *Religion and Society*, Vol. XI, No. 1, March 1964 p. 17. and James Massey: 'Presbyterian Missionaries and the Development of Punjabi language and Literature, 1834-1984.' in *Journal of Presbyterian History*, Vol 62, #3, Fall, 1984, pp. 258-261 who quotes Dhillon's thesis: *Pilgrim's Progress: The Translation and Punjabi of Padries*, Patiala, Punjabi University, 1969.

relatively few in number. In that the Sikhs had been considered the 'target' group the number of conversions showed the degree of response. Between 1834 and 1886 there were 183 conversions of whom 22 were Sikhs. Of these 4 were from Ludhiana, 2 from Jullundur, 2 from Ambala, 12 from Lahore, 1 from Hoshiarpur and 1 from Rawalpindi.[6]

By the 1880s the Presbyterians' attempt to evangelise the Sikhs had not brought the hoped-for success in significant numbers. This may be due to the lack of any clear distinction having been made between Sikhism and Hinduism by the missionaries themselves and, according to Webster 'the fact that the Sikhs were predominantly a rural community while the Presbyterians were an urban community throughout almost the entire nineteenth century.'[7] This analysis requires further reflection. It is likely that the attitude of the second group of missionaries would have been coloured by Swift's farewell address. Whilst his statement about the Sikhs has some positive elements with regard to the people themselves, there was also a dismissal of their faith together with Nanak's supposed methodology - 'Nanac (sic)...adopt (ed) the common method of pretended visions and miraculous endowments .... and confirm (ed his) arguments by the power of his miracles.'[8] The early Presbyterian missionaries were, therefore, dogged by an inadequate background knowledge of the faith of the people amongst whom they worked and seemed disinclined to support a specialist in the Sikh faith as they did, eventually, in the persons of Kellogg, Griswold and Ewing with regard to Hinduism and Wherry regarding Islam.[9]

---

6. Webster (1976) p. 273f gives a breakdown of the conversions from other faiths at this time: 76 were Muslims, 32 were unspecified, 22 were Sikhs, 20 Brahmins, 3 of other high castes and 30 of lower caste. Some indication of the reason for the higher number of converts from Islam may be found in the fact that by far and away the language favoured by the Missionaries for their publications was Urdu. Notwithstanding this, significant numbers of Old Testament and Gospel portions were printed in Gurmukhi Panjabi, but whereas there was a long catalogue of books for Muslims and Hindus, the Panjab Religious Book Society had no books specifically written with Sikhs in mind – see H.U.Weitbrecht: *A Descriptive Catalogue of Urdu Christian Literature* with a review of the same and a supplementary catalogue of Christian Publications in the other languages of the Panjab, London, Religious Tract Society and Lahore, Panjab Religious Book Society, 1886.

7. Webster (1976) p. 117.

8. Nanak firmly rejected such practices: 'I have no miracle to display save the miracle of the True Name.' Var 1. 43.

9. As will be seen later, it was not until the arrival of Clinton Loehlin that such a specialist in Sikhism was to be found.

Most of the missionaries lived in the towns with the result that there would be little contact with the Sikh community. The normal practice was for missionaries to learn Urdu if they were to work in towns and Panjabi were they to work in the villages. Thus whilst it was regular practice for missionaries to 'itinerate' during the cold season, their fluency in Panjabi, the language of the villages, may not have been as great as in Urdu, thus putting them at a disadvantage.

Such itineration, however, brought them into contact with that which they had not expected for they were to discover that theirs was not the first Christian presence and that this was the case far before the Nineteenth Century. Whilst there is a strong tradition that Christianity in India, particularly the South, dates from the First Century, claims are made that St. Thomas also founded several communities in the North-West, in Panjab and in Sind, but that over the centuries such communities dwindled considerably because of political turmoil, isolation and neglect.[10] However, during the Nineteenth Century there was said to have been a community of *Fakirs* in Thattah in Sind reputed to be followers of Thuma Bhagat - St. Thomas.[11] Whilst there is no written evidence in support of these suggestions, contact between Palestine and India was not unknown since both Strabo and Pliny wrote of the existence of trade relations between the Roman Empire and India during the First Century of the Common Era and that voyages were made at least once every year.[12] Bartholomew, likewise, is said to have visited India although there is no Indian tradition of this nature. Rather, it is Eusebius[13] writing of the journey made about 303 C.E. as far as the Indus by Pantaenus, the Alexandrian philosopher, who makes reference to a previous visit by Bartholomew to the Panjab. There Pantaenus found a community of Christians '...for Bartholomew, one of the apostles, had preached to them,

10. P.Thomas: *Christians and Christianity in India and Pakistan*, London, 1954, p. 21; Ganda Singh, *The Panjab Past and Present*, Vol. I, Pt. II, No 2, Oct, 1967, pp. 369 writes that G.M.Moraes in his *A History of Christianity in India*, Bombay, 1964, indicates that Christianity came to the Panjab as a result of the conversion of the Parthian king Gondophernes (Gondophoros) by St. Thomas, but that it disappeared because of the subversion of Parthian rule by the Kushans. See Anand Spencer: 'Church History of the Panjab: Some Overlooked Facts - A Case for Re-Study' in *Proceedings Panjab History Conference*. (May 1992, Part 1)
11. Ganda Singh *op. cit.* p. 369.
12. see M.K.Kuriakose: *History of Christianity in India: Source Materials*, Madras, C.L.S., 1982, p. 1.
13. Kuriakose (1982). p. 4.

and left with them the writing of Matthew in the Hebrew language, which they had preserved till that time.'[14] Such preservation, however, may have lasted longer, for in 1871 members of a sect following the teachings of one Hakim Singh of Rampur came to the American Presbyterians to buy copies of the Gurmukhi New Testament. The Rev'ds John Newton and E.M.Wherry of Ludhiana visited Hakim Singh's village and found him 'sat upon a bedstead. In front of him men and a few women sat crowded together, reverently listening to the reading of the 24th, 25th and 26th chapters of the Gospel of St. Matthew.' The missionaries learnt that Hakim Singh believed in the *Nishkalank Avtar*, the Sinless Incarnation, seemingly foretold in the *Dasam Granth Sahib* and fulfilled in Jesus Christ.[15]

A further suggestion of a possible early Christian presence or influence is made by Dr Anand Spencer who writes of Sadhu Sundar Singh's meeting a 'very old seer' in a Himalayan cave who prayed with the Sadhu and who ended his prayers in the name of Jesus. However, Heiler in his biography of the Sadhu holds that some would cast doubt about this matter.[16]

The fact that representatives of Christianity were in the Panjab before the Nineteenth Century is also attested by the reference, the earliest from a Sikh Panjabi source, made by Bhai Gurdas (1546-1637). He refers to the self-centredness and confusion of Christians in his *Var* 38. 11. It may be that he refers to a group of Jesuit priests who were invited to the court of the Mogul Emperor Akbar (1556-1605).[17] They

14. However, C.B.Firth: *An Introduction to Indian Church History* Madras, C.L.S., 1961, p. 19, indicates that whilst Jerome repeats this suggestion some doubt is cast on this matter by modern scholars like Mingana. He continues: 'It may be that scholars have dismissed too lightly the story of Pantaeus' visit and his discovery of a Gospel brought by Bartholomew.'

15. C.H.Loehlin: 'The History of Christianity in the Panjab' in *The Panjab Past and Present* Vol. VII, Pt. 1, April 1973, p. 187f.); J.G.Fraser: *The Golden Bough* Pt. 1 Vol. 1, p. 409f also makes reference to Hakim Singh's having 4000 followers in Patiala State. Rumour also had it that Jesus Christ himself paid a visit to the Panjab: 'There is still a persistent rumour that Jesus, the great Messiah of Western religion, visited with the saints and sages of India, to deepen his understanding, before returning to teach in the land Europeans call 'the Middle East." - Fatha Singh Khalsa (Toronto) '*Nanak Naam*' in *The Sikh Review*, Vol. 43. 10, Oct. 1995, No. 502, p. 9.

16. Spencer (1992) p. 250 and Heiler: *The Gospel of Sadhu Sundar Singh*, New Delhi, I.S.P.C.K. 1989, p. 71f.

17. James Massey: 'Christianity and Culture: Their Relationship in the 19th and 20th Centuries Punjab' in *Bulletin of the Christian Institute of Sikh Studies (BCISS)* Vol 17, No 1, January, 1988 p. 3; Douglas M. Thornton: *Parsi, Jain and Sikh*, Religious Tract Society, 1898 p. 74. 'It was in the last year of the Guru's life (Ram Das) that several Jesuit fathers from Goa were invited by Akbar to visit the Panjab.'

disputed with the Muslims when one of their number, Padri Rudolf, challenged one of the *ulema* to carry their respective scriptures through a fire to prove who had the true revelation.[18] There were also amongst the Jesuits some who were witnesses to the martyrdom of Guru Arjan during the reign of Akbar's successor, Jahangir. This is reflected in a letter written by Fr Jerome Xavier S.J. from Lahore on 25 September 1606 to the Jesuit Provincial Superior in Goa, Fr Gaspar Fernandes S.J.[19]

Newton realised that the hope for the conversion of the Sikhs he had in mind could not be established if it were confined to the work of the American Presbyterians. With that recognition the British Church Missionary Society entered the Panjab. In his *History of American Presbyterian Missions in India*, John Newton indicates what attracted missionaries from both America and Britain to the Panjab:

> After much consideration they chose the Panjab. No other section of India is so full of historic interest as this. It was from here that Hindooism spread over the whole Peninsula. It was here that the great battle was fought which is described in the Mahabharat. It was through the Punjab that every successful invasion of India has taken place, except the British. It was here that the tide of Alexander's victories was terminated.

> But such considerations had little influence on the first missionaries in the selection of their field of labour. This seems to have been due mainly to the fact that it was the land of the Sikhs - a people of fine physique, and unusually independent character; a people, moreover, who had already, in principle at least, discarded the old idolatry of Hindooism, and broken, in some measure, the bonds of caste; and therefore might be considered to be in a favourable state to be influenced by the preaching of Christian Missionaries.[20]

---

18. J.C.Archer: *The Sikhs in Relation to Hindus, Muslims, Christians and Ahmadiyyas.* Princeton, 1948, p. 165.

19. '[Jahangir] sent for the said Guru (Arjan) ... held him prisoner ... he gave every day new torments to (the) saint. He ordered to give him much torture ... he took away his food, he did him a thousand and one dishonours. In that way their good Pope died, overwhelmed by the sufferings, torments and dishonours...' E.R.Hambye S.J.: 'A Contemporary Jesuit Document on Guru Arjun Dev's Martyrdom' in ed. Harbans Singh and N. Gerald Barrier: *Essays in Honour of Dr Ganda Singh*, Patiala, 1976 pp. 113-118. Note the positive comment about the Guru made in what is probably the earliest extant material of Christian authorship regarding the Sikhs.

20. John Newton: *History of American Presbyterian Missions in India*, Allahabad, 1886 p. 4.

Such an understanding was echoed by a CMS leader:

We believe, that when converted to Christ, they (the Sikhs) will
become soldiers of the Cross, as brave and true and faithful to Christ,
as they have been to Muslim invaders, or Delhi Emperors, or to their
own Maharajahs, or to our English Queen. Our object is to enlist
these races in Christ's service, so that they may as Christians join
with us, and seek to win countries for Christ, even as they have
joined us as soldiers in Burmah, in China, in Delhi, in Abyssinia, in
Cabul, in Cyprus, and in Egypt, and have aided us in conquering
many countries and taking possession of their capitals for our Queen.[21]

Thus Robert Clark indicates an element in the motivation of British
C.M.S. missionaries in the Panjab and the close links which existed
between the governing authorities and the mission society. Whilst some
historians of the Indian Church would indicate that C.M.S. was invited
by the American Presbyterian John Newton to take in work in the
Panjab,[22] it would seem that Newton was actually the intermediary
between an anonymous officer in the East India Company's army who in
1849 sent a donation of Rs. 10,000 to the C.M.S. with the request that
they should begin mission work in the newly annexed Panjab.[23] The
links with the civil administration and an indication of that
administration's support are further seen by the letter of welcome sent to
the missionaries together with an annual subscription of Rs. 500 by the

---

21. Robert Clark: *A Brief Account of Thirty Years of Missionary Work of the Church Missionary Society in the Punjab and Sindh. 1852-1882*, Lahore, The Albert Press, 1883, p. 24. Note that similar military metaphors were still in use in Edinburgh 1910.

22. Ernest Y. Campbell: *The Church in the Punjab*, in ed. Victor Hayward: *Three Studies of North Indian Churches*, London, Lutterworth Press, 1966, p. 149.

23. Clark (1883) p. 3. A further aspect shown by this quotation is the considerable spirit of cooperation and respect which existed between the Anglicans and the Presbyterians: 'Whatever others may say, or think, we who are in the Punjab have seen, and therefore we bear witness, that God's grace is not confined to any one Church or people. Dearly as we love our own Church, we have seen that converts are not made only in the Church of England; and we have seen also that converts of the Church of England are not better Christians than those of other Churches.' (p. 4) He further pays tribute to 'Dr Duff and to the Free Church of Scotland in Bengal, who have sent to the Punjab many of the most influential and useful Native Christians, who are now labouring in the Punjab...' (p. 4) It is possible that the need to produce vernacular translations may have fostered cooperation.

then head of the Board of Administration of the Panjab, Sir Henry
Lawrence. At the first meeting of the Panjab Mission held in Lahore on
19 February 1852, supporters heard of a further anonymous donation of
Rs 10,000. A number of civil and military functionaries also offered to
be corresponding members of the Association.[24] This parallels and well
illustrates the policy taken by the British Government just over a decade
previously when Lord Glenelg, the then Secretary of State for War and
Colonies advised the new governor of Ceylon in 1837 to regard support
of missionary enterprise as his foremost concern.[25] Three reasons may be
given for this cooperation. Security was of primary concern. This was
both in terms of the need for personal security from possible attack and
in terms of freedom to propagate the faith. War with the Sikhs had only
recently come to an end and their fighting capability was both well-
known and much respected. Likewise the missionaries greatly valued the
change in policy from the days of the East India Company which restricted
missionary enterprise. The change in policy was noted and appreciated.
Of the administrators of the Panjab Clark wrote:

> Those were days...in which both the Bible and the Prayer Book were
> believed in; when magistrates thought it not only their duty to
> execute justice, but were diligent also to maintain *truth* (his italics);
> and were not ashamed to pray for grace to do it; when Rulers "inclined
> to *God's* will and walked in His ways"...[26]

Along with security Clark also indicates here the faith of the
government officials. Many, but not all, were of evangelical stock who
were more than ready to endorse missionary goals[27] and who reflected the

24. Clark (1883) p. 31.
25. On this matter see Prof. A.N.Porter's inaugural lecture delivered at King's College, London, 20
November 1991: 'Religion and Empire: British Expansion in the Long 19th Century, 1780-1914.
26. Clark (1883) p. 5.
27. See Ian Talbot: *Punjab and the Raj 1849-1947*, New Delhi, Manohar, 1988, p. 70 quoting
P. Woodruff: *The Men Who Ruled India*, Vol. 2, *The Guardians*, London, 1971, p. 37: 'Although
the Punjab Government adopted a policy of strict religious neutrality from the outset, many
officials openly supported missionary activity. The Lawrences likened their punitive expeditions
against the Sikhs to those of the Israelites against the surrounding heathen populations as they
entered the Promised Land. For them and many of their colleagues, 'the conversion of the
natives to Christianity was the greatest blessing our rule could confer .... and as far as human
reason could see, one of the greatest objects for which our rule was permitted."
Talbot (1988) adds that in the early years of British rule no government official moved his camp
on Sundays, nor did any regiment march or were any public works projects undertaken. By 1868

increased political weight of evangelicals in the U.K. The third factor was of a practical nature. It was considered that the 'heathen' would be better controlled if they were to become Christian.

Thus C.M.S. missionaries established a foothold in the Panjab and especially in Amritsar. It was a strategic position 'and the object and aim of the Society has been ever to occupy it and its neighbouring stations in strength,' wrote Clark. The site of the 'Golden Temple', was not only a place of pilgrimage where there were regular fairs, but also a commercial and social centre which 'attracts all who are specially concerned with everything that is purely Native.'[28] Mission houses, schools and churches were built, with considerable help 'from the very first' from government engineers. Encouragement was forthcoming from England including a letter from the Rev'd J. Tucker of Wantage who professed it was '...no common privilege to be permitted to hear the good tidings of the preparation there appears to be in the Panjab for the reception of the Gospel of our Blessed Lord.' Drawing on his experience in Madras he suggested a 'mission audit' - though not in those terms - a statistical analysis of the area, 'specifying population, i.e. the number of religions, character,' and whether it was agricultural, mercantile, etc. He further suggested three distinct missions be set up, one of which should be for the country where 'the Sikhs and the Hindoos prevail.'[29]

The attitude of many evangelicals was coloured by an article about the Panjab in the *Church Missionary Intelligencer* of July 1851 described by Tony Ballantyne[30] as 'a rather caustic assessment of the newly annexed

the Government was much more open in its support of missionary activity and granted 2,000 acres of irrigated land in Chunian to C.M.S. so that a colony could be established there.
Robert Clark: *A Brief Account of Thirty Years of Missionary Work of the Church Missionary Society in the Panjab and Sindh 1852-1882*, Lahore, The Albert Press, 1883, p. 216f, quotes Sir John Lawrence's opinion in a state paper after the Mutiny: '... all measures which are really and truly Christian can be carried out in India, not only without danger to British rule, but on the contrary, with every advantage to its stability. Christian things done in a Christian way will never alienate the Heathen.' Clark adds: 'We have seen that our Government have even in the most difficult circumstances and amongst the most fanatical population, ever been the strongest, where missions have been most encouraged.' He adds: 'The officers who most promoted the diffusion of Christianity were those who were the most trusted by the people... They were those who loved the people most, and felt most sympathy for them, and they were in return the most beloved by the people.'
28. *Ibid* p. 19.
29. Letter to R. Clark dt. 12 August 1853. C.M.S. archives.
30. Ballantyne, T (2007); *Between Colonialism and Diaspora*, New Delhi, Permanent Black, p. 51.

region' and 'as a battle cry for Christian proselytisation' with 'its starting point (which) was an attack on the desiccating effects of Sikhism: "The inhabitants of the Punjab are like the lands around them, which are laying waste for want of irrigation. The Sikh religion cannot benefit them. It has been tried and fond worthless."

Missionary attitudes towards Sikhism can be gained also from the CMS missionaries' Amritsar meeting of 3-6 January 1855. A debate arose regarding the time at which to baptise converts. Opinion had it that this should be 'as soon as the candidate has attained to a clear distinction *of the truth of Christianity and the fundamental errors of other systems, particularly of his own religion.*' (my italics) Thus no salvific validity whatsoever was considered to be present within the religious faith of others. Indeed, further to that such faiths were erroneous. It was recommended that the language, history and literature of the indigenous people be studied but when asked the strategic question 'How far is it necessary or desirable to make oneself acquainted with the systems of religions around us by the study of those books acknowledged by other religions for the purpose of meeting opponents on their own ground?', the reply was 'Desirable *as far as leisure permits.*' The conviction held by the missionaries in the salvific qualities of Christianity was also emphasised explicitly in a statement emphasising the self-evident nature of that faith:

> Will not God own His own...when put forth with the simple authority of 'Thus saith the Lord whether men allow it or not to be from God?...The word of God is undoubtedly 'the sword of the Spirit' and we may not use carnal weapons. We ought to rely much on the authentic declarations of inspired truth and show our hearers that we do so...[31]

However, a caveat was suggested ... 'but we may after the example of St Paul occasionally refer to their own writings also'.

With regard to Christian beliefs it was considered 'desirable to assert the doctrine of the Trinity, of the Divinity of Christ... though we must not be indifferent to the passions and prejudices of opponents'. 'The leading doctrines', it was suggested, 'need to be continually set forth:... the'

---

31. Report of Mission Conference 3-6 January 1855, C.M.S. archives. C I 1 0/7/1

office of the Divine Personality of the Holy Ghost... and... the resurrection of Our Lord.'[32] The latter was seen as a 'convincing evidence to the Hindoos of his mission.'

The order of importance of work was set as: 1) Preaching to the 'heathen', including writing and the translation of books; 2) teaching the Christian folk; 3) Educational work, especially schools.

Various techniques were employed in terms of preaching. The Rev'd William Keene, one of C.M.S.'s early recruits, wrote in his reports of preaching in the bazaar in Amritsar, though it was thought best to discontinue this practice after the 'Mutiny' of 1857.[33] Another technique was to visit villages with the intention of cultivating 'friendship and intercourse with respectable and educated natives.'[34] In one village Keene came under a barrage of bricks, to the extent that he sought the advice of a local magistrate as to whether he should prosecute.[35] From the perspective of written work, in the course of time C.M.S. missionaries joined their American colleagues in the preparation of translations of Bible portions, popular books and tracts which were published in Panjabi between the early 1860s and 1884.[36]

As to the teaching and methods of the missionaries, the technique used seems to be that of enabling local leaders to understand the faith better so that they may help in the up-building of others. The Rev'd Daud Singh was one such person, having been the first Sikh convert to Christianity. He was baptised by the Rev'd H.H.Perkins in 'Cawnpore' and later transferred to Amritsar in 1852. Ordained in 1854, his education

---

32. There is an anticipation here of 'The Church's Royal Charter', a pioneering theology of missions from the International Missionary Council at Willingen, Germany in 1952, see: Norman Thomas: *Readings in World Mission*, London, S.P.C.K. 1995, p. 103: 'For God sent forth His Son, Jesus Christ, to seek out, and gather together, and transform, all [persons] who are alienated by sin from God and their fellows. This is and always has been the will of God. It was embodied in Christ and will be completed in Christ. For God also sends forth the Holy Spirit. By the Holy Spirit the Church, experiencing God's active love, is assured that God will complete what He has set His hand to in the sending of His Son.'

33. Annual Letter to C.M.S. 24 Jan. 1858. C I 1 0/160/20

34. M.A.Sherring: *The History of Protestant Missions in India 1706-1821*, London, Truebner & Co., 1875, p. 220.

35. Keene: Annual Letter 24 Jan. 1858.

36. H. Weitbrecht: (1886)

continued under Keene who, for instance, translated for him from English an analysis of the letter to the Romans so that he might understand New Testament theology better.

The building of schools was considered an important early task. The City School was built in 1853, with help from the local Executive Engineer, and to these schools were attracted a number of indigenous boys whose major desire was to receive a sound Western education which, it was thought, would effect entrance to lucrative work within the civil administration. Keene was reluctantly employed as a teacher in the mission school and in his 1856 annual letter wrote that he gave a daily exposition of scripture in Urdu to the pupils yet...' I have not been privileged to witness any fruit to my labours. No conversion has taken place from either masters or scholars. Some are undoubtedly fully persuaded by the truth of the Bible and the falsity of their own systems, but yet there they remain, love of carnal pleasures of the world and the fear of men keep them away from Christ who alone can save them.'

It was Keene who later brought to the attention of C.M.S. the need for specialist missionary work amongst the Sikhs. He himself was to write a short account of the Sikhs, but it was not the first to come from the pen of a Protestant missionary. William Ward had earlier done so in his book on Hinduism.[37] Their work, together with that of Canon Edward Guilford, will be considered in the light of the consolidation of the Church Missionary Society's work in the Panjab.

It was work amongst the Sikhs which had attracted the American Presbyterians to the Panjab in the 1830s. However they mainly worked in urban areas and thus their contact with the Sikh community was limited. This was reflected not only in the low numbers of converts but also by the fact that they published very little regarding the Sikhs up to and just beyond the turn of the century. C.W. Forman published a short biography of Guru Nanak.[38] E.M. Wherry, who wrote a number of pieces on Islam, wrote only one essay on Sikhism. It was a review article of one

---

37. William Ward: *A View of the History, Literature and Mythology of the Hindus*, (2 vols.), 1817.
38. C.M.Forman: 'Who are the Sikhs?' in *The Foreign Missionary*, November 1882, p. 256. Webster (1976) p. 104, describes the piece as 'anecdotal' and Nanak as someone who 'obviously appealed to Forman.'

of the Ludhiana Mission Press's publications: *Hari Charitra* by Pandit Walji Bhai (reviewed later). In it Walji Bhai claimed that Guru Nanak received his inspiration from the New Testament and encouraged his Sikh readers to consider the Bible as the original source of the *Guru Granth Sahib*.[39]

The Church Missionary Society fared no better with regard to publications regarding the Sikhs after Keene's essay, for it was not until 1915 that Guilford produced his short work. However it was a time to attempt to consolidate their work among the Sikhs. The early years were fraught with difficulty for both new Christians and missionaries alike. In the 1854/55 annual report Fitzpatrick wrote:

> The pastoral charge at Bishop Ryder's church in Birmingham, where I was curate, did not leave me with more anxiety and prayer...The experience of the Mission, up to the present time, would seem to lead to the conclusion that the trials of converts from heathenism, however dreadful at the time of baptism, are not for one moment to be compared to the spiritual trials and dangers which await them after they have been baptised.[40]

Whilst Fitzpatrick does not go into detail on this issue, one of Keene's letters to the C.M.S. in London indicates the difficulties faced by both convert and missionary. Of one Sobha Singh, later baptized by the name Isai Das, he writes:

> Mr. Clark was heard to remark that as an enquirer, the manner in which he once spoke of the love of Christ was astonishing. His relatives made great efforts to get him back before baptism - they appealed to the Deputy Commissioner and eighteen of them sat for 22 hours in Mr Clark's compound, but all to no purpose.

He further illustrated the point:

> One of our teachers, a *Granthi*, and a young man in the school are also convinced of the Truth of Christianity, but as yet the world in

---

39. E.M.Wherry: 'Was Nanak a Christian? in *The Indian Standard*, March 1903, pp. 12-14. Pandit Walji Bhai: *Hari Charitra*, Ludhiana Mission Press, 1893.

40. C.M.S. Annual Report 1854/55, p. 100f.

the shape of relatives is too strong for them. The former now comes to Clark for instruction in Christianity, may grace be given for him to confess it.[41]

Fitzpatrick and his colleagues were grateful for the help, particularly pastoral, given by the Rev'd Daud Singh, formerly a Sikh and one of the earliest to be baptized by the Society for the Propagation of the Gospel in Kanpur nearly a decade earlier. The report went on to describe him:

He has great influence both with Christian and heathen, and had been already the instrument of bringing others to the knowledge of the truth. He is unacquainted with English, Greek and Hebrew; but the Bishop regarded his sterling qualifications as a native pastor to his countrymen as sufficiently proved by better tests than those of human learning.[42]

Some 14 years later Keene, who, in his early years, had read through a commentary on Romans with Daud Singh, indicated his gratitude for native clergy and pressed for their better training since they were of great value to the mission. Daud Singh's ill health may have led to the need for further indigenous help. However, a colleague, Mr Knott of Lahore, indicated his misgivings concerning those who thought that employment as a native clergyman would be a 'lucrative profession and an easy stepping-stone to worldly advancement.'[43]

Not all the missionaries considered this to be the case since one young man of a good Sikh family joined the Divinity School in Lahore in October 1890. After baptism in Amritsar he attended Baring High School. Weitbrecht expressed the hope that he would candidate for the priesthood since he had given up 'many inducements ... for a secular career ... for the claims of spiritual work.' However, there were other inducements:

It is also a hopeful sign that Malkhan Singh was encouraged to give himself to the ministry by the father of his future wife, who is one of our leading Christians.[44]

41. Keene: Letter to C.M.S. London. 8 April 1854. C I 1 0/160/2
42. C.M.S. Annual Report 1854/55, p. 101.
43. C.M.S. Annual Report 1869/70, p. 126f.
44. C.M.S. Annual Report 1890/91, p. 120.

Baptisms continued apace, by 1870/71 there were 166 native Christians in Amritsar. It was in that city that one of the privates of the 4th Panjab Infantry was baptised. Unlike the ostracism that some new Christians suffered it was reported in 1858/59 that although he was the only one of his regiment to be baptised while the regiment was stationed in Amritsar, '(at) his baptism many of his comrades were present ... (and) on his return to the lines he was received in the most friendly manner.'[45] He was not the first amongst soldiers to have been baptised since there had been a movement of Muzbee Sikhs towards Christianity in the late 1850s. In response to these formerly outcaste people the C.M.S. established a mission in Khairabad in support of those men from the then 24th Panjab Infantry who had enlisted in 1857 and who had proved loyal to the British at the time of the so-called 'Mutiny.' They 'evinced a desire to shake off their present religious bonds, which associated them with the very lowest class of Sikhs and Hindoos. Some of them through the study of Christian books which they found in Delhi, and through the instruction they received at various places from missionaries who visited their quarters, have in this regiment become Christians.'[46] Officers of the regiment had been active in arranging for missionaries to speak to their men and some officers were present, albeit in a private capacity, at their baptism. The Government, however, intervened and forbade any attempts at conversion. On hearing of this C.M.S. officials in London pressurised for the 'restoration of liberty of action to Christian regimental officers, in respect of unofficial Christian intercourse with their men', with the result that Christian clergy were given full access to huts and hospitals provided it did not interfere with duties.[47]

After roughly forty years of missionary work on the part of both the Americans and the British were the initial high hope and aspirations justified and fulfilled?

In terms of justification the Americans had come well prepared. Their planning had been reasonably thorough. They had learnt something of the

---

45. C.M.S. Annual Report 1858/59, p. 116.
46. Robert Clark quoted in M.A.Sherring: *The History of Protestant Missions in India 1706-1821.* London, Truebner & Co., 1875, p. 236.
47. Robert Clark: in Sherring (1875), p. 219f Government policy was that all Sikh soldiers should be *keshdari* with the result that the presence of new Christians may have undermined both policy and, for some, morale.

background and context of the Sikhs and the Panjab even before they left America, Lowrie and Reed's early letter quoted at the start of this chapter indicates such, as does Elijah P. Swift's farewell address to Newton and his peers. On reaching Calcutta, the then capital of British India, they received further encouragement from both missionaries and highly placed civil servants and were given to understand that the Panjab presented them with a seemingly open door to both conversion and commerce. Further to this was their understanding of the Sikhs as a group of people who were willing to question and challenge the theology, beliefs and practices of their Muslim and Hindu compatriots, who might, therefore, grasp the opportunities to embrace the truth of the Gospel as the missionaries saw it.

Newton must have been further encouraged when Maharajah Ranjit Singh invited him to discuss further the possibilities for English medium education for his people. One can imagine the high hopes held by Newton and, for that matter, the Maharajah, though the hopes and motivations differed.

Perhaps such still maintained hope gave rise to Newton's later invitation to the British Church Missionary Society to work in the Panjab. The fact that an invitation was given, and with the backing of an officer in the East India Company's army strongly motivated the CMS who worked principally from Amritsar and Lahore. This was a time when an evangelical spirit was to be found amongst political leaders in both India and Britain, thus providing missionaries with a sense of security and support.

Above all, however, hope was undergirded by the utter conviction of the truth of the Christian faith and the rejection of the 'fundamental errors of other systems.'[48] With this in mind the work of missionaries continued in the Panjab, building on and consolidating the work of the early pioneers.

To such consolidation we must now turn.

---

48. Such an attitude was typical of that engendered by the classical Princeton theology of the time, dominated by Archibald Alexander, Charles Hodge and his son, Archibald Alexander Hodge. It was based on the authoritative nature of revelation, as opposed to religious experience; the inerrancy of the Bible and the veracity of the biblical record which meant that the inspired scriptures provided 'the infallible standard of all religious knowledge.' Thus '(t) he missionaries reckoned they had everything to teach and nothing to learn from Indians who 'as proponents of human systems, were expected only to accept the missionaries' truth with repentance, faith and thanksgiving – or reject it to their eternal peril.'

2

Consolidation, Understanding and Indigenization

Whilst those of us who are presently engaged in interfaith dialogue would make every effort to understand the faith of those with whom we speak, sometimes to the extent of learning the language of their scriptures or reading their theology, we have seen that the convictions of many missionaries in the Nineteenth Century led them to believe that such study was not a part of the missionary's duty. That a knowledge of the language, history and literature of the people among whom they worked was needed was not denied, but when, as happened at a missionary conference in Amritsar on 3-5 January 1855, the strategic question was asked, 'How far is it necessary or desirable to make oneself acquainted with the systems of religions around us by the study of those books acknowledged by other religions for the purpose of meeting opponents on their own ground?', the reply was 'Desirable *as far as leisure permits.*' (My italics.) One missionary who probably found this somewhat unacceptable was the Rev'd William Keene. It was he and a few like him who attempted to establish some form of understanding of the Sikh faith. This was more for reasons of conversion than academic study, but the result was a less aggressive form of evangelism and for some of Keene's successors a burgeoning appreciation of the Sikh faith. In the next fifty or so years, to just past the turn of the century, we find a period of consolidation, understanding and, to an extent, limited forms of indigenisation.

Whilst many had taken the line that an understanding of indigenous faiths was not necessary, there were some exceptions among missionaries. One such early exception was William Ward, one of the three renowned Baptist missionaries in Bengal. Ward published *A View of the History, Literature and Mythology of the Hindoos* in two volumes in 1817 with a new edition of three volumes in 1822. He based his work on secondary sources, in particular the *Sketch of the Sikhs* by John Malcolm whose political duties on behalf of the East India Company had taken him to the Panjab in 1805. Ward, however, added material from independent sources, most notably a Sikh who was an employee at the mission printing press. In doing so he differs from Malcolm in his theological evaluation and according to one modern Sikh reviewer compared with Malcolm 'is more close to the Sikh experience.'[1] His account deals mainly with Sikh theology rather than politics and also has a description of the lives of the Sikh Gurus and their contributions to the development of Sikhism. He is considered to be the first Western writer to give an account of the Sikh scriptures, including the Japuji of Guru Nanak. Unlike later Christian writers who saw Sikhism as an attempt to syncretise Islam and Hinduism, Ward indicated the rejection of both systems by Guru Nanak and his dislike of 'barren speculations and religious shews' whilst favouring 'attachment to forms of devotion.'[2] The account further deals with the festivals and rites of passage of the Sikh community and finally paraphrases passages from both the *Guru Granth Sahib* and the *Dasam Granth*.

Ward's comments are few, if any. It is an account which is not clothed in the rhetoric of the dismissive missionary, but rather reflects with some degree of accuracy the faith of the Sikhs as it was presented to him and, by the standards of the day, is sympathetic. Ward was not in a position to do much more than that, for he never visited the Panjab, but had probably come into contact with the several Sikh communities in Bengal and Assam which had grown since the visits to that part of India by Gurus Nanak and Tegh Bahadur.[3]

Whilst not a missionary an evangelical who wrote about the Sikhs was Robert Needham Cust who produced the first biography of Guru Nanak in English. He was a judicial commissioner in the Panjab who made it his business to understand Sikhs and Sikhism. He regarded Nanak as one through whom God worked ... 'We cannot but admit, that he was one of those, on whom the Almighty has vouched safe special

---

1. Darshan Singh: *Western Perspective on the Sikh Religion*, New Delhi, Sehgal, 1991, p. 142.
2. Ward (1822) p. 448f.
3. See Khushwant Singh: *A History of the Sikhs*, Vol 1, Delhi, O.U.P., 1977, pp. 33 & 72.

blessings ... he laboured unceasingly ... to reform the lives and religion of his countrymen, to break through the tyranny of Priestcraft, outward ritual, and Caste. He taught that purity of thought, word and deed, abstinence from Lust, Anger and Avarice, were better than feeding Brahmins, or making offerings at Temples.'[4]

It was not until the arrival of William Keene in the Panjab that we find another missionary like Ward who took a similar interest in the Sikh faith. In Keene one finds a missionary who bucked the system, who went to India with the express intention of witnessing for Christ in 'Satan's land', who was frustrated by the lack of converts after years of work yet who seems also to reflect a reluctant admiration for those who followed Guru Nanak in their search for spiritual fulfilment.

Sent by the C.M.S. for work in Amritsar, Keene was ordained priest by the Bishop of Calcutta in January 1854. On arrival in the Panjab he found himself engaged variously in bazaar preaching, itinerant work in the villages and teaching in the school. Within a year of his arrival, that strategic question was posed with regard to the need to study the religious faith of the indigenous people. The reply in terms of its desirability but only during leisure time must have echoed in his mind as in various annual letters he indicated his sheer frustration that he had not seen any converts of his own making. By 1858 he complained: 'Are conversions the invariable result of a faithful ministry or not? If so (as far as I am aware) I am either no true missionary or an unfaithful one.'[5] Within the next four years he was to study Sikhism in an attempt to understand the faith of his hearers and the fruit of that labour was a presentation at the Panjab Missionary Conference held in Lahore in December/January

---

4. Cust, R.N. (1859): *The Life of Baba Nanuck, the Founder of the Sikh Sect of the Hindu Religion in the Panjab: For the Use of Schools*, Lahore p. 7. Tony Ballantyne in his *Between Colonialism and Diaspora*, New Delhi, Permanent Black, 2007, p. 47f, points out the manner in which commentators of the time painted the Sikh faith in terms of their own Protestant, and perhaps, Reformed, tradition. He further points out that this 'underscores not only the intersections between British and Punjabi histories but also the ways in which the construction of cross-cultural affinities (between Sikhs and Britons, for example) actually rested on the 'othering' of other communities ... The construction of cross-cultural affinities was a power-saturated strategy, one that produced a host of 'others' in the drive to delineate the common ground between the colonizer and a particular colonized group.

5. Annual letter 24 January 1858. C I 1 0/160/20

1862/3.[6] The title of his essay, '*The Sikhs: all that can be said about them from a missionary point of view*,' illustrates Keene's conviction of the need to present the Christian faith in the light of the beliefs of his hearers. He acknowledged the deep desire of Guru Nanak to find freedom 'from every earth-born trammel' but maintained that it is 'the Son (who) makes you free.' Like Cunningham,[7] he portrayed Guru Nanak as one who rejected the current practices of Hinduism and followed that by a relatively positive presentation of the Sikh understanding of the Godhead; their rejection of 'idolatry' and caste; liberation through grace; God's forgiveness and the futility of an outward show of religiosity through ceremonial ablutions. He carefully drew a distinction between iconoclastic Sikhism as a reforming faith and 'the gross errors of the popular Hindu belief' in which people 'prostrate (themselves) before senseless stone, and believe the Divine Being to be in such idols.'

Years before Farquhar and his colleagues were to suggest Christianity as the fulfilment of other faiths, Keene suggested that Sikh teaching is, 'all in favour of the Christian missionary.'[8] Further he pointed out that the Guru Granth Sahib abounded in passages which struck common accord with Christian belief and asked if, like the teaching of Moses and the prophets which was designed by God to prepare the Jewish people, the teaching of Nanak might prepare Sikhs 'for the reception of Christianity'. In effect he was proposing the Guru Granth Sahib as the Sikh's 'Old Testament' and thus implying the preparation of the Sikhs *by God* for the Gospel. Thus God was at work amongst them before and outside the missionaries' activities.

He spoke further that some would argue that Sikhism had done nothing to prepare for the reception of Christianity, judging by the

6. See: *An account of the Panjab Missionary Conference held in Lahore in December/January 1862/63*, Lodhiana, American Presbyterian Mission Press, 1873, pp. 261-268.

7. J.D.Cunningham: *A History of the Sikhs*, (1849); Delhi, Low Price, 1994, p. 41. Cunningham was officer in the Indian army who took it upon himself to write about the Sikhs, against whom he had fought but whom he was later to command. Keene cribbed much of his pamphlet from Cunningham's book, the latest introduction to the faith published a short time before Keene left for India.

8. *An Account of the Panjab Missionary Conference held in Lahore in December/January 1862/3*, Lodhiana, American Presbytern Mission Press, 1873, pp. 261-268.

behaviour of certain people and 'thereby fallaciously drawing a universal conclusion from a particular premise.'[9] Others, he claimed, would suggest that the very purity of Sikh teaching may gave an adverse effect because 'it is more difficult for a moral, upright man to come to Christ than one who is openly profligate'.

Keene drew to the end of his paper by making a number of suggestions:

1. Missionaries should take up 'a particular line of study' and, further, that there should be distinct evangelists for Muslims, Hindus and Sikhs;

2. Itinerating missions should be established and those missionaries dedicated to work amongst the Sikhs should work in the villages of the Manjha and the Malwa - the Sikh strongholds.

3. Such evangelists should have a thorough knowledge of Sikhism, the lives of the Gurus and the Vedanta system of philosophy which he considered to be of influence on Sikhism.

4. The substance of preaching must be the person and work of Jesus Christ through the distinctive doctrines of Christianity, otherwise Sikhs and Hindus will claim that they have just as good teaching in their own systems.

5. '...the most effectual preaching to the heathen is the power of a holy, loving, Christ-like life.'[10]

The text of Keene's paper draws out the tension between his evangelical fervour and his appreciation of certain elements of the Sikh faith. His obvious frustration at the lack of converts as understood through his annual letters indicates his belief that that was his primary task, but unlike other missionaries of his day he does not reject Sikhism outright. Judging from borrowed phrases, it is possible that he derived such a view from reading Cunningham's book. Cunningham's work, still appreciated by Sikhs today, is sympathetic towards their faith and may

---

9. p. 265.
10. p. 267f.
11. See: *An account of the Panjab Missionary Conference held in Lahore in December/January 1862/63*, Lodhiana, American Presbyterian Mission Press, 1873, pp. 261-268.

have contributed to the tension within the Keene's mind. But while one may recognise Cunningham's influence one may also suggest that it was not impossible that Keene may have met Cust and taken courage from Cust's positive attitude.[11]

However, there may well have been some who listened attentively to Keene since the work in Amritsar continued apace as was seen in the previous chapter a regiment of Muzbee Sikhs had taken Christian baptism. One suggestion made by Keene, that of drawing in specialist missionaries may have been considered to have been taken up in the appointment of a German Lutheran by the name of Ernest Trumpp. But his was hardly a success story. Born in Northern Württemberg in 1828, Trumpp trained for the ministry at Tübingen. He was a very proficient linguist who, whilst working at East India House, was approached by C.M.S. with a view to his helping in their work of providing grammars and dictionaries of modern Indian languages. Thus he went to Karachi in 1854 but as a result of his own ill-health and the death of his first wife shortly after childbirth he returned to Europe. He had a second period in India, returned to Europe again after becoming ill and, most significantly with regard to relations with the Sikhs, was invited in 1869 by the British Government in India, not C.M.S., to translate the Sikh scriptures into English.

Trumpp's work has been analysed by a number of scholars[12] and thus must be dealt with here in terms of the influence or otherwise he had on his one-time fellow missionaries.

Trumpp rarely failed to make a derogatory remark about either Sikhs or Sikhism, thus he portrayed the faith as on the wane and soon to belong

---

12. Trumpp had published an incomplete translation of the Sikh scripture: *The Adi Granth*, London, W.H.Allen, 1877, to which he added an introduction and which was criticised by e.g. M.A.Macauliffe: 'The Holy Scriptures of the Sikhs' in *Asiatic Quarterly Review*, Oct., 1919, pp. 1-2; N.G.Barrier: 'Trumpp and Macauliffe: Western Students of Sikh History and Religion' in *Historians and Historiography of the Sikhs*, pp. 169, 170; Darshan Singh: *Western Perspective on the Sikh Religion*, Delhi, Sehgal, 1991, p. 34ff. See also Trilochan Singh: *Ernest Trumpp and W.H.McLeod As Scholars of Sikh History, Religion and Culture*, Chandigarh, International Centre of Sikh Studies, 1994, p. 53: 'From the view-point of ambitious Christian Missionaries and the Imperialists his presentation of the work was remarkable in its ability of running down this heathenish religion, Sikhism, which they were sure was decaying and dying and could easily be replaced by Christianity whose superiority he had reflected in all the pages of his work.'

to history.[13]   He considered it to be founded by one who was not an
independent thinker, Guru Nanak, who 'followed in all essential points
the common Hindu philosophy of those days.'[14]   Nor, indeed, claimed
Trumpp did Guru Nanak make any attempt to prove that he was divinely
appointed[15]. The final human Guru, Gobind Singh, he accused of leading
a relapse into Hinduism and of being personally addicted to the goddess
Durga and of encouraging the adoration of minor deities.[16]   He further
objected to the nature of Sikh theology which he believed to be akin to
the 'pantheism' and 'atheistic pessimism' of Buddhist doctrine.'[17]

Trumpp's negative view of Sikhism was also matched by his arrogance
and academic posturing.   In his attempt to translate the *Guru Granth
Sahib* he first enlisted the aid of several Sikh *Granthis*.   According to
M.A.Macauliffe whose major work on the Sikhs was written to do better
justice to Sikhism than did Trumpp's, Trumpp explained to the *Granthis*
that he knew Sanskrit better than they did and then lit up a cigar as he
read the *Adi Granth* which lay on a table before him. 'Tobacco being an
abomination to the Sikhs, the priests fled in consternation, and left Dr
Trumpp to plume himself on his display of learning and originality.' He
then depended for further translation on a poorly educated Sikh described
as being of 'loose character.'[18]   Further help he misguidedly sought from
better educated Brahmins[19] but they were probably ignorant of the Panjabi
language of the *Adi Granth* written some three hundred years earlier.
The publication in 1877 of his translation was greeted by the Sikhs with
consternation, disgust, horror and outright rejection.

---

13. Trumpp, 1877, p. vii. cf the attitude of triumphalism typified by the title of Johannes Warneck's
    book, *The Living Christ and the Dying Heathenism*, (1909) and the calculation made by the
    Norwegian Lars Dahle who, by comparing the numbers of Christians in the Third World in
    1800 and 1900, worked out a mathematical formula by which he 'confidently predicted that by
    the year 1990 the entire human race would be won for Christianity.' (David J. Bosch: *Witness to
    the World*, London, Marshall, Morgan and Scott, 1980, p. 6.)

14. Trumpp, 1877, p. xcvii.

15. Trumpp, 1877, p. cviii.

16. Trumpp, 1877, p. cxii-cxiii.

17. Trumpp, 1877, p. cv-cvi.

18. M.A. Macauliffe: 'The Holy Scripture of the Sikhs' in *Asiatic Quarterly Review*, Oct., 1919, fn 42.

19. Trumpp, 1877, p. vi.

Would the missionaries ever find anyone who could repair this horrendous breach of understanding and communication? Fortunately this was the case in the figure of the Rev'd Ernest Guilford.

In 1881 at the age of 28 Guilford was ordained Deacon by the Bishop of London and joined the C.M.S.'s work in the Panjab some eighteen years after Keene's call for a specialist to take up evangelisation work amongst the Sikhs. He was ordained Priest by the Bishop of Lahore on Trinity Sunday 1882 and thereafter prepared himself for work among the Sikhs by searching for a suitable base. He wrote to supporters of the society explaining his aims and requesting help:

Tarn Taran ranks second amongst the sacred places of the Sikhs. It has a population of about 6,000 souls, with over 300 villages surrounding it, containing 261,676 people. As a centre for missionary work it stands second to none in the Punjab; every month there is a *mela* (fair) held there, to which thousands of people flock from all parts. It is obvious, then, that the head-quarters of the mission should be fixed among the people themselves. To carry on the work from Amritsar is impossible, with any great hope of success. To do so would involve the loss of 7 months in the year, besides incalculable advantages derived from daily contact with the people. Having made two tours through the district in the last cold season, I can myself testify to the hearty desire of the people for Christian teachers. Everywhere we have been received most warmly, listened to most attentively, and pressed to come again soon.

The cost of establishing our headquarters at Tarn Taran, and of erecting a small bungalow there, cannot be less than Rs 5000. We earnestly appeal to our friends to assist us in this great work. We believe that it is a work which lies very near the heart of our Divine Master. Nothing was so prominent in His life upon earth as his tender solicitude for the poor and the ignorant amongst men. We believe that he still has the same love now for the people in the villages of the Punjab, that He had, when He was on earth for the villages of the Holy land. We believe that Christian work in the villages will strengthen our work in the towns, and that the work in the towns will again react with the work in the villages. We believe that it is more for the interests of Christianity to occupy thoroughly one whole neighbourhood, than to scatter our efforts abroad at great distances from one another.

At the present time there is not, we believe, any other English Missionary of our Society in the Punjab who is able to devote himself specially to the villages. Our Church Missionary Society have now made over this special work to my hands, and I ask for your kind assistance to enable me, in dependence of the Divine help to seek to do it well.'[20]

Like Sir Donald McLeod a civil servant in the Punjab who supported C.M.S., both Guilford and Clark were in favour of work in the villages since it was there that 'the power and strength of the country lies.'[21] Guilford's task was seen to be essentially with the Sikh village dwellers, not with the Muslims or Hindu Babus of the towns - a significant move away from the normal habit of trying to convert members of a high class/ caste through work in the larger towns. It shows Guilford's willingness to challenge the accepted missionary methodology of his mission society peers. He won the confidence of many people in the town through regular contact with them and it is probably this which forced him not to make an outright rejection of the faith of others. This may be illustrated by a description of a 'strange prayer meeting for rain' - a heading given to the description by an unknown C.M.S. headquarters secretary:

We had some heavy showers of rain here last week amounting in all to some 2.32 inches of rain. Thirty-six hours before the rain fell, we had a remarkable prayer meeting for rain on the open place in front of the C.M.S. house. We numbered 500 in all comprising Christians, Hindus, Sikhs, Moslims and Chuhras, and a representative from each of the first four mentioned religions offered prayer, all being extempore prayer, except the Sikh's which had been written for the occasion.

---

20. Quoted by Robert Clark 1883 p. 66. Oberoi: The Construction of Religious Boundaries, Delhi, O.U.P., 1994, p. 321, describes the nature of the monthly fairs to be such that they were detested by the Singh Sabha who were determined to clean up the place which was said to be full of drunken gangs of 'ne'erdowells and prostitutes freely (dancing) and (singing) vulgar songs' at the main gateway of the *Gurdwara*. Given the nature of the evangelical Christianity of the day, this was probably an added incentive for the establishment of a mission.

21. Clark 1883, p. 67.

The whole crowd listened very attentively to the address which I gave at the beginning of the meeting, and then repeated after me the first six verses of Psalm 130 and the first eight verses of Psalm 143.

It was a remarkable meeting and the people were much astonished at the speedy answer which we have received to our united prayer for at the time the heavens were as brass and they had been for many weary months.[22]

The fact that Guilford uses the term 'united prayer' would seem to indicate that although he obviously led the occasion it was not a trial of spiritual strength, as it were, nor were people of other faith considered by him to be mere observers. This was an *act* of inter-religious dialogue, of cooperation in life issues.[23] In the light of his experience amongst Sikhs Guilford was asked to write about the them and while he had intended to write at length - 'giving more in detail the results of his studies in the Granth and of his intimate experience and knowledge of religious and social life among the Sikhs' - he was able only to complete a short introduction.

Weitbrecht indicates in his Preface to the introduction that 'this is no mere academic essay' but something which arises out of the fact that '(h)is whole life...has been spent in intercourse with the Sikh peasantry, gentry and priesthood, and his great and beneficial influence over them' had been honoured by the government but...' (b)etter still, a Christian church has been gathered in the town and villages of Tarn Taran, which includes a number of Sikhs who have become soldiers of Christ.'[24]

Guilford wrote his short book on Sikhism after Edinburgh 1910 and was influenced by that conference. However, in certain issues he retains his own interpretation which was at odds with his peers at Edinburgh, perhaps reflecting the fact that he lived and worked among the Sikhs in their own heartland.

---

22. Letter from Guilford to the Rev'd Ireland Jones, 21 July 1900, G214/0/1900/281.
23. Cf the third principle of Dialogue outlined in *In Good Faith*, London, CCBI, 1991[2]: Dialogue makes it possible to share in service to the community.
24. E. Guilford: *Sikhism*, London, 1915, *Preface*.

His account opens with a short history of the Sikhs much of which is appreciative of their fighting qualities and of the 'wonderful man, Maharaja Ranjit Singh,' pointing out that it was the Sikhs who 'took up arms on behalf of England in the Mutiny of 1857.' Relevant to the period of writing (1914/5) was his appreciation of the Sikh regiments fighting on the side of the Allies in France.

He was critical but not dismissive of Sikhism and appreciative of many Sikhs. Whilst some fell short of Nanak's ideals, in his opinion, 'yet the influence of his teaching has been such to mark the Sikhs, as a nation, as being far in advance of any other people of India in spiritual conceptions, and in moral ideals and aspirations.'[25]

Unlike many of his colleagues, both at Edinburgh and elsewhere he regarded Sikhism as a distinct religion but also recognised the presence and practices of popular Hinduism amongst the Sikhs of his day, 'for they are still bound by the grave-clothes of Hindu superstition, and by the iron rules of caste...'[26] Like Farquhar he realised the need for a thorough-going study of the religion of the people amongst whom he worked and recommended that as being vital in the presentation of the Gospel. 'There are many gems to be found in the *Japji*, but they need to be diligently dug out and searched for amidst a mass of unedifying matter. The labour is, however, well worth the best efforts of the Christian missionary, for it will yield not only a few points of contact with the great truths revealed in Jesus Christ. The *Shabd* of the Granth is in truth no other than the Eternal Logos.'[27]

The same quoted sentence further reveals Guilford's conviction of the centrality of Jesus Christ in the Gospel message and likewise indicates his taking seriously the question which was asked of delegates to the Edinburgh conference: 'What are the elements in the said religion or religions (i.e. that of the people amongst whom one works) which present points of contact with Christianity and may be regarded as a preparation for it?'[28] Guilford answered this in terms of the 'gems which may be got from Guru Nanak's teaching' and lists them as:

---

25. Guilford, 1915, p. 29.
26. Guilford, 1915, p. 29.
27. Guilford, 1915, p. 28.
28. The question list is given as an appendix in J.J.E. van Lin: *Protestante Theologie der Godsdiensten van Edinburgh naar Tambaram*, Assen, van Gorcum & Comp. B.V., 1974.

1. The Fatherhood, the love, the mercy, and the justice of God.

2. The brotherhood of man.

3. The necessity of obedience to the inward divine voice.

4. The unerring working of divine justice.

5. The necessity of a divine Teacher.

6. The existence of One who can put away sin, under the name of Hari. (Interpreted by him to mean the 'One Who puts away'.)

7. The folly and sin of idolatry.

Many of these suggestions for an apologetic to the Sikhs indeed take their origin from Guru Nanak's teaching, but it would be advisable to add a note of caution with regard to the matter of 'Hari' since Guilford may be placing an overly Christian interpretation on the meaning of this word.[29] None the less, Guilford certainly lays the foundations for an apologetic to the Sikhs.

Such was Guilford's experience that he recognised the difference between the beliefs of Sikhism as outlined by the Singh Sabha movement and the claims made by the 'common people' who considered the Gurus to be 'ten different incarnations of the One all-pervading Spirit' which claim he indicates cannot be substantiated by the sacred books. This reflects the attitude of such people generations later when Clarence O. McMullen conducted his interviews which showed that 79.4% of the people asked believed that Guru Nanak was an incarnation of God.[30]

Guilford arrived in India five years after the publication of Trumpp's translation of the Sikh scriptures and partly influenced by the translator's low opinion of Sikhs and Sikhism - they both had worked for the same mission society - he described the legends of the birth and childhood of

---

29. Here Guilford utilises the questionable hermeneutic suggested in Pandit Walji's *Hari Charitra* p. 73, where the meaning of 'Hari' is said to be 'the one who takes away sin, sickness, pain and everyday calamity and saves.' However, 'hari' is also the third person singular of the verb *hiri*, meaning to 'snatch,' 'take away by force,' and thus is probably too strong an action to uphold Walji's suggestion.

30. See: Clarance O. McMullen: *Religious Beliefs and Practices of the Sikhs in Rural Panjab*, London, Jaya Books, 1989, p. 83, Table 4.13.

Guru Nanak to be 'of a very puerile nature' and went on to quote Trumpp's opinion that Nanak was 'by no means an independent thinker.'[31] For Guilford '...the religion of Nanak seems to be a serious attempt at ...establishing a religion that could embrace both Hindus and Mohammedans,' which he describes as a 'compromise' ...'which shares the weakness common to all compromises.'[32]

Rejecting the 'dreary round of transmigration', he bemoans the loss of identity involved in the Sikh concept of *moksha* (liberation) which he felt 'held out no more hope of future personal bliss than is afforded by Hinduism.'[33]

Here one finds the inevitable conflict between the Christian search for personal salvation and the Sikh rejection of such individualism since it reflects the egocentricity of *haumai* (self-centredness).

In common with many Christians who seem to claim a monopoly of spiritual truth he suggested that the only explanation of the presence of such truths is through Guru Nanak's having come into contact with Christianity '...for there are many things in his writings which have a Christian colouring, and which seem inexplicable, except on the hypothesis that Nanak had some personal knowledge of the faith', a hypothesis which he felt was strengthened by the existence of a sect of descendents of people converted to Christianity by the preaching of St Thomas. '...These men have in their possession both the Gospel of St Matthew and the writings of Nanak, and they render equal honour to both.'[34]

In a gentle manner Guilford rejected the thesis of Pandit Walji that Nanak was 'a convinced Christian who taught, but in obscure language the whole doctrine of the Life of Christ'. That said, his affirmation that Guru Nanak was a seeker after truth and his high opinion of the Guru's life-style are high praise indeed for one who sought the conversion of the Sikhs.

---

31. Guilford, 1915, p. 7.
32. Guilford, 1915, p. 7.
33. Guilford, 1915, p. 8.
34. Guilford, 1915, p. 9.

Nanak, in Guilford's eyes provided a *preparatio evangelica* for the Christian missionary, for although he 'laboured with many grand truths he was unable to give form to any. He was a great and saintly soul, and one who stood out beyond all others of his time in India.'[35] Guilford encouraged his fellow missionaries to search the Sikh scriptures 'for it will yield not a few points of contact with the great truths revealed in Jesus Christ.'[36] Perhaps most surprising is his claim that the *Shabad* of the Granth 'is in truth no other than the Eternal Logos - "The true light that lighteth every man coming into the world..."

Guilford showed that he was familiar with the work of the Singh Sabha movement in that he writes of the variety of sects to be found within Sikhism as then practised in the Panjab. He was well aware, as were many of his generation, of the danger of Sikhism being lost amidst an all-embracing Hindu environment.

Finally he acknowledged that 'the Sikhs are a noble race and ... their religion compared with the religions of some other peoples of India, is of a high order, and one worthy of study.' But to what end? It is so that Sikhs may be persuaded to 'accept the Christ of God as the Guru "sent from God" who 'lighteth every man coming into the world'. Using his recognition of the similarities of 'shabad' and 'logos' Guilford encouraged his readers that Christ alone is the 'One Mediator', confessed by Guru Amar Das when he told his followers "Seek such a one for your Guru who is able to reconcile you to God."[37]

Like his older colleague Keene, Guilford was convinced that the goal of his ministry must be conversion. Even the headed note-paper later used by him and his wife declares their address to be the *Gurdwara* or 'The Door of the True Light' - *Sat Gur Ka Dwara*; and using vocabulary familiar to those who read the Sikh scriptures they indicated by the heading on the opposite side of the page their belief in the 'Sinless, Eternal Being - Praise be to the Lord Jesus.'

However, a clearly perceptible development had taken place from the time of Keene with regard to the attitude taken to Sikhism. Keene was

---

35. Guilford, 1915, p. 28.
36. Guilford, 1915, p. 28.
37. Guilford, 1915, p. 12.

inclined to the belief that the theological ideas embraced by Guru Nanak, even though at best, inadequate, and at worst, false, could be used as a foundation for reception of the Gospel message. Meanwhile, thanks to the climate of opinion developed after the publication of Darwin's *On the Origin of Species by means of Natural Selection*, Guilford was able to make use of its theological corollary, that Christianity could be presented as the fulfilment of Sikhism. Guilford's book was published at a time when the Fulfilment School normally associated with J.N.Farquhar[38] was popular amongst missionaries. Max Mueller's work also helped in the development of this understanding of the role of other faiths for although he did not make any claim for the supremacy of Christianity he maintained that the non-Christian religions could be considered as 'part of the divine education of the human race.'[39]

However, the idea of Christian superiority, benevolent or not was considered by him to be inappropriate.[40] Perhaps the greater influence on Guilford was that of Monier Williams who had suggested it may be the case that some of Christianity's 'grandest and most essential dogmas...and its root ideas, do indeed lie at the root of all religions'. He asked, 'Is it not a fact that all gropings after truth, all the religious instincts...find their only true expression and fulfilment - their only complete satisfaction - in Christianity?'[41] True that Monier Williams rescinded his view in a well received address at the 1887 C.M.S. anniversary meeting, but Guilford was by then in the Panjab and had possibly experienced at first hand elements of Sikh spirituality which may have given him a more positive view. In keeping with the fulfilment theologians of his day, Guilford's attitude to Sikhism emphasises sympathy whilst at the same time declaring its inadequacy. Thus Guilford conceived of the Sikhs' faith as a *preparatio evangelica*[42] as is illustrated by the final words

38. Notably *The Crown of Hinduism*, 1913.
39. *Introduction to the Science of Religion*, 1909 p. 151.
40. *Chips from a German Workshop, I*, p. xxi.
41. Monier Williams: *Modern India*, p. 234, quoted in Sharpe: *Not to Destroy but to Fulfil*, Uppsala, Gleerup, 1965.
42. A similar attitude is struck by a Panjab lady missionary (unnamed) quoted by F.W.Youngson in his *Forty Years in the Panjab of the Presbyterian Missions of the Church of Scotland*, Edinburgh, R.& R. Clark Ltd, 1896, p. 50. Of the Sikhs she writes: 'Their religion is most interesting and

of his book in which he states that the 'Christ of God' is the true 'Inward Light' for whom they search, the true 'Shabad' (Word) by which all things were created.[43]   Guilford also had the benefit of the growth of knowledge in the West of the scriptures of India, thanks to the work of Monier Williams, Mueller, and, in the case of Sikhism, Trumpp's translation of the *Guru Granth Sahib*, for all its deficiencies. Further, the reforming movements within Hinduism such as the Arya and Brahmo Samajes and the growth of the influence of the Singh Sabha within Sikhism enabled a new climate of opinion which was less inclined to reject all that was seen of Indian religions as satanic and crude. That being the case he was not opposed to contact with the Sikh community, rather he contributed to possible bridge building by the weekly series of lectures on the New Testament which he gave at one of the Sikh 'theological colleges' in Tarn Taran, given, it must be stated, at the request of the college authorities.[44]

So by the turn of the century it had become obvious that there were the beginnings of mutual understanding as is evidence by a comment from one of the students in a Bible class about missionaries' methods:

> It appears to me that all you preachers go about things the wrong way. They all preach far too much about the Trinity and the Atonement, subjects which do not appeal to the people of this country. Why do they not preach more about Christ and His teaching? The people of this land naturally turn to teachers such as Christ. If you once get them interested in Him, then they will in time themselves ask what relation such a teacher holds to God, and how it is possible for us, who fall so far short of His standard, to be 'at one' with God.[45]

The quotation is significant not only in terms of the request for a Christocentric message, but also as an indication that this particular

---

touching to those who study it: it has so many strange insights and foreshadowings of the Great Revelation - as yet to come to them - .... Surely they are a chosen people, meant to inherit the gift of eternal life, with many other nations who shall at that day be found saved, and walking in the light of the Lord.'

43. Guilford 1915 p. 39.
44. C.M.S. Gazetteer for July 1910.
45. C.M.S. Annual Report 1999/1900, p. 261.

student was willing to recognise the Christian claim that there is a shortfall in human character as compared with the claim made by both Sikhs and Hindus that human-beings are essentially good by nature. Further, some elements of a spirit of cooperation with the Sikhs were evident. They illustrate a change in attitude on the part of missionaries from condemnation - of the 'heathen' practices in 'Satan's land' to a willingness to be involved in dialogue, not so much to create mutual understanding, but to witness to faith. This is evident not only in the 'strange prayer meeting' for rain held outside Guilford's home in Tarn Taran in July 1900, but also in the significant development of joint meetings held in Amritsar District, reported on with enthusiasm by the C.M.S. missionaries:

The Annual Report for 1906/7 demonstrates a softening of attitude taken by CMS missionaries:

Indirect signs of the spread of the Gospel have been numerous, particularly the remarkable testimony to Christ borne by a leading Sikh teacher at the 'Love Assembly' at Amritsar. In 1906, as in previous years, a *Prem Sangat*, or 'Love Assembly,' was held in the Autumn. Christians and Sikhs meeting in a friendly way to allow preachers of each religion to give public addresses. The Rev'd R.H.A. Haslam of the Canadian C.M.S. who was present writes of the remarkable gathering:

'A significant feature of the gathering was the large percentage of the Sikh and Mohammedan religious teachers of the surrounding country and it is true to say that 'as go the religious leaders in India so follow the people.'

At ten o'clock in the morning of the *mela* those present sat down under a huge *shamiana* (tent), the Christians at one end to the number of twenty, the Sikhs numbering some 300; on one side, near them the various branches of the neo-Hindu community; and at one end 150 Mohammedans.

When we had been sitting on our crossed legs for about an hour and a half there was a slight excitement in the camp. Asking what it was I was told that Kesar had arrived. Almost immediately all gave the greatest respect and reverence to an old man - grey-headed, wearing a fakir's garb, with hair standing straight out all over his head, who stepped into the Assembly. He stood a moment with outstretched hands, with his followers behind him, and thus began in Panjabi this striking utterance - striking because coming from a nominal heathen, a Sikh fakir, and also because of the contents of the message, and the almost apostolic boldness with which it was delivered:-

'There is one Prophet.
'There is one Living Prophet.
'There is one *Guru* (teacher).
'There is one living *Guru*.

'The *Guru* is not *Guru* Nanak.
'The prophet is not Mohammad,
'*Guru* Nanak is dead;
'Muhammad is dead.

'The living Prophet is Jesus Christ.
'The living *Guru* is Jesus Christ.'

This man Kesar is one of the leading Sikh teachers in that district. He heard of Christ some four years ago, and has since been reading the New Testament. The result is that he is going about the country still as a Sikh (though at heart a Christian), and is being received by the people as such, and yet I am told that he has made Christ the subject of his teaching.

That night at 10.30, when I was in my tent, and had just prayed, 'O Lord, if there is a Nicodemus in this camp tonight, send him here and give him a knowledge of Christ', the flap of my tent was opened, and in walked the chief disciple of Kesar, a man by name Sohan Singh, who, before leaving that night, definitely and intelligently accepted Jesus Christ as Lord and Saviour, and the following morning and day confessed Him openly before the whole body of Sikhs and Mohammedans present.

On the first evening, at the close of a meeting on the hospital verandah, after an address given on 'the true nature of the love demanded by God', the high priest of the Sikhs in that district got up, and, after a striking testimony to the lives of a deceased missionary and an India *Padre*, as those who reflected the life and love of Jesus, he said, 'I have a request to make of all present (some sixty to seventy Sikh teachers). All pray from this night forward that the kingdom of Jesus may make speedy advance in this whole district, and in all India.' This man had treated Christians very scornfully as recently as a year ago.

I interviewed night visitors until about 12.30 a.m. All of them were enquirers about Christianity, and many very near the kingdom.'[46]

The passage is quoted in full since it raises significant matters with regard to the missionaries' activities and attitudes.

It must be noted that sufficient trust, or interest, or both, had been established by the turn of the century between the missionaries and the Sikh populace to hold such joint meetings. The missionaries believed this to be the case and illustrated this by the way in which some Sikhs had considered British rule favourably even since the 1860s.[47]

The meeting represents an early form of dialogue, but more akin to that of Paul in Ephesus rather than the dialogue of the present time. The Christian understanding of the meeting was that it was a means of witness for conversion. However, it did run the risk of being turned into a dispute since the people present were not by any means inarticulate. They were religious leaders and teachers and would have been well able to voice their opinions and criticisms of Christianity without hesitation.

It is evident that conversion to Christianity continued to bring with it personal difficulties such as ostracism or persecution. Thus enquirers were inclined to visit the missionary under cover of darkness and the missionary expected this to be the case.

The statement regarding the figure of Jesus Christ made by the Bible-class student, and quoted above, is borne out by the 'testimony'

---

46. C.M.S. Annual Report 1906/7 p. 196f.
47. After his return from furlough in 1863 Fitzpatrick reported that he found 'striking improvements in the temper and bearing of the people.' One Sikh whom he had known for many years told him 'that his nation are now so impressed with the wisdom, power and justice of the English, that it is a common saying amongst them, that God imparted a sixteenth portion of Himself to them.' C.M.S. Annual Report 1863/64. p. 141.

made by Kesar Singh who was obviously struck by missionary teaching regarding the 'Living Christ', whom he possibly regarded as being of a more personal nature than the 'Living Guru' which is the *Guru Granth Sahib* itself. (This must also be seen in the context of the reverence for certain human 'living Gurus' of the various Sikh sects of the time.)

Kesar Singh may have indicated his appreciation of Jesus Christ and spoken of him in reverential terms, but it is significant that at this stage there was no indication of his thinking that aligning himself with the Christian Church was necessary. Similarly the 'high priest' had little difficulty in encouraging prayer for the 'Kingdom of Jesus' but not for the conversion of India to Christianity.

Whilst this may well have been the case for Kesar Singh and many of his peers, there were others who had responded to the extent of their conversion to Christianity and subsequent baptism. Amongst these were a number of people, albeit small, who were to make significant contributions to the indigenisation of Christianity and to a burgeoning apologetic to Sikhs. Among these we may include Sadhu Sundhar Singh about whom so much has been written, but who confronts us with a dilemma. He has been so often paraded as the convert from Sikhism to Christianity. Yet was this the case? Of his Christian faith there is ample evidence, the issue at hand is whether he was a Sikh. An exploration of this matter cannot be exhaustive here, but it may be enough to question the tradition that has been built up. A paragraph from Eric Sharpe's overview of the various biographies, perhaps, hagiographies, may suffice:

Sundar Singh was born into a relatively rich Sikh-Hindu family at Rampur[48] (northern Punjab) on September 3, 1889. The precise balance of his family's Sikh and Hindu elements must remain conjectural, though his mother, from whom he received whatever religion he learned in his early days, was quite clearly more Hindu than Sikh. At the same time, though, in the 1880s the boundaries between the two traditions were by no means as clear as later textbooks would suggest, and we would be greatly wide of the mark if we were

48. One wonders if this was the same Rampur mentioned above as the village of Hakim Singh whom Newton and Wherry visited in 1871. If so, was he still alive at the time of Sundar Singh and did he or his followers influence Sundar Singh's spirituality?

to follow Friedrich Heiler in seeking for Sundar's characteristic spiritual heritage in the world of the Sikh gurus. His own words were: "I was born in a family that was commonly considered Sikh, but in which the teaching of Hinduism was considered most essential..."

It would seem that had had learnt by heart the Hindu *Bhagavadgita*, and was reputed to have known both the Guru Granth Sahib and the Qur'an, yet nowhere does he quote from either or 'left any obvious trace on his mature mind', to quote Sharpe.[49]

Little is recorded of the work of other Indian converts, since reports to mission societies normally spoke of expatriate missionaries. As with so many other parts of the world, there must be thousands of unsung mission heroes, often ignored because they were not of Western origin. However, here we name four such people.

The first is Pandit Walji Bhai. Nearly a decade after Guilford arrived in Tarn Taran Pandit Walji Bhai's *Hari Charitra* or Comparison Between the *Ad Granth* and the Bible was published.[50] For many years Panjabi Christians had indicated that passages in the *Granth* bear remarkable resemblance to the Bible, so much so that Pandit Walji Bhai suggested that Guru Nanak was a Christian who presented Jesus Christ as *Hari*, the saviour of humankind, the *Sat Guru*, True Teacher, also known as *Isa*,[51] whose followers were Sikhs or disciples.

Walji's methodology was first to attempt to undermine the status of the Sikh Gurus whose biographers gave 'undue praise and ascribed excessive glory to their Gurus'... 'by mixing up wonderful myths with their writings so that it became a great difficulty to distinguish truth from falsehood'. He saw the biographers of Nanak Sahib as being no exception, since

---

49. Sharpe, E.J. (2004): *The Riddle of Sadhu Sundar Singh*, New Delhi, Intercultural Publications, p. 29 – both quotations.

50. Lodiana Mission Press, 1893.

51. See: S.S.Kohli: A Conceptual Encyclopaedia of Guru Granth Sahib, New Delhi, Manohar, 1992, p. 158: 'There is no direct reference to Jesus Christ in the *Adi Granth*, but the usage of the word 'Kateb' (Books) refers to the Christian scripture *Injil*, which contains revelations made by God to Jesus. But some Christian Missionaries have mistook (sic) the word *Isai* used in the *Adi Granth* for Christ, though it is a derivative from Sanskrit 'Ish', which means Ishwara or God (A.G. p. 1072, Maru M. 5).

'truth was hidden in false words.' But of Nanak himself, Walji writes '... Nanak Sahib was wise and godly and he put on many guises as of sadhoo and fakir and wandered in search of salvation.' Further Nanak 'became acquainted with *Sat Guru Hari* and began to worship him, heart and soul and also showed real repentance by confessing his sins.'[52]

However he asserted that the followers of Nanak possess no good qualities by which they can be saved, thus according to him only through the righteousness of *Hari*, for which one should read 'Jesus, the Son of God' can they find salvation. Such a one Nanak revered, according to Walji, and spoke of as the 'one Krishna who is the God of gods'... 'I am the servant of him'[53] He further suggested that this is not the Krishna of Indian legend since Nanak 'does not believe in this Krishna,' but 'the real truth is, that Krishna, whom Nanak calls God of gods is Christ, the Son of God.'

Walji believed he had discovered in the text of the *Guru Granth Sahib* a number of Christian doctrines which he hoped would 'prove' his case. Thus he finds texts which support his belief that the world was created by 'God and His son *Hari*;'[54] that God is one, the True Guru and also known as Allah;[55] that *Hari* is the Son of God who, born as a child, took the form of a Servant or *Sadhu*;[56] that *Hari* means 'one who takes away sin, sickness, pain and every calamity and saves'[57] and that he is to be identified with *Isa* - Jesus.

He also claims to find references to the atoning death[58] and resurrection of *Hari*;[59] that baptism was practised together with the

---

52. Walji Bhai, 1893, p. 4.
53. A.G. p. 1353. Since such standard page numbering of the *Guru Granth Sahib* was not established until the Twentieth Century Walji's references to a hand-written text cannot be easily verified. Only where he quotes in full, in Panjabi, is there any possibility of finding his quoted text by means of a concordance.
54. Walji Bhai, 1893, pp. 14, 58.
55. Walji Bhai, 1893, pp. 48, 58.
56. Walji Bhai, 1893, pp. 12, 106.
57. Walji Bhai, 1893, pp. 28, 73.
58. Walji Bhai, 1893, p. 170.
59. Walji Bhai, 1893, p. 181.

laying on of hands, washing of feet and the 'Lord's Supper.' *Hari* also is said to triumph over the serpent or Satan[60] so that the righteous may enter heaven.[61]

Walji concludes his work with the somewhat exaggerated claim that the:

above chapters clearly show that Nanak Sahib and his followers taking many things from the Bible inserted them in the Ad Granth in an altered form. All these Biblical texts shine in the Ad Granth like a star shining in darkness. The Sikhs appear satisfied with this glimmering light and consider their *shashtra* and their knowledge to be perfect, but if one were to look at things without prejudice he will have to acknowledge that the Ad Granth has the Bible as its original source. The Bible is the perfect treasure for salvation so our readers will make a comparison between it and the Ad Granth, and when they find where the truth lies they will accept it with a true heart, for by so doing they will be abundantly profited both for this world and the world to come.[62]

Thus, for Walji, Nanak was akin to an anonymous Christian who had been touched by grace and who possessed some form of natural

---

60. Walji Bhai, 1893, p. 201.

61. Walji Bhai, 1893, p. 193.

62. Walji Bhai, 1893, p. 215. Pandit Walji Bhai developed this thesis in another small publication of 1895 in which he alleged that Nanak had been considerably influenced by Kabir whose sect was founded, according to Walji Bhai, by a secret sect called 'the Jesuits': 'On the plan of the Jesuits many sects were founded in India, one of which was the Kabir Panth which from its religious books clearly seems to have originated from the Christian religion .... Kabir Panthists are real Jesuits.' Pandit Walji Bhai: *The Dawn of Nanak Saheb's Religion*, Bombay, The Andra Vernacular Press, 1895, p. 5. A similar view of Nanak's followers being sympathetic towards the Christ figure is to be found in Youngson's *Forty Years of the Punjab Mission of the Church of Scotland*, p. 50, in which he claims that 'Sikhs seem to have advanced to that point where they should appreciate the Christian faith and acknowledge Jesus as Sat Guru, the True Teacher, in whose hand is the key, and beside whom none is able to open.' Walji Bhai, however, was not the first to associate Christian concepts of the deity with the figure of Hari. Clinton Loehlin in his *The Christian Approach to the Sikh*, writes of 'A Christian lady missionary, Miss Charlotte Marie Tucker, who learnt Punjabi and studied the *Adi Granth* in the original (who) wrote in 1848, " As far as I have read, the Guru Granth is wonderfully pure and spiritual. If you could substitute the name 'Almighty' for Hari and Lord Jesus for Guru, it might almost seem to be the composition of hermits in the early centuries, except that celibacy is not enjoined. One might call the Granth the book of learning and I feel humiliated that I with Gospel light, stand in spiritual contemplation and longing for the closest communion with the Deity.' (*Life and Letters of A.L.O.E.*, [A Lady Of England - Miss Tucker's *nom de plume*], p. 209.

knowledge of God, yet who, with his followers, needed to be brought to a fuller understanding of what was already within their scriptures. Whilst there are shades of a 'fulfilment theology' at work here, Walji's technique of imposing his own theology on what amounts, from a Christian perspective, to an alien system is highly dubious, not only in terms of the technique itself but also because of the suspect nature of his scriptural quotations and his misreading of history.

Yet one must recognise that Walji was attempting to take his readers one stage further from the concept, beloved of many Indians, of Jesus the Teacher. The fact that he chose to write about doctrine is an attempt to break away from the Indians' demand for the 'Christ of India' in favour of a more traditional Christology. Thus can be seen the tension within the process of indigenisation. For Walji indigenisation necessitates exposing the already present Christ figure but imposing a 'Western' Christian expression of faith and theology, whereas for other Indians the need is to free the Christ figure from the shackles of Christian theology thus to be interpreted in Indian rather than 'Western' Christian terms. Walji's work must also be seen in terms of an attempt to build bridges between the two faiths. It also shows that he refused to accept the otherness of Sikhism.

A second local Christian to whom one must pay tribute is Padri Daud Singh. Whilst reports were written of his pastoral work[63] by C.M.S. missionaries no mention was made of his writings. It is significant that mission history is not local church history viewed and written from an indigenous perspective. Consequently there is often more concentration and greater value placed on the work of expatriate missionaries than indigenous Christians.

Padri Daud Singh, to give him a title used by his Panjabi fellow Christians, published in 1873 a translation of Matthew's Gospel under the title of *Mangalsamachar*. It was no simple translation but a poem

---

63. Of Daud Singh, H.M.Clark wrote that he was of 'good bearing, stature and manner but also as an ex-devotee he was well-versed in the holy books, maxims and philosophies of the Sikhs. He was of simple faith and transparent sincerity, and he was untiring and eloquent in fervent preaching of the Gospel.' *Robert Clark of the Punjab - Pioneer and Missionary Statesman*, London, Andrew Melrose, 1907, p. 101.

written in verse according to strict poetic forms. His task was doubly difficult since not only was he to translate accurately but also obliged to conform to set poetic principles. In addition to his poetic contribution his was a very early attempt to use Panjabi expressions and phrases to articulate the Christian faith. Thus he uses the term *paramatama* - 'the supreme or universal soul' for the Holy Spirit and *Is* to represent 'Lord' rather than Jesus. Those of his day who read the poetry of Guru Nanak would have found familiar vocabulary.[64]

We find a similar contribution on the part of Tahil Singh who, in 1910, published his story of Jesus Christ in Panjabi verse under the title of *Sat Swami Nihalank Autar Prabhu Jisu Masih* (The True Master and Sinless Incarnation, the Lord Jesus Christ).[65] In it he makes reference to his own faith as a Christian by stating that the blood of Jesus - *Jisu ka khun* - redeems a person from sin. He further describes himself as a *kavi*, a poet, and someone who searches the scriptures - *khoj anjil*. He uses a particular form of poetry called *cand*, a term rooted in the Sanskrit *candas*, linked with the verb 'to praise.'

His major contribution to an indigenous Christology is his use of titles for Christ which come directly from Sikh theology. Thus he calls Christ the True Master (*Sat Swami*); Sinless *(Nihalank)*; Incarnation (*Autar*), Lord (*Prabhu*); True Teacher (*Satigur*); King (*Raja*); Internal ruler who guides humankind (*Antarjami*); Teacher (*Guru*); Chief (*Sardar*). He also introduces various Christian doctrines articulated in a Panjabi mode e.g. Jesus having paid the ransom (*jamni*) for humankind; Jesus as incarnation (*autar*); the incarnation as being truly human (not a shadow, as, he suggested, *avtar* is portrayed in the Indian traditions); the need for new birth and the incorporation into the 'true congregation (*sat sangat*) and the final judgment.

---

64. See: James Massey: 'Literary Heritage of Panjabi Christians: An Analysis', in *Bulletin of the Christian Institute for Religious Studies,* Vol. 21, No. 1, January, 1992. pp. 10-23. Padri Daud Singh: *Mangalsamachar*, Ludhiana, Mission Press, 1873. James Massey, the erstwhile General Secretary of the I.S.P.C.K., has managed to collect a number of tracts and booklets, many of which would otherwise have been lost. Indeed the literary heritage of Panjabi Christians is mainly forgotten by the Panjabi Christians themselves – Massey, 1992, p. 11.

65. Published by Panjab Religious Book Society, Anarkali, Lahore, 1900.

Thus Daud Singh and Tahil Singh from a one-time Sikh perspective, together with their colleagues Imam-ul-Din Shabaz, Musa Khan 'Khan'[66] and Jawahar Das from erstwhile Muslim and Hindu perspectives, opened up Christian theology to expression in Panjabi thought forms eminently familiar and deeply rooted in the religious traditions of the Panjab.

On a practical note we move to the legacy of Shauman, the erstwhile Kaiser Singh, at which point we have to recognize that the process of indigenisation is not confined to theology. Sikhs are immediately recognisable by their outward appearance and, similarly, a Sikh *Gurdwara* can been seen from a considerable distance away by the *nishan sahib* - a pennant - flying above the place of worship and hospitality. So it was that a 'flag for Christ' eventually was flown over the roof-tops of Amritsar. This was the dying wish of this first convert baptised in Amritsar by the C.M.S. missionaries on 3 July 1853. Kaiser Singh was previously a *granthi* who, on baptism, took the name Shamaun - Simeon. It is reported that in the mid 1860s as he lay dying Shamaun said, 'I see many flags for many gods and religions all over the city, but none for the Truth. Take my property, and let there be raised a flag for Christ, that my countrymen may know He too has come to Amritsar.' Eventually Shamaun's house and jewellery were sold and a hall built over which was flown his 'flag for Christ', a white cross on a red ground.[67]

Whilst Pandit Walji Bhai refused to accept the 'otherness' of Sikhism and began the work of building bridges which Tahil Singh strengthened by his use of a familiar theological vocabulary. Kaiser Singh's contribution, though, not on an intellectual plain, was nonetheless significant in the first steps in the process of the indigenisation of the faith particularly with regard to the Sikh milieu. Yet these qualities were rarely appropriately recognised by the English missionaries. So, for instance, in summing up the work of the Rev'd Daud Singh it was acknowledged that whilst 'he knew no English, to say nothing of more recondite Latin, Greek or Hebrew ... (he) was lamentably deficient in the merest rudiments of

---

66. 'Khan' composed a love story written in a Persian tradition based on the book of Esther. The nature of its presentation would have been familiar since the form used was that of the much loved *Hir-Ranjha* story.

67. H.M.Clark: *Robert Clark of the Panjab - Pioneer and Missionary Statesman.*, London, Andrew Melrose, 1907, pp. 67 & 246f.

education, as that term is understood in the Occident. But for all that he was equipped and gifted with attainments of a far higher character for work amongst Panjabis.'[68] The attainments are not defined, no mention is made of his translation work. It is no wonder that James Massey opens one essay with he words: 'The literary heritage of Punjabi Christians is both ignored and forgotten. It is ignored because scholars (of the) Punjab - local as well as outsiders (including missionaries) - have not taken into account the contribution made by Punjabi Christians towards the development of their mother-tongue, Punjabi. The focus has always been on the contribution of missionaries and Europeans to the Punjabi language. Even if any reference is made to the works of Punjabi Christians, these have been included as part of the missionaries' works.'[69]

By the turn of the century, indigenous Christians had presented a Jesus figure who was clothed in Sikh apparel: the 'True Teacher', the 'Chief'; the 'Internal Guide'. In effect they portrayed a Nanak substitute, who, they hoped, would appeal to their Sikh peers. It is a process not dissimilar to the sanskritisation of Indian theology which some commentators may say is an attempt to justify to fellow Indians the decision to become a Christian. Was this too close to syncretism for their expatriate missionary colleagues? Is this one reason for their theological contribution's being virtually ignored?

This situation is even more exacerbated if one considers the scant preparation undertaken by missionaries. This is fairly well illustrated by the discussion at the World Missionary Conference held in Edinburgh in 1910. There strategies were discussed including the preparation of missionaries. In words which echoed the call made by Keene for specialist workers, many acknowledged the inadequacy of their training. The Report of Commission V makes this clear. The experiences of the participants were printed anonymously and reflect great frustration:

> I went to India without any knowledge practically of the people I was among. I was obliged to pick up anything I have learnt by degrees, through intercourse with the people in ordinary work. I have always felt this to be a great disadvantage.'

68. Clark, 1907, p. 101.
69. Massey, 1992, p. 10.

'Men thus prepared (through the normal theological education of the day) are not armed to meet the exceedingly complicated problems which face the Christian Church in every part of India. If they do succeed in solving them, they do so more by happy practical genius than through understanding them. The average missionary of today has no reasoned conception of the relation of Christianity to other religions, except the good old contrast of one truth and many errors. He is not prepared in any sense for estimating an alien faith. He is not in a position to appreciate spiritual excellence or moral character if they are on lines other than his own; too often he does not know even where to find the information necessary for understanding the barest elements of the civilisation around him; nor has he been introduced to those large social questions which inevitably arise when a people is passing over from one religion to another.[70]

In the light of this calls were made for much more adequate training for new missionaries. Indeed prior to the conference J.N.Farquhar responded not only to the questionnaire sent to all delegates, but also made recommendations with regard to the 'Study of the Field'. He suggested that at home the missionary study Old and New Testaments; Systematic Theology; Growth of the Kingdom; Philosophy of Religion; Apologetics. On arrival 'he' should be encouraged to study the Religions of the World and the religions, history and civilisation of the particular field, also the classical language if there be one.[71]

Had such a programme of missionary formation been established for those working in the Panjab there would have been a better understanding of the Sikh faith. Sadly such understanding was inadequate or reflected the particular manifestation of the Sikhism of the day, for at Edinburgh in 1910 there was a tendency to make little distinction between Sikhism and Hinduism. This may have been due in no small way to the response to the above-mentioned questionnaire made by C.F.Andrews. In preparation for Edinburgh, Andrews talked with a Sikh:

70. World Mission Conference 1910 Report of Commission V, *The Training of Teachers*, Edinburgh and London, Oliphant, Anderson and Ferrier, p. 165f.
71. Report as above pp. 280 & 283.

I asked a leading Sikh Priest in Delhi if his religion was a separate religion, or if he would wish to be reckoned in with Hinduism, and to my surprise he said he would wish to be reckoned with Hinduism.[72]

Likewise other delegates were inclined either to fail to distinguish between Sikhism and Hinduism or present Sikhism as an attempt to 'unite' Hinduism and Islam.[73] Thus Wherry on being asked what elements of the faith of others might be considered a bridge which may aid the presentation of the Gospel indicated that amongst Sikhs were such matters as 'faith in a personal God, their rejection of Brahmanical rule; their faith in Incarnation and hope for the Sinless One, and much in their beliefs which seem to have been learned from Christian teachers.'[74]

Whilst such a phrase as 'their faith in Incarnation' may reflect Wherry's lack of understanding, it is only proper to point out that at this time Sikhism was undergoing a period of upheaval and disorientation to the extent that one leading Sikh, Baba Gurbaksh Singh Bedi, the son of Baba Sir Khem Singh Bedi, made a public statement that Sikhs were Hindus and Bhai Autar Singh[75] 'maintained in a couple of tracts published a year later, that the Sikh Gurus had worshipped gods and goddesses, accepted no Muslims as their followers and maintained the distinctions of castes.'[76]

Among the delegates from the Panjab there was a variety of opinion as to the theological stance which missionaries might take. Wherry, whose work was not primarily with the Sikhs, was of the opinion that

---

72. World Missionary Conference typed reports for Commission IV, Vol. 2. p. 31, courtesy of WCC, Geneva. Andrews' response to his Sikh interlocutor is not without reason. He knew Sikhs well - 'Some of my most cherished days in all my religious experiences of the East have been spent amongst the Sikhs.' He sympathetically reported the events of the Jallianwala Bagh massacre and even went to Vancouver to advocate citizens' rights for Sikhs in Canada. That he should have taken the stand he did seems most uncharacteristic. (See: Daniel O'Connor: *The Testimony of C.F. Andrews*, Madras, 1974.)

73. e.g. Farquhar portrays Nanak as the disciple of Kabir who tried to 'create a doctrine which both Hindus and Mohammedans could confess'. W.M.C. typed reports for Commission IV, Vol. 2 p. 247. W.R.James who had previously worked in Bengal but who responded from Shimla described Sikhism as 'a cross between Mohammedanism and Hinduism'. - typed reports, Vol. 2 p. 516.

74. W.M.C. typed reports for Commission IV, Vol. 3 p. 540.

75. Bhai Autar Singh was a protege of Baba Sir Khem Singh Bedi, a member of an influential Panjabi family and founder member of the Amritsar Singh Sabha.

76. J.S.Grewel: *The Sikhs of the Punjab*, New Cambridge History of India, Cambridge, 1990, p. 146. The implications of this matter are dealt with in greater detail in a following chapter on the response of Sikhs to the missionaries and their faith.

'the principle of destructive criticism is bound rapidly to undermine the faith of Hindus and Moslems in their own sacred books. A struggle is sure to come, and that soon, which will shake the faith of many, but the result will be the establishment of the Bible upon the ruins of Veda and Qur'an!'[77] Yet by the same token it was also Wherry who said that the 'Christian preacher should manifest toward the people the Spirit of love which characterizes his Master's Ministry on Earth. It is love that wins.'

W.R.James took a less aggressive line than his American counterpart and suggested, 'By general admission on the field, missionaries, and especially native evangelists, erred in the past through indulging too much in denunciation of other faiths. A more excellent way is the rule of today. Our Lord did not tell his disciples when he sent them out into all the world to preach to denounce any system. What he told them was to preach the gospel.'[78]

Given the input made by C.F.Andrews and the lack of its being contradicted by fellow missionaries the opinion taken towards Sikhism by the participants of Edinburgh 1910 is that it is a sect of Hinduism which is on the wane. A reference given in the Report of Commission IV - *The Missionary Message in Relation to Non-Christian Religions* is not by any means positive:

> Even in those thorough-going forms of theism which arose from contact with Islam, we see the power of the environment dragging down the higher tendency. Thus, for example, one of the most hopeful protests against idolatry and in favour of monotheism was that made by Nanak, the founder of the Sikh religion early in the Sixteenth Century. Today, however, in the Golden Temple in Amritsar, the Granth, i.e. the sacred book of the Sikhs, is accorded reverence which can scarcely be distinguished from idolatry. It is fanned by priests all day long, and offerings of flowers are brought to it by the people. It is interesting to know that there is some hope that a reform movement may develop in the Punjab, the object of which would be to lay renewed emphasis upon the monotheistic teaching of Nanak.[79]

---

77. Wherry: W.M.C. 1920 Comm. IV typed reports, Vol. 3 p. 541.
78. James: Typed Reports p. 523.
79. W.M.C. 1910, Report of Commission IV, *The Missionary Message in Relation to Non-Christian Religions*, Edinburgh, Oliphant, Anderson & Ferrier, p. 184.

Nevertheless, there arose a positive note from Edinburgh 1910 which represents an attitude similar to that of the call made by both Keene and Guilford for the study of the faith of the people among whom missionaries work. W.H.T. Gairdner wrote with regard to world religions that there was

> ....a general consensus that, representing as they do so many attempted solutions to life's problem, they must be approached with very real sympathy and respect; that they must be *studied*, if only to bring the evangelist in touch with the minds of his hearers. More than that, the conviction has grown that their 'confused, closed-world' will be found to be 'shot through and through with the broken lights of a hidden sun'. And, these things being true, another conviction has dawned - Christianity, the religion of the Light of the World, can ignore no lights however 'broken' - it must take them all into account, absorb them all into its central glow.[80]

Such a general consensus could not have taken place had attitudes to other faiths remained unchanged from those taken by sending agencies. The history of the encounter of individual missionaries with Sikhs well illustrates the development of this attitude. By change of circumstances, however, witness among the Sikhs was no longer to be the dominant work of the Panjab mission. The first hints of a change of direction was to be found in the C.M.S. Annual Report for 1884/85 in which a Mr Bateman reported that:

> ....(t)here is a movement among the lowest classes, many hundred of whom have been baptized in the neighbourhood by the Sialkot missionaries (American Presbyterian). Most of them are exceedingly ignorant, and are likely to be a stumbling block to their better-born neighbours, but on that very account they claim our sympathy and effort.[81]

80. W.H.T.Gairdner: *Edinburgh 1910: An Account and Interpretation of the World Missionary Conference*, Edinburgh, Oliphant, Anderson and Ferrier, 1910, quoted in Kenneth Cracknell: *Justice, Courtesy and Love*, London, Epworth Press, 1995, p. 264.
81. C.M.S. Annual Report 1884/85 p. 112. 'A lame, dark man', to quote Andrew Gordon, *Our India Mission*, Philadelphia, 1888, p. 422, was baptized by the Rev'd S.Martin. Following Ditt, were hundreds of thousands of people who came from the lower classes and who thus turned the church's attention to work to uplift the 'Untouchables'.

H.U. Weitbrecht also reported the baptism of an 'old man named Kanda' in Batala[82] and missionaries from other societies found themselves caught up in what became known as the mass movement of so-called 'Untouchables' to Christianity. It was a timely occurrence as far as some were concerned since missionary zeal was in need of renewed hope:

> Some societies at home, made somewhat timid and unfaithful by the constant demand of their adversaries for large success, and by their own ignorance of the tremendous difficulties in the way of conversions among Hindoos proper, are showing symptoms of weariness and diminished zeal...[83]

Such a new direction of work brought converts in numbers beyond expectation or previous experience. This was an about-turn in missionary direction from the challenge of Sikhs whose faith gave them personal dignity and security and who were, therefore, difficult to convert, to a much more responsive group of people who felt they had everything to gain by turning to Christianity. The interest expressed by the Dalit community in Christianity meant that many missionary societies sent significant numbers of missionaries with the result that there was a change in emphasis. Sikhs were no longer seen as the target group.

---

82. C.M.S. Annual Report 1884/85, p. 115.
83. M.A. Sherring: *The History of Protestant Missions in India, 1706-1821*, London, Truebner & Co, 1875, p. 232, writing of the situation after 1860.

3

Burgeoning Cooperation

Thus far we have seen one particular trajectory, that which starts with the high hopes of the missionaries and the suspicions of Sikhs who were the original target group. As with any interaction of people there are varieties of attitudes taken, much dependant on the relationships established. We have seen a burgeoning respect for Sikhism on the part of Keene and Guilford. Certainly that was the case with regard to Macauliffe, but Trumpp coloured Sikh attitudes with his arrogant dismissal of their faith. Small wonder that suspicion and concern dominated so much of their response.

Yet this is not the whole story and to that we must turn. We have noted already that Sikhs were not dismissive of missionary tactics. Indeed they began to use the same forms of communication. We have seen the manner in which missionary activity was the genesis for the foundation of the Singh Sabha and the consequent reformation of the Sikh faith. Whilst there was undoubtedly a sense of competition, there was also a burgeoning cooperation and more positive interaction.

For this we must return to the 1920s and thus begin to recognise a process of development from competition to cooperation and mutual understanding. During that time the greater part of missionary work in the Panjab was among the so-called outcaste groups. However, not only Christians but Sikhs also were engaged in attempts to attract followers from the same social groups. The Singh Sabhas, the Chief Khalsa Diwan and the Akalis were all receiving new converts since Sikhism offered a rise in social status without the disadvantage of possible persecution or leaving the Indian tradition.[1] Thus by this time Sikhs were seen by

---

1.   N.Gerald Barrier: *The Sikhs and Their Literature*, Delhi, Manohar, 1970, p. xxxii.

Christian missionaries as competitors. Since most missionaries were involved with the 'mass movement' of Dalits to Christianity few gave themselves to an attempt to understand the Sikhs.[2] There was one major exception.

Clinton Loehlin

Clinton Loehlin was an American Presbyterian missionary who must be regarded as playing a most significant role in bringing about an atmosphere of mutual understanding and an appreciation of dialogue between people of the two faiths. He went to the Panjab in 1923 as a Princeton graduate and from then until his retirement forty-four years later worked in Lahore, Moga, Ludhiana, Jullundar, Tarn Taran, Amritsar and Batala. Much of his time in the early years was spent in itinerant village mission work in areas which were the Sikh heartland and it was then that he recognised the paucity of written material about the Sikhs which would enable the Christian missionary to understand their faith.

He wrote in the International Review of Missions of the difficulties faced by those who read the scriptures such as the lack of divisions between words in copies of the Guru Granth Sahib and the reluctance of Sikh Granthis to separate the words of the text since it was 'cutting

2 In his PhD thesis published later as *The Christian Community and Change in North India (1834-1914)* John C.B. Webster mentions (p.187f) an essay by C.W Forman and the work of Walji Bhai as being the only pieces of a scholarly nature to be published regarding the Sikh faith. This reflects the greater interest in the so-called 'lower classes'. However, whilst many were involved in the work amongst such people, some continued to seek the conversion of Sikhs:

"Among my prized possessions I have a lock of hair. But it is not that of any flaxen-haired child; it is from a grey old man who asked me to cut it.

Dyala was nearing 65 and, true to Guru Nanak, the founder of the Sikh religion, he had never allowed a razor to come near his head. But his friend Garibu often passed that way, and as they squatted together and gurgled at the water pipe, there was aroused a restlessness in the old man's being by tales of a certain Jesus of Nazareth who both saved and satisfied. And when the neighbour rose, yawning and stretching, he was always urged to come back and tell more.

One day the travelling preacher came and propounded the question: 'What doth hinder thee from being baptized?' Then there were deliberations and conferring with relatives until at last the day of readiness arrived. The missionary was called, the little upper room, reached by ladder outside, was set in order and there in the calm of an Indian evening three generations bent their heads to the Christian shears and their necks to the yoke that is easy.

What a time of rejoicing it was! As the long locks fell to the ground, a great burden rolled away. Father, son and grandson had cut off not only their hair but all connection with their fruitless

into pieces the body of our Guru'[3]; the multiplicity of languages used in the Granth's poetry; its largely obsolescent language; the lack of a dictionary of the Guru Granth Sahib and suitable commentaries. Quoting Macauliffe's opinion that the 'Granth Sahib thus becomes probably the most difficult work, sacred or profane, that exists...' he indicated this was 'probably the reason why there are among missionaries almost no authorities on Sikhism such as we have on Islam and Hinduism...'[4] Thereafter describing the nature of the Sikh scriptures, Loehlin briefly outlined Sikh theology, emphasising the doctrine of grace, asked significant questions relating to Sikhism's nature and the lack of knowledge of the faith outside the Panjab, the effects of modern textual and historio-grammatical criticism on the faith and finally asked: 'Is Christianity in any sense the crown or fulfilment of Sikhism, or are the two mutually incompatible? Does Sikhism contain the truth and spiritual power essential to eternal salvation? What teachings of Jesus would appeal directly to Sikhs?' He provided no answer at that stage in his career, rather he called for 'contemporary contributions to the solution of the living and vital problem of Sikhism and the Sikhs.'[5] As with Keene's similar suggestion, the request fell on fairly deaf ears since from the specific perspectives of church or mission related sources little material regarding Sikhism was published. Even the exception of the work of Loehlin's friend, the Yale scholar John Clark Archer, must be seen as coming from an academic rather than an ecclesial background and was more an exercise in comparative religion taking Sikhism as a model. He described Sikhism as an attempt to reconcile the Hindu and Muslim religions which eventually developed into 'an independent and conspicuous order of its

---

past. During prayer the revered family leader with his son and son's son bowed with hands clasped and heads shorn, and when the intercessor, unacquainted with all the names of those now for the first time to be remembered before the Throne, stumbled and searched, Dyala quietly supplied him the names, loath to let a single one left out. He had abandoned the vow of the Nazarite for the love of the Nazarene.' Howard E. Anderson: *Gospel Romance in the Huts of the Punjab*, New York, Revell & Co., 1925, p. 17f.

3.   The fact that critical methods demand an almost letter by letter analysis of the text of scripture means that if the same technique is used on the Sikh scripture, revered as it is as Guru, one is in effect dissecting that which is the Word, as much to be avoided as dismembering not simply a live human-being, but a saviour-figure.

4.   C.H.Loehlin: 'The Riddle of Sikhism' in I.R.M. Vol. 27, 1938, p. 227.

5.   Loehlin (1938) p. 232.

own'[6] and in so doing confirmed Loehlin in his recognition of the distinctiveness of Sikhism, which faith he continued to study.

Loehlin was also engaged in a translation of the Bible into Panjabi published in 1959. He reflected on this work in a paper presented to the Punjab History Conference in March 1968. In it he rehearsed the many difficulties inherent in cross-cultural communication and indicated the need for translation work to be always done by a committee. Two Sikhs are said to have sat on one such working group to enable translators to express themselves in a Panjabi cultural idiom.[7] The resulting translations, like those into other Eastern languages, Loehlin claimed, became more vivid and meaningful than is the case in Western languages. Similarly because many Panjabis are farmers they would have well understood the Hebrew Bible with its closeness to daily pastoral life.[8]

Loehlin's later working life coincided with that of many who contributed to the S.C.M. 'Christian Presence' series and much of his nature reflects their philosophy.[9] Whilst his work in the Panjab started in the 1920s, from our perspective his most significant contributions were made after Indian Independence in 1947 when the Church recognised that it existed in a new situation in which the Christian faith was to be distinguished from its past with its association with Western political, economic and cultural aggression. Likewise, in deep humility, many Christians were able to recognise that God had not left 'him'self without witness so that one could approach other faiths in the expectation that the love of God could be discovered in and through others. Though one may disagree with one's partners in dialogue one has to respect his/her integrity. In his editorial Introduction to William Stewart's *India's Religious*

---

6. J.C.Archer: *The Sikhs in Relation to Hindus, Moslems, Christians and Ahmmadiyyas: A Study in Comparative Religion.* Princeton U.P., 1946, p. v. This statement is not as clear-cut as what he had heard in an interview with Bhai Vir Singh at his house in Amritsar on 1 June 1937. In his diary entry he quotes the Bhai: 'Sikhism is not an eclecticism, as the Western books all say, not an attempt by Nanak to combine Islam and Hinduism. Its mission is and was purification...' Cathaline Alford Archer: *John Clark Archer – A Chronicle,* Hamden, Connecticut, private publication of three diaries of visits to India in 1917/18, 1937 & 1946/7, 246 typed pages, Dec., 1959, p. 79.

7. Conversation with the Rev'd Rashid Choudhury in Batala, April 1994.

8. C.H.Loehlin: 'The History of the Gurmukhi Punjabi Bible' in *Proceedings of the Punjab History Conference,* Vol. III, March 1968, pp. 187-190.

9. e.g. George Appleton; Kenneth Cragg; Raymond Hammer; Peter Schneider, William Stewart.

Frontier, Max Warren writes: 'We have to try to sit where they sit, to enter sympathetically into the pains and griefs and joys of their history and see how (they) have determined the premises of their argument. We have, in a word, to be 'present' with them.'[10] Loehlin's manner was a fine example of this approach, to the extent that he won many friends among, and was trusted by, the Sikh community.

His period of work covered the time of Independence when millions of people were displaced. But the very evils which were inherent in Partition also brought a new impetus for reconciliation. Since the 1880s when the mass movements of 'outcastes' were searching for a more meaningful place in society, both Sikhs and Christians had tried to attract them into their respective folds. 1947 saw many Christians actively supporting Sikh refugees from Pakistan through the work of the mission hospitals. There were, of course, some Christians who continued to maintain old rivalries but Loehlin was convinced that hostility could not be the attitude Christians should take. He rejected aloofness or separation and wrote of the discontinuity inherent in some of the attitudes of the Tambaram Conference of 1938 that this ... 'attitude breeds communalism, which is rampant in India. Its dangers were dramatized in the Partition rioting of 1947. Enough of it.'[11]

In Loehlin one sees a missionary who has taken a step beyond the 'fulfilment' theory to an attitude of cooperation. He recognised that some may see Christ as the 'True Guru', the 'Sinless Incarnation' but also had to acknowledge the failure of the Church: 'Where is the Sermon on the Mount fulfilled in the Christian Church? With the Sikhs, at any rate, who judge by the fruit of the tree, and who even might claim that Sikhism is the fulfilment of Christianity, being later in time, we might as well abandon fulfilment as an immediate approach, however much we may believe in it as the culmination of all history.'[12]

Taking his lead from Archer,[13] Loehlin was convinced of the need to venture into the field of cooperation, not knowing what the future

10. William Stewart: *India's Religious Frontier*, London, S.C.M., 1964, p. 15.
11. C.H.Loehlin: *The Christian Approach to The Sikh*, London, Edinburgh House Press, 1966, p. 71.
12. Loehlin (1966) p. 72.
13. In July 1918 Archer had written in his diary: 'I am very excited over the big idea that came through last night, *Inter-Religious Cooperation* as a field of Christian activity ...it (the idea) has

would be but leaving that 'in the hands of him whose Will both faiths acknowledge to be the supreme guide in life.'[14] Given that both faiths emphasise the working out of God's purpose within history, Loehlin suggested that the Christian's emphasis must be on a kingdom-centred theology. 'Surely a realm,' he wrote, 'where brotherhood, justice and love predominate will appeal to those who daily pray, 'Help us to meet those beloved in whose fellowship Thy Name may come to mind... By Thy favour may there be welfare for all.'[15]

As one of few people whose experience enabled him to write about the Sikhs for readers of English, Loehlin produced three books significant for this study. *The Christian Approach to the Sikh*[16] was based on, and is better presented than his earlier *The Sikhs and Their Scriptures.*[17] The latter book was well received by the Sikh academics Ganda Singh and Pritam Singh who wrote in their preface: 'It is an objective study and an admirable introduction to the subject... The author has dealt with his thesis with just appraisal and sympathetic understanding....'[18] However, it is a short introduction and by its very nature cannot include detail or depth. Loehlin deals with the geographical setting of the Gurus; the racial roots of the Sikhs, Sikh characteristics, the history of the development of Sikhism after the death of Guru Gobind Singh, the Sikh Scriptures, both the Adi Granth and the Dasam Granth, and the official book on worship and discipline. A short chapter on Sikh theology was contributed by Dr Jodh Singh and an addition on Christianity and Sikhism as 'religions of grace' was made by Loehlin. The final chapters deal with the development of devotional religion (bhakti); Sufism and Sikhism; the Sikh orders; notes on some Sikh holy places; some

---

now broken on me with tremendous power.' [Cathaline Alford Archer (1959) p. 96.] Further Archer wrote: '... This cooperation recognizes as sincere the best claims made by the best non-Christians regarding their systems, lets them evaluate and recognises their evaluation. Yet argumentation is not ruled out, it is, in fact made way for in friendly spirit ... By this method I no longer fear to speak good of other faiths ... I am not theorizing in a closet. And I am systematically re-reading the New Testament for light on the subject. My whole thought is directed towards the problems of Christian missions...' p. 97.

14. Loehlin (1966) p. 73.
15. Loehlin (1966) p. 74.
16. London, Edinburgh House Press, 1966.
17. I.S.P.C.K./LPH, Delhi, 1958, 1974².
18. Loehlin (1958) Foreword to the 1958 edition.

translations from the two Granths and appendices of tables of the dates of the Gurus; other contributors to the scriptures and similarities and differences between Sikhism and Christianity.

Loehlin's Ph.D. gave rise to his third book: *The Granth of Guru Gobind Singh and the Khalsa Brotherhood*.[19] His purpose was to question the perception of many that Guru Gobind Singh whilst a warrior was not militaristic. The book essentially deals with issues relating to the study of the Tenth Guru and his writings and, therefore, whilst adding to the Western appreciation and understanding of the Guru is not primarily concerned with relations between the two faiths. Two issues are, however, significant. He gave notice of the founding, in 1967, of the Department of Comparative Religion at Punjabi University, Patiala and the development of the 'Christian Institute of Sikh Studies' at Baring Christian College in Batala. Secondly, he made a very strong plea for careful textual critical study of the Kartarpuri Granth, widely believed to be the manuscript dictated by Guru Arjan. Likewise he supported calls from Sikh scholars such as G.S.Grewel and S.S.Bal for research on historical as well as textual problems within the Sikh tradition.

Shortly before he retired, Loehlin's acceptability within the Panjabi Sikh community was such that in December 1965 he was invited to speak at a meeting held to celebrate the birthday of Guru Gobind Singh at the 'Golden Temple'. He spoke on Guru Gobind Singh and the Emperor Aurangzeb and was appreciated by the congregation. Moved by the experience he wrote: 'I felt I had been through a unique experience, which indeed it was, for they told me that this was the first time a Christian missionary had been asked to speak in the Golden Temple. I was pleased that I was introduced to the audience as a Christian missionary, for this was another evidence that Sikhs and Christians are coming closer to each other.'[20]

Loehlin's contribution does not, however, remain at this point. He and his wife chose to move to California in retirement, to live in Marysville (Yuba County). This is in the light of the significant numbers of Sikhs who had settled in the Panjab-like Central Valley of California. He was

---

19. Lucknow Publishing House, Lucknow, 1971.
20. Unpublished 'Letter from Batala', February, 1966.

invited to support the foundation of a local Sikh Gurdwara and regularly contributed to a Panjabi language programme on Radio KUBY.[21]

Loehlin left as his heritage a number of valuable resources. First was the goodwill he established with Sikhs, including leading scholars who recognised his sincere attempt to understand the Sikh faith as far as anyone of another faith is able to do. Secondly, his explorations into the comparative field established a number of areas of theology in which Sikhs and Christians would be able to find common ground for dialogue and further exploration. These were: the Nature of God; the place of Grace in salvation/liberation; the quest for religious reconciliation; missionary service and the future life.[22]

Thirdly, he was closely involved in the establishment of the Christian Institute of Sikh Studies at Baring College in Batala. Within Loehlin's own working life-time relationships between many people of the two faiths moved from suspicion and competition to cooperation.

The Christian Institute of Sikh Studies

It was in Batala that Mian Sadiq, a trusted local Christian opened a mission on behalf of C.M.S. The Church of England Zenana Missionary Society thereafter opened five schools for young women in the city and these were followed by the opening of a boys' school by the Rev'd Francis Henry Baring in 1878. Baring Union Christian College developed from Baring's original boys' school and it is within the college grounds that the Christian Institute of Sikh Studies is to be found within easy reach of Amritsar, some 25 miles distant. Its constitution was adopted in 1966 and states as its purpose:

a)   to engage in study and research in the field of Sikh history, religion and culture;

b)   to encourage interest in the study of Sikhism and the Sikhs by the Christian Church, and to impart an understanding of Sikhism, both historical and contemporary, to members of the Church;

---

21. Data sourced through a copy of a diary written by Loehlin's wife, Eunice and kindly sent by Dr John Loehlin and his sister, Margaret Shafer.
22. C.H.Loehlin: 'Guru Nanak's Religion with Special Reference to Christianity.' in *Studies In Sikhism and Comparative Religion*, Guru Nanak Foundation, New Delhi, Vol. 1, #1, October, 1982. Also published in (ed) Gurmukh Nihal Singh: *Guru Nanak - His Life, Time and Teachings*, Delhi, Guru Nanak Foundation/National Publishing House, 1969.

c) to stimulate and maintain dialogue and communication between Christians and Sikhs;

d) to produce and distribute relevant literature.

Whilst most of the members of the Managing Committee were Christians three members could be co-opted, some of whom were distinguished Sikh scholars and leaders, thus formally establishing the cooperation which the Rev'd Dr Clinton Loehlin, its first Director sought and inspired.[23]

However, the establishment of the Institute was not universally greeted with pleasure. Some Sikhs questioned the Christians' motive for studying Sikhism and Hindus wondered if Sikhs and Christians were attempting to join forces against them. There were also Christians who thought that the Institute would be a centre for Sikh worship and thereby undermine the Christian character of Baring Union College.[24] Suspicion and mistrust were not far away.[25] An explanation for the former criticism may be found in the fact that in the Nineteenth Century many Christians studied other faiths in order to refute them. However, later, as is evidenced by the work of Guilford and Loehlin, and giving rise to the foundation of the Institute, a new understanding may have come into play as indigenous Christians refused to reject their entire cultural and spiritual heritage. 'These scholars believed that Christ was not the refutation of the Indian heritage but its proper fulfilment. Some even saw that Christ who provided this fulfilment was not the Christ who had been defined in exclusively western terms. This theological outlook, which saw Christ

---

23. Dr Trilochan Singh writes of the period of 1930-1960, roughly coincidental with Loehlin's work: '....relations between Sikhs and Christians were at their best.' Trilochan Singh (1968) p. 72.

24. *Bulletin of the Christian Institute of Sikh Studies*, Vol. 3 No. 1, January 1974. Welcome address by John Webster to the conference on 'Popular Religion in the Punjab Today' p. 6.

25. See: Gurdarshan Singh Dhillon: 'The Sikhs and the British' in Punjab Past and Present Vol. XXIV No. II, Oct. 1990 p. 454: '...the British allowed, under the protection of their wings, free play to the Christian missionaries to attack the identity and ideology of the Sikh religion, its history and institutions. These missions were located in the heart of the Sikh areas like Batala. The purpose and work of these missions are well known. The journalistic work of McLeod, who has for long years been a functionary of the Batala Christian Centre, can be taken to be typically representative and revealing of the aims and objectives of such centres.'

at work redemptively in and revealing himself through Hindu, Sikh and Muslim religion, led to a more positive appreciation of and a greater willingness to learn from religions other than Christianity.'[26]

Prior to the formal opening of the Institute, Baring College hosted a colloquium of Sikh and Christian leaders in October 1963 sponsored jointly with the Christian Institute for the Study of Religion and Society in Bangalore. In keeping with the practical nature of Sikhism, the Director of CISRS suggested that people of both faiths share a common humanity and that they must both respond to seek ultimate meaning and destiny in life and share the task of building a society in which all can realise their dignity and enter mutual service. Differences between the faiths were not to be overlooked but explored to facilitate better understanding. The tone of the report[27] gives the impression of much discussion, but a rather one-sided debate in which the majority of papers presented were with regard to Sikh themes. Of the two recorded papers by Christian authors Loehlin's deals with the history of the Church in the Panjab and the need for Sikhs and Christians to work together in nation-building and that of the Rev'd Dr Herbert Jai Singh takes up the issue of the commonality of both faiths but goes on to develop a specific Christian theology of approach to Sikhs. He suggested that whilst people of both faiths share a common humanity, the two religions are distinctive and thus there is need for a mutual search for understanding. Both faiths recognise sin, but do not share the same concept of sin, both must eschew communalism and seek freedom from prejudice. Yet dialogue does not preclude clear articulation of the distinctive message of the two faiths. Jai Singh hoped that mutual understanding would lead to mutual help in theological formation.[28]

At this early, if not first, post-independence meeting between the two faiths, it is significant that Herbert Jai Singh points out three issues:

- the distinctiveness of Sikhism, thus recognising the integrity of the faith;

---

26. Webster (1974) p. 7.

27. See: Religion and Society - Bulletin of the Christian Institute for the Study of Religion and Society, Vol. XI, No. 1, March 1964. pp. 1-7.

28. Herbert Jai Singh, Religion and Society, Vol. XI, No. 1, March 1964, pp. 103-107.

- the common role in nation-building, thus making an important claim for both Sikhism and Christianity, in particular, as legitimate Indian religions;
- the need for minority faiths to be mutually supportive.

The conference laid down the foundations for future collaboration in terms of the foundation of the CISS.

From its early days the institute organised a number of conferences and seminars, the papers from which were often later published as books such as: *Popular Religion in the Punjab Today*, 1974, *The Nature of Guruship*, 1976, *Rituals and Sacraments in Indian Religions*, 1979, *Marxism and the Religions of India: Spirit and Matter*, 1979, *The Concept of Guru in Indian Religions*, 1982, *The Problem of Death and Suffering in Indian Religions*, 1983. All but the first, which was edited by the Rev'd Dr. John C.B.Webster, were edited by his successor, Dr Clarence O. McMullen. As their titles indicate the conferences, and thereby the books, dealt with a wider dialogue than that between Sikhs and Christians. The work of publication and the education of Christians together with attempts to foster mutual understanding was also reflected in the publication of a history of *The Amritsar Diocese*, by McMullen, Webster and Caleb; of Webster's *The Nirankari Sikhs* and James Massey's *Christianity, An Introduction* in Panjabi. There were other shorter publications such as Dr Ganda Singh's translation of the Sermon on the Mount, and a report of *Religion and Status of Women in the Panjab*. Twice yearly the institute published a Bulletin.

In the 1970s the members of the Institute wished to publish a book on Sikh and Christian theology and to this end a seminar was held. The project, however, was considered too ambitious at the time and was abandoned since some manuscripts were never completed. However, the abandonment of the project may be as much due to differences in the way in which Sikhs and Christians reflect theologically. Sikhs are far more interested in religious experience than dogma. Indeed at a seminar on personal religious experience in March 1974 many participants came to the conclusion that doctrines, dogmas, rituals and religious organisation, rather than being expressions of, and vehicles for, the transmission of religious experience tend to smother it.[29]

---

29. Director's Report 1974/75 CISS Archives.

Yet notwithstanding the regular publication of helpful material, dialogue between church members and their Sikh counterparts remained minimal. The education and involvement of the church was regarded as being the 'weakest area' of the Institution. The Church was described as 'not really interested' and many members regarded dialogue as being 'elitist.'[30] Some explanation may be found in the low self-image of the Panjabi Christians, coming, as most of them do, from a low caste background, some having gained a good education, but the vast majority being employed as landless labourers.[31] John C.B. Webster's work [32] gives further explanation. In the villages he surveyed Christians and Sikhs have very little to do with each other except in terms of work relationships where the Christians are at a disadvantage being the landless labourers on the Sikh landlords' lands. The life-style of the village was such that Christians were usually regarded as being of low rank, but where in some cases Christians found themselves on a sound financial basis they were often regarded as assertive. Members of both faiths had little knowledge of that of the other and considerable lack of interest. Indeed the term 'Christian' or 'Sikh' would very often be more a social label than one of religious identity. Where there was any dialogue it was between Christians and Mazhabi Sikhs whose equally lowly status meant that they were considered to be social equals. Webster in his tentative conclusion differentiates between the opportunities for encounter between the faiths in rural and urban contexts: 'Cities offer far more opportunities to break out of the pattern of relations set by custom than do villages. This makes inter-faith dialogue based on individual equality possible and allows knowledge, ideas, and spiritual insight to play a significant role in that dialogue.'[33]

As the work of the Institute evolved so a change in emphasis can be detected. Perhaps this is best reflected in two reports published in 1975 and 1983. Both were on Gospel themes, the former arising out of a

30. Director's Report, 1974. CISS Archives.
31. Clarence O. McMullen: 'The Self Image of the Christians in the Punjab' in *BCISS* Vol. 6 No. 1, January 1977, p. 17, quoting James Massey's paper 'Historical Background of the Self Image of Punjabi Christians'.
32. J.C.B.Webster: BCISS Vol. 6, p. 27 Special Number, 'Christians and Sikhs in the Panjab: The Village Encounter', pp. 24ff.
33. As above, p. 27.

working party of Pastors and Lay People on 'The Gospel for the Punjab' and the latter found its genesis in a seminar on 'Jesus Christ-The Life of the World: The Punjabi Context'. Both dealt with the centrality of the Cross, with the need to strengthen the faith and resolve of the Church and its need for commitment to the life of the Panjab. There are, however, significant differences.

In the former report the need for the educational programme for women and their involvement in the communication of the Gospel is stressed. This must be seen within the context of a Sikh milieu which encourages the equality of the sexes. Foremost, however, is the recognition that the Gospel is presented to people of other faiths and thus there are preconditions:

> One is prayerful preparation. Another is a genuine respect for and appreciation of them as persons (rather than as objects or targets) as well as the faiths they profess based on knowledge, understanding and sympathy. A third precondition is a knowledge of our own faith and an ability to relate it imaginatively to ideas, values, and world-views of our neighbours.[34]

The pamphlet concludes with a note encouraging 'deeds of love, service, reconciliation, as well as in striving for justice, especially for the poor. Christians need not perform such deeds only privately or through exclusively Christian agencies but should also join gladly with others in joint efforts for the common good.'[35] Thus the presentation of the Gospel is seen in both practical and strongly dialogical terms.

A change is to be found in the material published in 1983 on the WCC theme of 'Jesus Christ - the Light of the World'. The report of the discussions of this theme reflects the perception that the Church in the Panjab was weak, not reflecting the dynamic work of Christ,[36] which needs to show Christ's love through cross-bearing, root its rituals in the Panjabi culture and come out of isolation.[37] The pamphlet concentrates

---

34. 'The Gospel for the Punjab', pamphlet published by CISS, 1975, p. 3.
35. Webster: BCISS Vol. 6, p. 4.
36. 'Jesus Christ - The Life of the World: The Punjabi Context', pamphlet published by CISS, 1983, p. 2.
37. Webster: BCISS Vol. 6, pp. 2-4.

on the nature and role of the church and reflects little of the plural milieu in which it is to be found. Dialogue is scarcely mentioned, the core message is one of aligning the Church with those who are poor and persecuted, searching for the 'true Jesus who identified with the oppressed, hungry and exploited.'[38] Thus the concern of the seminar and, for that matter, the Church was with regard to the majority of its members and their peers - the Dalits.

This change in emphasis of the work of the Institute was not only reflected in the publication of the two pamphlets but also in terms of seminars conducted and the interests of one of the Directors, John C.B.Webster who was 'inclined to broaden the scope of the Institute to include all Punjabis, past and present'[39] However, a virtual moratorium on Christian-Sikh dialogue was essentially caused by the political and social developments of the 1980s, particularly resulting from the events which surrounded the invasion/liberation of the 'Golden Temple' in 1984. The Director's Report for 1987/88 indicated the dilemma:

> An uninhibited atmosphere is essential for a free flow to open and sincere exchange of ideas. Dialogue between communities involves mutual understanding, critical appreciation and balanced judgement. Punjab for the last several years has become a place where different religious communities as well as political authorities have been reinforcing each other's insecurities. Insecurity, as insecurity without access to genuine spiritual resources always does, leads to suspicion and consequently to closing of minds and hardening of hearts. These circumstances have not been conducive to the programmes of the Institute. It appears that if the situation in the Punjab does not improve, the Association must either seriously think of changing its location or bring some fundamental changes in its objectives. We are trying to diversify the programme for the Institute.'[40]

Subsequent reports reflect much the same state of affairs in terms of difficulties in holding seminars in Batala. By 1990/91 Clarence McMullen's was writing:

---

38. Webster: BCISS Vol. 6, p. 4.
39. BCISS Vol. 3, No. 1, January 1974, p. 8. Welcome address to the 'Popular religion in the Punjab Today' conference.
40. Director's Report, 1987/88.

The changed circumstances in the Punjab ... have made the idea of interfaith dialogue not only extremely difficult, but as virtually ineffective and inconsequential. During the last six years most of the seminars organised on interfaith dialogue generated more heat than light... One hopes that things are beginning to change and people are beginning to realize that it is better to sit together and talk about problems, hurts, struggles and aspirations than to let the distance between people and the consequent distrust and antagonism grow. [41]

By far the major emphasis was in terms of support for the Church in the Panjab and Christian Dalits in particular. This was also reflected in a change in the name from 'Sikh Studies' to 'Religious Studies' since ...'under the present circumstances in the Punjab the Institute is not in a position to do very much in the direction of interfaith dialogue - at least not through a structured and formal programme.'[42] Within a year, however, an optimistic note crept into the Institute due to the beginning of a return to normal life in the Panjab and hope was expressed that a programme of dialogue could be resumed as well as Dalit supporting work continued. This was partly due to the fact that by that time Dalit Presbyters of the Church of North India were in a position to convince the Diocese of the real need for Christian witness in the Panjab to be through social involvement in support of the oppressed classes.

Whilst not directly part of the work of the Institute one development within Sikh-Christian relations is more than worthy of mention, for it demonstrates the type of encounter encouraged. In the early 1990s a group of Sikhs from Village Baba Bakala near Beas approached Bishop Anand Chandu Lal of the Diocese of Amritsar with a request that an English medium school be opened in the village. Four teachers, Miss Shabnam Haque, M.A., B.Ed., Miss Veena Masih, M.A., B.Ed., Miss Anita Newton and Mrs Violet Gill, from Alexandra Girls High School in Amritsar were appointed to establish an 'extension' of the school and to teach there. Each day they travelled to the village, a distance of some 43 kms, by a car supplied by the Sikh village headman. Established in May 1993 with 58 pupils, both boys and girls, the number rose to 73 within

41. Director's Report, 1990/91.
42. Director's Report, 1991/92.

one year. At first 4 classes were established from Lower Nursery to Reception, but it was hoped to increase by one class per year. Few of the parents were educated and represent a cross-section of earners, but they made high demands of the teachers in terms of standards. On being asked why they wanted Christian teachers they responded that Christians are honest and hard-working and they wanted their children to be like that. Said Shabnam Haque: 'My prayer every day is that we will not betray their trust.' Each day all the children joined in Christian morning prayers. There were no R.E. lessons but the teachers are keen not to give a 'bookish' education only because life-style is important.[43]   Sadly within the new millennium the school was to close because of decreasing financial support.

The history of formal dialogue during the last thirty years of the Twentieth Century is evidently influenced considerably by three major factors. The first is with regard to personal relations. Loehlin had spent much of his missionary life in daily contact with leading members of the Sikh community. Many of them were the academic and intellectual elite, the security of whose breadth of vision and understanding enabled them to welcome the exploration of faith that interfaith dialogue represented. Those Christians who were involved were of a similar nature, such as John C.B. Webster and Clarence O. McMullen, whose writings have been the basis of much of the historical record of this period. However, this first factor was later outweighed by the political realities of the time, particularly during the 1980s when the Panjab was in turmoil. During such a period interfaith dialogue, particularly if it is mainly in terms of theological exploration, would have been regarded as having little relevance to social and political realities. Had interfaith dialogue been regarded as the search for an understanding of the partner's philosophy of life, then possibly such dialogue could have been an inherent part in the process of the search for communal peace and thus worth pursuing. The third factor to have influenced the encounter is that of the low self-regard of the Christians particularly and their almost constant struggle to find sufficient income to maintain family life. In such circumstances dialogue is perceived as not so much a luxury more as an irrelevance.

---

43. Details from a conversation with the teachers, Amritsar, 25:April:'94.

4

Increasing Understanding

We have seen how Clinton Loehlin's work established a pattern of cooperation and mutual understanding appreciated by many Sikh academics. This, however, was not the case for all and the development of the Christian Institute for Sikh Studies, even though it was devoted to the encouragement of dialogue, was viewed with suspicion on the part of some Sikhs who considered it to be an agent for proselytism. Whilst no Christian evangelical writers commented on its work, nevertheless there were some who saw it as their task to write of their faith in a way which, they hoped, Sikhs might respond by conversion. Thus there was within the Christian fold the familiar tension between those who sought mutual understanding through dialogue and those who felt it their duty to seek conversion. We turn first to a series of post – Independence evangelical writers and the nature of their witness to Sikhs of their Christian faith.

Each of the five evangelical Christian writers considered here presents Sikhism in a positive, if unfulfilled, light. K.V.Paul Pillai[1] writes of Sikhism as ...'one of the most dynamic of all Indian religions (which) comes nearer than all other religions to the concept of one God who reveals Himself through His prophets...'[2] In a similar vein the Rev'd Inayat Khan[3] attempts to show that similarities between the faiths do exist and considers the purpose of his booklet to be that of proving this to be the case by references to the scriptures of both faiths. E. Ahmad-Shah[4] holds Sikhism in a similarly positive light and like Pandit Walji Bhai of the previous century he attempts to find references to Christ in the Guru Granth Sahib.

---

1. K.V. Paul Pillai: *India's Search for the Unknown Christ*, New Delhi, Fazl Publishers, 1978.
2. Pillai (1978) p. 93.
3. Rev'd Inayat Khan: *SHABAD in Christianity and Sikhism*, Pub. by author, Ferozepore Cantt. c. 1961. p. 1.
4. E.Ahmad-Shah: *Sikhism and Christian Faith*, Lucknow, Lucknow Publishing House, n.d.

For each of the authors under consideration the starting points are
the similarities and common ground between the two faiths. However,
each defines such common ground in differing ways. For Khan it is to be
found in the concept of *shabad*/logos, present at Creation as its agent.[5]
Ahmad-Shah writes, in much more general terms, of the influence on
Nanak's way of life of the Roman Catholic Orders such as the
Benedictines, Franciscans and the Sisters of Charity and Mercy. Such
influence, he claims, increased during the time of Akbar the Great.[6] For
Pillai, 'Sikhism is very near liberal Christianity. There are many teachings
in Sikhism which are very similar to others in the Bible. The Sikh
concept of God is almost the same as that of the Hebrews.'[7]

All three suggest that Sikhs search after the truth, which, for Khan
and Ahmad-Shah, can partially be found in the Sikh scriptures if one
were to recognise in them, they argue, references to Jesus Christ. Pillai
takes a different line of argument suggesting that Guru Nanak comes
close to establishing the truth but does not declare it.

Khan discovers a hidden Christ through what might be considered
the misappropriation of the Sikh scriptures. He quotes the Guru Granth
Sahib to the effect that it is the *shabad* which is the agent of creation
and is personal.[8] He further suggests, through the misuse of the term
'three *gunas*' which are more correctly 'modes of being which govern
worldly existence,'[9] that the doctrine of the Trinity is to be found. He
also 'reveals' to Sikh readers the Third Person of the Trinity:

The Spirit is God, and the world is his handiwork.

God is Spirit and Spirit is in God and this recognition is given as a
gift by our true Guru.[10]

---

5. Khan (1961) p. 4f.
6. Ahmad-Shah, (n.d.) p. 87f.
7. Pillai (1978) p. 94.
8. *A.G.* p. 117.
9. *A.G.* p. 1003. Definition from C.Shackle: *A Guru Nanak Glossary*, London, SOAS, 1981, p. 101.
10. Khan (1961) p. 6; *A.G.*. p. 764, 1153. Of these passages, the former indicates the Sikh doctrine
    of panentheism where the Ultimate Reality is said to pervade the entire universe, and the latter
    is more accurately a reflection of the 'Brahman-Atman synthesis'.

Khan then develops the part supposedly played by the *shabad* in the quest for salvation claiming that:

> If *shabad* may die then we always have peace. Govind the true Guru has done sacrifice for us.[11]

He makes great play of the word *'Govind'* which usually refers to Krishna or God, but which he claims is a 'shepherd of cows' and '...(i)n India cows, like sheep in Palestine, stand for harmless and innocent people and the word 'shepherd' means one who looks after such people. Such was Christ.'[12] The death of *shabad* he claims is 'the gateway to victory over death for all men.'(sic): '(If) *shabad* may die then death will be no more. How can purpose be fulfilled without his death?'[13] Ahmad-Shah uses a similar technique to Khan in his attempt to demonstrate the Christ 'hidden' within the Sikh scriptures. Having given a short introduction to Sikhism, he establishes by a plethora of quotations from the Bible the Christian analysis of the human condition and its consequent remedy through Jesus Christ and follows this with the claim that Christ is presented as the goal of the Sikh search because:

> according to your (i.e. Sikh) scriptural version He carries in himself the supremacy (*sraisthya*), the sovereignty (*svarajya*) and the overlordship (*adhipatya*) over all beings. He is *prabhavapyari* (beginning and end). He is *Isa* (the lord), *Prabhu* (Potentate) and *Mahesvra* (the mighty Lord). Though so mighty and great, He is *samvatsyatha* (dwells with us) and is *atmasanstha* (indweller in the self)[14]

His confidence is such that he claims that Guru Arjan made a 'famous and far reaching significant statement concerning Jesus Christ' in his *Sukhmani,* a *var* (ballad) of which, Ispedi, he quotes as hailing 'Isa

---

11. Khan (1961) p. 10. supposedly quoting *A.G.* p. 364 which is better translated: 'He who dies in the Word, is for ever in bliss. He is united with (lit. meets, comes to) the true Guru, God.'

12. Khan (1961) p. 10.

13. Khan (1961) p. 11. Again *shabad* is not the subject of the verb 'to die', but rather it is the human being who dies 'in the Word' and does not die again for without dying in the Word one cannot reach liberation. The reference is with regard to the concept of *jivan mukta,* that is, the believer who is liberated whilst still alive.

14. Ahmad-Shah: p. 123.

(Jesus) as the king of all people, the destroyer of all forms of evil, protector and sustainer of the poor and needy and above all the conqueror of the Devil by putting him to death.[15]

By contrast with Khan and Ahmad-Shah, Pillai whilst acknowledging the similarities between Christianity and Sikhism, does not attempt to 'find' the Christ figure in the Sikh scriptures but maintains the 'otherness' of Sikhism reflected in the sentence: 'But what they do not have is the Saviour and Lord.'[16] Again for him there is a shortfall in Sikhism in which, whilst Guru Nanak recognises that salvation/liberation is possible only through the grace of God through faith in the Name, he does not name the Name whom Pillai declares to be Jesus Christ: 'To find out in clear terms about this Name we should go to the Bible where it is categorically stated about the name of Jesus.' [17]

All three writers finish their works with a call to faith - in Christianity. Khan recognises that the Sikh is less interested in the Church than in the figure of Jesus Christ and thus writes:

The reader of this booklet may have felt the attraction of his personality and the winsomeness of his love. This is his gentle knock. He is saying to you, "May I come in? I love you. I will save you and keep you for eternal life."[18]

Ahmad-Shah makes a similar plea: 'Come, O my Sikh brethren. Listen to Him and experience Him and find your salvation in Him.'

---

15. Ahmad-Shah:p. 124f. *Dudhya jan so koi arkar, kat deo us tujh nara naharkor.* Consider a messenger like (precious) milk, one who cuts off that fiery godless (devil). *Pun rakhshas ka kata sisa, shri asket jagat ke Isa.* At once he cut off Rakhshus's (devil's) head, the holy unique Isa (Jesus) of the world). *Popan bhishat gagan te bhai, sab ne an badhai dei.* Heaven's showered flowers from above, everyone came and congratulated Him. *Dhan dhan lokan ke raja, Dushat andah, gharib nawaza.* Blessed, blessed (Thou art) the King of all people evil destroyer and protector of the poor). *Akhil bhawan ke surjan hare, das jan mohe, lahu ubhare.* Creator of the undivided world (Thou art), consider me your servant (slave) my blood declares.

16. Pillai (1978) p. 94.

17. Pillai (1978) p. 95f. See also: 'The Biblical terms for God make the faithful Sikhs feel at home. However, this clear vision of God is dimmed and totally misdirected as they come to the teachings concerning their Gurus. Instead of the clear vision of God leading to the supreme Guru, the Lord Jesus Christ, who is the only one in whom God became man and dwelt among men, the seeking and searching mind of the Sikh leaders entered into the wilderness of deification of human beings who were totally deprived as anybody else in the world.' p. 97.

18. Khan (1961) p. 16.

Pillai dreams: 'How wonderful it would really be if the True and Eternal Guru, the Lord Jesus Christ, enters into the heart of a Sikh and becomes the life and the life-giver...'[19]

Two characteristics are to be found among the three authors considered:

- All impose on Sikhism their Christian understanding of the nature of humanity and humanity's relationship with God. They make little attempt to answer the problem as the Sikh sees it, i.e. human ignorance and the need to be liberated from *samsara*. They rather impose the need to find salvation from sin.

- Khan and Ahmad-Shah misappropriate Sikh scripture attempting to find within its pages references to Jesus Christ. It is as if they cannot acknowledge that truth cannot be found other than in the Christian Church's understanding of the figure of Jesus Christ.

The Sikhs are a target for mission not only in the Panjab, but in some parts of the Sikh diaspora, notably in the United Kingdom where in October 1994 In Contact Ministries wrote in terms of 'Regaining a Vision for the Sikh Community.'[20] A short description of Sikhs and Sikhism, especially in the British Isles, introduces readers to the need, as the above authors perceive to be the case, to witness to Sikhs which they claim...

> ... is in one way easier (than) witnessing to Muslims because Sikhs tend to recognise and be open to spirituality from all religions. On the other hand they are reluctant to be committed exclusively to Jesus. Furthermore, the Christian concept of basing a person's acceptance with God on the death of Jesus rather than on the merit of the person is a 'stumbling block'.

The quotation indicates the author's lack of knowledge of the Sikh faith since time and again the Gurus write of the futility of searching for liberation through merit since only through the Guru's grace can liberation be found. As with their Indian counterparts evangelicals in Britain stress Jesus as the 'only way' only to find that as being entirely unacceptable in Sikh understanding.

---

19. Pillai (1978) p. 98.
20. *In Contact Ministries* newsletter for October/November 1994.

James Canjanam Gamaliel

Back in India, Gamaliel responded to a request for a book written to enable the Sikh community to understand Christianity. With great honesty he makes no claim to be an expert in the field of Sikh studies and consequently makes use of his understanding of Hinduism in his presentation. Many Sikhs would dispute, for instance, his claim that '[m]any religious forces and trends of Hinduism and Islam met and converged in Nanak.'[21] Likewise the description of Sikhism as an 'amalgamation'[22] and 'syncretistic'[23] would be vehemently rejected. That said the short introduction to the Sikh faith should be seen as an encouragement to read further on the issue.

Gamaliel's interpretation of the Sikh understanding of God seems not to take into account the recognition on the Sikhs' part of the ineffable nature of the divine. Rather this is dismissed in terms of the god of the Adi Granth being 'a vague abstract power who is not concerned about the world, his creation. Such names as Sat Nam or Truth are abstractions. God's nature is described as omnipresent, as one who hides himself, manifests himself, deep, intense, unfathomable, limitless, infinite. What do these attributes mean for man (*sic*) in his problems, perplexities, in life situations? None can grasp [his] abundance. Is it not a negative description?[24] Sadly the author has failed to recognise not only God's infallibility but also humanity's limitations. Gamaliel's presentation of the concept of *jivanmukta* (one who is liberated whilst in this human life)[25] also presents difficulties.

Sikh readers would be distressed to see their faith as something which has 'sunk to the level of polytheism.'[26] To offer as an alternative a Gospel message which is essentially Western in nature does not do full justice to the original quest, that is, 'to reveal the one God which Sikhism is seeking.'[27]

---

21. Gamaliel, J.C. (1997) *The Gospel of God to the Sikh*, p. 15.
22. Gamaliel, J.C. (1997), p. 16.
23. Gamaliel, J.C. (1997), p. 17.
24. Gamaliel, J.C. (1997), p. 52.
25. Gamaliel, J.C. (1997), p. 67.
26. Gamaliel, J.C. (1997), back cover.
27. Gamaliel, J.C. (1997), back cover.

In contrast with the previous evangelical writers Gamaliel depicts Sikhism in far more negative terms and offers not a Gospel message couched in the culture of the Panjab but an uncompromising Western Gospel which takes little or no account of the Sikh faith's founding context.

The Rev'd Jitinder Jeet Singh

Jeet Singh, as his title implies, is a minister of the Church of North India whose knowledge of Sikhism is thorough and first hand, thanks to his having been trained as a Sikh *Granthi.* He became a Christian, is a convinced evangelical and, in effect, this research paper is a testimony to his own faith. In preparation of a Master's degree he wrote a research paper entitled '*The concept of "Guru" in Sikhism and its fulfilment in Jesus Christ 'the Satguru.'*[28]

His first sections deal with various Sikh theological concepts before he begins to deal with the figure of Jesus Christ whom he sees as the *Satguru.* One 'sees Him as if He is walking through the pages of the *Sri Guru Granth Sahib.*' He further makes the claim that there are references in the *Guru Granth Sahib* 'where it is explicitly said that (except) through *Satguru* Jesus Christ one cannot attain salvation:

'The true *Satguru* (God) has sent the child. The long-lived child has been born by destiny. When he came and acquired the abode of the world, his mother's heart became very glad, the Son, the Saint, of the world, the Lord is born. The primal writ had become manifest among all. In the tenth month, by the Lord's command, the baby had been born. Sorrow has left and great joy has become manifest. The Sikhs sing the *Gurbani* in their joy.'[29]

Jeet Singh continues in this manner, dealing with the *hukum* (will) of God which he sees lived out in the life of Jesus – the Master (*Swami*) of all and complete divine being, through whom God speaks. Further he sees Jesus as the embodiment of *Sabad* (the Word) and takes up a theme of Sadhu Sundar Singh with the claim that 'God to help man had to

---

28. Singh, Jitinder Jeet (n.d) unpublished M.Div research paper: *The concept of "Guru" in Sikhism and its fulfilment in Jesus Christ 'the SatGuru'.* Southern Asia Bible College, Bangalore.

29. *Guru Granth Sahib: So Dar, Rag Asa, M.V.* (4-7-101) p. 396. Singh's translation. Quoted in Singh J.J. p. 34.

become incarnate. The Word of life was made flesh. He will carry those who want to cross the river of this world to heaven... we can see the living incarnation of *(Satguru)* Jesus Christ.'[30]

For Jeet Singh it is Jesus who leads one to become a *jivanmukta*, one who is liberated whilst in this life. He is the voice of God, the True Guru, who through his grace destroys self-centredness *(haumai)*. In him God shifts from the transcendent *(Akal Purukh)* to the immanent *(Satguru)*, the one who is God's gift to humankind, the only one through whom one can comprehend the nature of all that is related to God.

There could hardly be a greater contrast to Gamaliel's methodology. Where Gamaliel views the Sikh faith negatively, Jeet Singh sees the positive influence of his upbringing as a Sikh and attempts to define his new-found faith using Sikh categories and terminology. Drawing on the Fulfilment School of J.N.Farquhar, he sees his erstwhile faith as a preparation for the Gospel in which he finds fulfilment and deeper understanding of the ways of God through Jesus the *Satguru*. But whilst Christians may rejoice at this process of Panjabi contextualisation, Sikhs express their misgivings about this methodology. In recent years Sikh websites, in this case, *Sikh Information*, have indicated severe misgivings about this methodology:

> Because of the strong adherence to tradition by Sikhs, missionaries have attempted to repackage Christianity. Jesus is called "Satguru," church is referred to as "Satsang" and choir singing is called "Kirtan." Choir boys in Panjabi churches wear turbans to attempt to minimize the variation between Sikhism and Christianity. However, despite these attempts to disguise Christianity as a version of Sikhism, missionaries still cannot hide their intent: to destroy the Sikh faith.[31]

I do not believe that is Jeet Singh's intention, but one recognises the concern and the potential for severe misunderstanding.

The Rev'd Dr Anand Spencer

Theologians involved in interfaith dialogue are inevitably both time and culture-bound reflecting the context in which they work. Anand

---

30. Singh J.J. p. 36 quoting Streeter and Appasamy, *The Sadhu*, Delhi, K.M. Mittal Pub. 1987, p. 57.
31. See: http://www.info-sikh.com/PageChris1.html

Spencer is no exception. He is an Indian ordained into the American Episcopalian Methodist Church in North India who taught at Panjabi University in Patiala. His responsibility was to teach Christian studies in the Department of Religious Studies where he was the only Christian on the staff. He has produced invaluable material on Panjabi church history and on the issue of the Christian-Sikh encounter since it is for him a daily occurrence.

In a paper entitled 'Inter-faith Dialogue: Some Basic Presuppositions'[32] he lays down ground-rules or guidelines for dialogue which reflect not only his own experience and irenic nature, but the context of being of a minority faith amongst a people of another minority faith. He suggests:

1. The equality of all religions demands that no religion can claim superiority since where equality does not exist dialogue becomes impossible. 'Each religious tradition has its own ethos and values which must be mutually respected and loved.'[33]

2. There must be a 'disclaim of absolutism'. 'A strict adherence to the absolutistic tendencies closes the door for looking beyond itself into infinity, into truth, and into the Absolute...Confining the truth to rigidly defined formularies is to limit the scope of its infinite meaning and its universality.' 'If a religion encloses itself and refuses to see any possibility beyond its marked boundaries, it becomes static.'[34]

3. The uniqueness of all religions must be respected so that each religion is recognised in its individuality and autonomy. Dialogue enables one to 'attain a deeper understanding of the truth through mutual awareness of one another's convictions and witness.'[35]

4. Openness and Emptiness are vital, by which he means the possibility to change and the ability to understand the other from within him/herself. This does not mean a betrayal of one's own faith but the ability to widen one's understanding of that faith.

---

32. Type-written, no date, but post 1975 - the date of the latest books quoted. It draws on material used in Chapter II.C of his Ph.D. thesis, see below.
33. Spencer thesis p. 1.
34. Spencer thesis p. 1f.
35. Spencer thesis p. 1f.

5. Reciprocity enables a true dialogue to take place so that it does not become a meeting in which one speaks and the other listens, but an occasion when ...'(e)ach partner finds his own presence in the other, finds his ideals and values in the other...'[36] (so that the other does not become a stranger and where the universality of one's faith is affirmed.

6. Through appreciation and appropriation one discovers that the other religious tradition is not entirely contradictory and thus breaks down isolationism. Further one is able to assimilate the spirit of others whilst preserving one's own faith's individuality.

7. If one recognises in the other the 'imago Dei' then one also must recognise the universal presence and work of God. Echoing Max Warren, Spencer suggests that '(i)n listening to the other, one listens to one's own self. The God of the other becomes 'my' God.'[37]

8. Dialogue is not simply a discussion about religious systems, but one must deal with the faith dimension which touches the partner's basic core, the deepest levels of religious experience.

9. The response to the dialogical urge means that we seek fellowship of both our fellow human-beings and God, 'experiencing the revelation of God being manifested through the unfolding of the religious experience of the partner.'[38]

10. One's dialogue leads to an understanding of our common humanity and, therefore, the need for inter-dependence and inter-relationship.

11. There can be no ulterior motive in dialogue. It does not aim at proselytising, but is an occasion for witnessing and unfolding one's own faith.

These guidelines are not merely academic reflections but reflect Spencer's own deeply held beliefs and experience of dialogue with

---

36. Spencer thesis p. 4.

37. Spencer thesis p. 4. and Max Warren: 'A Theology of Attention' in *Face to Face*, London, The Highway Press, 1971, p. 19: 'And if we listen very carefully ... it is likely that we hear him speaking to us through the lips of a Hindu, a Muslim....'

38. Spencer thesis p. 6.

colleagues who asked searching questions about the deeper meaning of faith. It is in the light of Spencer's criticism of the monological nature of a conference on 'Theology: Christian and Sikh', held at Batala in October 1972[39] that he began his search for an issue or concept which would provide a mutually understood basis for dialogue. The result was his 1979 Ph.D. thesis on *The Concept of Word in Christianity and Sikhism*. He sought to employ an approach which was 'objective and detached from the standpoint of personal conviction and also from the standpoint of theological and philosophical value judgement.'[40] To this end he analysed: the Comparative Study of Religions and its relationship to Interfaith Dialogue with particular reference to Christian-Sikh dialogue; the concept of the Word in Christianity, both in the Bible and later theological thought; the concept of the Word in Sikhism in the Guru Granth and as understood and interpreted by Sikh scholars; and finally a comparative study of the Word and prior to his conclusion a study of the Word in Christian-Sikh dialogue.

Spencer draws out significant parallels in terms of the Word as divine Word; pre-existent entity; as an idea, eternal, everlasting, pure and as truth, life and light; as power, creative, sustaining, destroying, healing, blessing and cursing; as a vehicle of revelation; as the means and end of salvation; as being of God and as message of God; as teacher or Guru; as divine entity; as Scripture; in relation to worship and devotion and finally he contrasts the Christian understanding and Sikh rejection of the Word as divine incarnation.

His thesis posits the idea that the concept of the Word should take one beyond the confines of Christian dogma to an understanding of something far wider and universal:

The Word represents truth and is not confined to cultural, geographical or traditional boundaries. It does not belong to

---

39. Anand Spencer: *The Concept of Word in Christianity and Sikhism*, unpublished Ph.D. thesis, Patiala, August 1979, p. 335 f.n: 'No effort was made to exchange views and to understand the other point of view. It was rather a monologue as it consisted of one party speaking while the other was listening.'

40. Spencer (1979) p. 12.

41. Spencer (1979) p. 343.

Christianity or Sikhism as such; it belongs to God. The Word or
truth is no one's monopoly. Religions are expressions of a certain
comprehension (experience) of the same Reality. But Reality remains
transtemporal, above space and time. The Word being Divine Reality
is not the exclusive possession of any one religious tradition. It is
universal in nature.[41]

Thus, suggests Spencer, there can be a firmer basis for dialogue between
the two faiths since a dialogue which takes the 'Word' as a starting point
is grounded in mutual understanding. Anticipating objections to this
from a Christian perspective he suggests ... 'The Bible says, "The word
of God is not bound," which clearly indicates that the revelation of God
is not bound to any single tradition.'[42] This is not to suggest that he
overlooks differences that exist between the faiths, primarily in the Sikh
rejection of Incarnation in the case of his analysis of the 'Word.'[43]
Notwithstanding this, dialogue is possible and that on a deep level for ...
'A Sikh who believes in God and also in the theology of the Sabad is
already an 'Imago Dei', and he has thus every right to be listened to by
a Christian. He is a fellow believer, a fellow pilgrim to the same sacred
destiny.'[44] In taking such a step, the Christian, Spencer suggests, will be
able to see the presence of the Word beyond Christian confines,

> to see the larger Christ in the universal and cosmic setting.
> Consequently, he is enabled to broaden the meaning of his faith ...
> (and) include his Sikh partner not as 'other' but as a fellow participant
> and sharer in the same heritage... A feeling of *ananyatva* 'un-otherness'
> ... begins to emerge. One realises one's essential relatedness to the
> other.[45]

---

42 Spencer (1979) p. 344, quoting 2 Tim. 2. 9.
43. Spencer (1979) p. 313.
44. Spencer (1979) p. 355.
45. Spencer (1979) p. 358. For many Christians this would be a dangerous and unacceptable theology,
     but it is a challenge which interfaith dialogue lays before those who participate. The theology
     of both the macrocosmic and microcosmic natures of Christ must be explored by the Christian.
     Spencer quotes in a footnote (p. 359) Murray Rogers who received a letter from one of his Hindu
     partners in dialogue who wrote: 'I must be brave enough to tell you all my thought. I am afraid
     you have minimized your Christ by insisting on the unique claims of Jesus. This absolutization
     of the conditions of his manifestation in human history, added to the lack of real interiority in
     the lives of most Christians, is the greatest stumbling block to us. When you have discovered

Yet Spencer is no easy-going syncretist since he indicates that whilst Christianity and Sikhism meet in Word or *Shabad* 'they uphold the tenets of their own faith and remain faithful and loyal to their beliefs and convictions.'[46]

Spencer's work takes further the encounter of Christians and Sikhs. The experience of cooperation between members of both faiths is extended from the practicalities of nation building and the creation of good communal relations to a deeper spiritual search possible because, as Spencer suggests, there is a mutually understood basis for theological dialogue in terms of the *Shabad*/Word.

The Rev'd Dr James Massey

James Massey was the General Secretary of the Indian Society for the Promotion of Christian Knowledge, a Dalit, he is Presbyter of the Church of North India and, whilst not a Sikh, has received Granthi training - one of few CNI Presbyters to have received such. He is a prolific writer whose recent major works are in the field of Dalit studies, but who has written numerous articles on Panjabi church history. Two books are significant with regard to the Sikh-Christian encounter. His Ph.D. thesis formed the basis of The Doctrine of Ultimate Reality in the Sikh Religion published in 1991. It is not a comparative study but an analysis of the Sikh understanding of the divine being. It is noteworthy that Guru Nanak was not a systematic theologian, for him, as for his followers, what is more important is spiritual experience of direct encounter with Ultimate Reality, a unique being of which 'there is no second;' one who is 'Lord,' 'creator,' and 'king,' to use descriptions of the personal aspects of the divine. However, there are other aspects which should be noted, those of oneness, of being omnipresent, omnipotent, invisible, infinite, inaccessible, imperceptible, self-existent. These are experienced and known only through the divine's favour, mercy, compassion, and will, that is through the grace (*gurprasadi*) of the divine.

---

the inner Christ in the light of the spirit within, then we shall gladly come forward to share with you our own experience of the interiority of God.' (From Murray Rogers: 'Hindu-Christian Dialogue Postponed' in Dialogue Between Men of Living Faiths, Geneva, W.C.C., 1971, pp. 27f.)

46. As above p. 363.

Massey's contribution to the encounter is not only in terms of opening up Sikh theology to an English-reading, often Christian, constituency but also in presenting Christianity to Panjabi readers whilst at the same time encouraging Panjabi Christians to take seriously their own Panjabi history and Culture. In 1976 he published *Masihiat ik Parichay* (Christianity - An Introduction (in Panjabi)[47] which he claimed was the first publication of its kind to be produced in that language. By this he means that it is not written in the style of an evangelical tract, the likes of which have been published previously, but it is an attempt at an academic introduction. It is still apologetic in nature and introduces the fundamentals of the Christian faith in a simple manner. Since it is written with a Panjabi readership in mind Massey avoids much of the history of the development of Christianity in the West since overemphasis on the divisions within Western Christianity would be entirely counter-productive.[48]

In his Foreword Massey encourages his fellow Christians to take seriously the rich literary heritage of the Panjabi language since it is through this that they can actually learn about their own faith through that of other people of faith. As examples he cites such concepts as *Gur Prasad* and *Sach Guru* which are to be found throughout the *Guru Granth Sahib* e.g. in the *Japji Sahib* and *Siddh Gosht* or the *Sri Rag*:

I have tested all, and found that no one but you alone saves us by your grace. (A.G. p. 74)

Similarly Massey points out as further examples: in *Japji* 1[49] showing that the rift between the Ultimate Being and humanity can be overcome and liberation attained: Through good deeds we go into the next birth, liberation comes through grace; *Sachkhand* - the place of the Ultimate Reality who is without form yet who lives and looks upon creation

---

47. James Massey: *Masihiat ik Parichay* (Christianity - An Introduction (in Panjabi)), Amritsar, Faqir Singh & Sons, for the Christian Institute of Sikh Studies, Batala, 1976.

48. This raises the question as to whether our image of Christianity is wide enough. There is a tendency for Western Christians to envisage their understanding of the faith to be normative and Christian history to be essentially European. I recall an argument in Nes Amin, Israel/ Palestine (28 November, 1984) when Pakistani Christians objected to their being implicitly included in what they saw as Western Christian responsibility for the Holocaust.

49. Massey (1976), p. 4.

with happiness. In *Siddh Gosht* one reads of the fellowship of the saints through which one receives the True One.

Such examples show distinctly parallel beliefs. Massey's technique is at one and the same time an attempt to witness to his own faith as a Christian, but also an encouragement to his fellow Christians not to turn their backs on their Panjabi heritage even if it is to be found within the milieu of another faith community's scriptures.

A further point is made in terms of his suggestion that Christian concepts are used within Panjabi literature. So, for example, two Panjabi authors use Christian imagery to illustrate concepts of suffering, sin and resurrection. Suffering and sin are to be found in the writings of Mr Justice Pritam Singh Safeer who uses the concept of the Cross, particularly in terms of taking up the cross oneself, to illustrate personal suffering. By the same token he recognises the propensity towards sin when he writes that sin has become so rooted among people that it would appear to be a profitable means worth exploiting, to the extent that even though one recognises the presence of sin one continues to live a sinful life (cf. the good that I would not...)

Another classical illustration is taken from the poet Waris Shah in which Ranja is beaten up and left half-dead by his paramour, Hir's, relations. Hir vows that she will go to him and 'like Jesus will resurrect him from the dead.'

Massey's final point is that the recognition of such illustrations from a Christian background within Panjabi literature can be an invaluable help to the Church in establishing its *bona fides*.

His first chapter - *Pit-bhumi* (Background) - deals with the history of the Church in India in which he maintains that it can be proved that St. Thomas came to the Panjab but tradition has it that he went to South India. Reference is made to the Jesuit priests who were in Akbar's court but a major step in the Panjab was made with the arrival of the first American Presbyterian missionary on 5 November 1834. Thereafter the story is well recorded, but particular significance is given to the conversion of Ditt and the beginning of the mass movement of Dalits to Christian faith. Into this equation is placed the story of Sadhu Sundar Singh whose background is in the land of the Gurus but who is portrayed as the Panjab Church's gift to the whole world.

Turning to the theology of the Incarnation in his second chapter - *Sabd Guru* ('Word' Guru) - Massey deals with the *logos* theology of John's Gospel using only Panjabi terms and thought forms. The main point he makes is to distinguish between Christian and Hindu concepts of incarnation in which the former comes once and for all whereas the latter are repeated manifestations. Massey suggests that the Hindu *avtars'* function was to destroy, whereas in John's Gospel the Word becomes flesh for much more positive reasons, coming not to destroy but to save. Massey goes on to point out that the divinity of the *Sabd* is because Jesus Christ was not a human-being through the wife of a god. Rather this was the same Word which came from God and not a creation. His proof text is taken not from the Bible but from *Japji 16* which he translates as: He entered the world by speaking once. This, however, is understood by other translators as indicating the single act of creation by the one word and thus indicates the basic unity of the universe since it is from the same source.

The Guru concept is introduced through the story of Nicodemus who came by night and addressed Jesus as 'Rabbi', the nearest translation of which in Panjabi is *'Guru'*, a title Massey claims is most suitable for Jesus. For the Christian, Massey writes, the Guru is not a human-being, but the *Sabd-Guru*, a term which he leaves untranslated but which one may understand to be 'Word-Guru'. To bring this chapter to the present day, Massey discusses how Christ is experienced through the Holy Spirit, the *Sat-Atman* - the Spirit of Truth, to use both Panjabi and Biblical language. The Spirit is in action through every human-being and is a universal power. Thus God's hand is always extended, a person only has to accept that fellowship. This metaphor is a significant one in a country where hand-shaking is as prevalent as in Germany.

Itiasih Sat - Historical Truth, is the title of the third chapter in which Massey explores the human nature of Jesus of Nazareth, emphasising the human name Jesus who is also the *Masih*, the 'Christ', the anointed one. So whilst the name 'Jesus' is used to represent the historical basis of faith, the term *Masih* is a symbol of the faith itself. Massey's emphasis on historicity is important for the Sikh faith is based on the historicity of the human Gurus. Massey is also aware of how the name Jesus Christ can also be interpreted along lines which remind the Sikh of the nature of the *Satguru* who is God since he portrays the *satguna* aspect of God in Jesus and the *nirguna* aspect in the term Christ. Further proof of the existence of the historical Jesus of Nazareth is shown through non-biblical sources and he follows this with material from the Gospel accounts.

Massey's fourth chapter - *Puran Manukh* - Perfect Man - is a life of Jesus Christ which once again stresses the historical nature of the birth of Jesus of Nazareth whilst at the same time acknowledging difficulties in its dating. His childhood is described in a fashion after the *Janam Sakhis* of Guru Nanak and the later baptism of Jesus by John is described in a way that reflects Indian practice. In keeping with the Sikh stress of *seva* as being an inherent part of religious life, the loving service of Jesus Christ to all is highlighted. Illustrations from everyday life in the parables are shown to be of a similar nature to those found in the writings of the Gurus.

Jesus Christ is portrayed as the perfect man through whom one meets God as a father who is always ready to forgive his children.

Using a common Panjabi expression meaning 'There is always enmity between truth and evil', Massey maintains that this reflection on human nature may be an explanation for the crucifixion of the one who was the Truth. Finally in this section he deals with the death and resurrection of Christ discussing the attitudes to the death of Jesus taken by Muslims such as the suggestion that the body was removed or exchanged and that Jesus did not die. He claims that none of these can be upheld. As to the resurrection, Massey suggests three testimonies of proof:

- the existence of the Church;

- there was no literature to dispute this, rather the Gospels came into existence;

- the significance of the first day of the week as maintained for worship by Christians throughout the world.

These 'testimonies of proof' are significant for Sikh readers. The first signifies the question of historicity, an important issue for the Sikh in contrast to the popularly held view of Hinduism's little concern for historical evidences. The existence of both the Church and the *Khalsa* are seen to support the validity of the messages they hold central and the historicity of their founders. Massey's second point demonstrates that in both faiths scripture takes on a primary authoritative nature. The third matter of the significance of worship on the first day of the week is the demonstration that it gives to Sikhs of the universality of the faith, its unity in comparison to the *Khalsa* and the fact that the major day of worship was changed shows the significance of the event which took place on Easter Sunday. This leads Massey to his next chapter.

The Central Message - *Kendri Sundesh* - is the subject of Massey's fifth chapter. For him every person's *real life* (his emphasis) starts at the foot of the cross which is seen not as a barrier but as the symbol of God's salvation. The Cross is not simply the event at Golgotha but the whole life of Christ from Birth to Ascension. Christ's teaching about the cross is to point out the need for his followers to take up the cross themselves. The Panjabi context in which Massey writes determines his expression seen here in two instances. First the term 'real life' may reflect the Sikh concept of *jivan mukti* - liberation whilst living in this world. It is, therefore, significant that Massey stresses the necessity of the individual's taking up the cross presently in his or her own life-time. Secondly, the issue of taking up the cross may also reflect the dictum of Guru Nanak that one must free oneself from *haumai* - self-centredness. The real meaning of the Cross is seen to be in terms of Christ's personality, his giving himself in both life and death for, and in, the service of others, and as such he is portrayed as he ideal human being sought by the Gurus.

Illustrating a Reformed influence in Massey's thought is his chapter on Divine Grace - *Diva Kirpa*, in which he suggests that if the Cross and taking up the Cross is the central message of the Gospel then the centre of that message is the grace of God revealed through the Cross and that only through grace can humanity find its salvation. But why is grace needed? Massey suggests first because of the disobedience of human beings as seen in Genesis and secondly the consequent distance between God and the human, between the Self and the self. This latter theme uses Panjabi terminology regarding *haumai* - self-centredness - which would be readily understood by his readers.

He discerns different meanings of grace and links it with love. Grace is primarily seen acting in the life of Jesus Christ and can be discerned by Christ's followers as was evidenced on the road to Emmaus. Secondly, grace is seen in the letters written by, and to, believers. Both letters and believers become living testimonies to God's grace. But what is the role of the human-being in all this? Indeed is there a role? His answer is dichotomous. No, because grace is the basic gift of God. Yes, because faith is needed. Through a concept not dissimilar to the Hindu idea of *sphota*, Massey indicates the spontaneity of recognition of the role of grace in one's life when he quotes *Japji* to the effect that at the moment one realises one's true state in the world, God's grace intervenes and carries one forward. It is that grace, an aspect of the divine plan which is for all, which enables human-beings to escape from the state of sin.

Links are made with the Sikh concept of the *jivan mukta* in Chapter Seven entitled *Anant Jivan - Eternal Life*. The goal of the Cross, through grace is to liberate the human being and give him/her eternal life. Here is the essential message of the Christian faith expressed by Massey in Sikh terminology. For example, in the first three chapters of Genesis, Massey explains, God created human beings with his own breath and before the Fall they lived in *sach khand*. After the Fall, the condition of life was such that humans had to learn not to be overcome by self-pride, *haumai*. This had happened to Adam, writes Massey and in so doing humankind loses life in the realm of *sach khand*.

The Christian faith is portrayed as the means of the whole of humanity returning to *sach-khand*. The terminology is deliberate since *sach-khand* in Panjabi culture is the equivalent of eternal life which in both Christianity and Sikhism begins on earth and is attained through God's grace. Massey's Reformed background is demonstrated in his next supposition, that the response to such grace is the expectation on God's part of humanity's complete faith in him.

Eternal life cannot be portrayed in its spiritual dimension only. Both Christianity and Sikhism recognise the need for the practical manifestation of faith in *seva*, service. Thus Massey writes that eternal judgement there may be, but one can fulfil one's faith through serving the needy as is shown in Matthew 25.

In his eighth chapter Massey explores the Believing Community - *Viswas Sanghat*. He points out that differing names were given to the Christians in the early days, but from the Second Century the term 'Christian' was used. Within the Indian sub-continent Christians are often named by Muslims 'the followers of *Isai*'. This reflects the Muslim name for Jesus - *Isa* - which Massey suggests is an inadequate name since it reflects only the humanity of Jesus Christ. He argues the case for the more adequate term 'followers of Masih' - the followers of the Christ, the anointed one.

Thereafter Massey writes that the *ecclesia* is one, the foundation of the believing community having been by means of the selection of the 12 disciples and it is through the gift of the Holy Spirit that a common life was established as demonstrated in Acts. Not without significance he points out that the Early Church members had to work in order to eat, a quality espoused and greatly valued by his Sikh readers. Three further points are made: all members are seen as the limbs of the same body; one becomes a member of the new creation which one becomes a Christian and finally Massey writes of the two main sacraments of Baptism and the Lord's Supper, although he points out that for some denominations there are more than two sacraments.

For a readership for whom the written Word of God is significant and the authoritative root of their faith, Massey's final chapter is entitled the Holy Bible - *Pavitra Baibel*. Here he indicates the nature and history of the formation of the Bible and gives a summary of its contents. Note that he uses the term 'holy' indicating reverence for the Bible which is every bit as great as that of Sikhs for the *Guru Granth Sahib*. Thus he shows that it is not simply any book but a most important one. Of the Gospels he uses the term given to the biographies of Guru Nanak - *Janam Sakhis* and in order to explain the apparent contradictions of the Gospels indicates that each of the Gospel authors wrote with particular readers in mind and from their own perspectives. He points out that the Bible was written because people go astray.

Finally he gives an indication of the history of the Panjabi Bible translations from Carey to those he was himself involved in producing e.g. the New Testament which was completed in 1975 and published in 1976. The techniques and principles of translation are discussed.

Unlike his fellow Indian Christians Massey makes no attempt whatsoever to find the 'hidden' Christ within the *Guru Granth Sahib*. That is not his task. His genius is in terms of the presentation of the Gospel in terms of his own Panjabi cultural milieu, finding parallels but pointing out the differences between Christianity and Sikhism. Like Spencer, Massey's work is not by nature syncretistic but a matter of acculturation. It creates a dilemma, however, for the presentation of Christianity to younger Sikhs in the Sikh diaspora, many of whom would have experienced the practice but read little of the theology of the Sikh faith. Nor indeed would they have experienced Panjabi culture at first hand to appreciate Massey's apologetic technique.

The Rev'd Dr Godwin R. Singh

If one lives side by side with people of other faiths it is inevitable that one's spiritual search will not be outside such a context. For a number of years the Christian Conference of Asia has been involved in the search for 'an authentic Asian spirituality undergirded with indigenous theological reflection...' thus '...in the midst of (the) religious and cultural pluralism of the Asian environment, concern for the mission of God must include (the) active role of being a facilitating agent for promoting dialogue and a theology of dialogue.'[50] To this end the Rev'd Dr Godwin Singh was asked to write on the Sikh concept of *Gur Prasad* - (Divine) Grace. The concept is central to Sikh thought and could be said to sum up the whole of the Sikh scriptures since God's grace would be considered to be immanent in the daily lives of the devout in their attempt to follow the dictates of the divine will. Like Anand Spencer, Godwin Singh provides another basis for dialogue since divine grace is held by both faiths to be the sole source and means of salvation/liberation.

As with James Massey's study of 'Ultimate Reality', Singh's study is not of a comparative nature. It brings an 'interfaith perspective' inasmuch as it deals with the Hindu and Muslim milieux of Guru Nanak's time and thereafter demonstrates the manner in which the doctrine developed as Sikhism evolved into a distinctive faith. Thus he deals with the historical

---

50. Godwin Rajinder Singh: *Gur Prasad*: Sikh Doctrine of Divine Grace: An Interfaith Perspective, Hong Kong, The Christian Conference of Asia, 1992: Preface by Bp. D.C.Dutton, p. ix.

antecedents of the doctrine; the understanding of grace found in the *Adi Granth*; in the *Dasam Granth* and, prior to his conclusion, amongst members of the *Singh Sabha* and other movements.

In that the book is designed to help Christians reflect upon their own faith his conclusion is in keeping with Spencer's claim that one would not be alienated by the otherness of Sikhism but recognise the 'un-otherness', one's essential relatedness to the partner in dialogue.[51] Of the Sikh concept of grace he writes:

> *Gur Prasad* is the basic and fundamental component of the creedal formulation of the Sikh faith'...(It is a) belief in the divine self-revelation and gift of unmerited favour ... a bestowal made on divine initiative. It is not preconditioned by any human endeavour' ...(nor does it) 'mean an arbitrariness in its bestowal. The gift of *gur prasad* is a divine mystery ... Thus the formless, ineffable and the unknowable becomes the knowable. He cares for his creation through the relation *of prasad*. Its ascendancy over all human striving has been acknowledged as essential in the path of salvation. Only human ego can obstruct the path of receiving the gift of *gur prasad*.[52]

Singh does not overlook the difference with Christianity, however, in that he indicates that the gift of grace is not mediated through an *avatar*. Notwithstanding this he contributes an added basis for the dialogue between Sikhs and Christians through his study of *gur prasad*.

Dr Clarence O. McMullen

As Director of the Christian Institute of Sikh Studies, later Religious Studies, Clarence McMullen was editor of the institution's Bulletin together with numerous books arising out of the conferences held in Batala and listed above.

McMullen's monograph, *Religious Beliefs and Practices of the Sikhs in Rural Panjab*, is valuable to the matter of Sikh-Christian encounter not in terms of a comparative study, for that it is not, but because it is a reminder that those who are involved in what little dialogue there is in Panjabi villages may not always encounter normative Sikh religious beliefs.

---

51. Spencer (1979) p. 358.
52. Singh (1992) p. 133.

Similarly inasmuch as the field work for this study was done prior to the invasion/liberation of the 'Golden Temple' in Amritsar, answers given and therefore the results are liable to be influenced by the changing generally held opinions of the day.

Whilst it may be expected that belief in God and monotheism would be central, the fact that 52% of those questioned claimed to believe in *avatars* and 79.4% declared Guru Nanak to be God is interesting in the light of Godwin Singh's theological study and the encounter with Christianity. Given that the *Singh Sabha* movement was established partly as a response to the challenge posed by Christian missions McMullen's conclusion that Sikhs 'seem to be familiar with the basic tenets of their faith and subscribe to them faithfully',[53] then the movement seems to have met with a deal of success. Likewise his finding that of the sample taken 96% visit the *gurdwara* either daily or at least twice a week is indicative of loyalty to their faith and a willingness to take their religious obligations and duties seriously. To put it in somewhat crude terms, in the light of such findings evangelical Christians could have little reason to believe that the Sikhs would be easy targets for conversion.

Dr W. Owen Cole

Sikh studies in the diaspora, particularly in the United Kingdom have been brought to peoples' attention through the work of Owen Cole and the late Piara Singh Sambhi. One of their early works *The Sikhs: Their Religious Beliefs and Practices*[54] was for many years one of the few basic introductions to Sikhism available in the United Kingdom. Cole augmented this with the publication of his theses[55] but the book which is of greatest concern to the encounter of Sikhs and Christians is the last one he wrote in collaboration with the late Piara Sambhi and which the latter described as one which symbolised many aspects of their work together.[56]

53. McMullen: *Religious Beliefs and Practices of the Sikhs in Rural Panjab*, London, Jaya Books, 1989, p.113.
54. W. Owen Cole and Piara Singh Sambhi: *Sikhism and Christianity: A Comparative Study*, London, Macmillan, 1993.
55. W. Owen Cole: *The Guru in Sikhism*, London, D.L.T., 1982; *Sikhism in its Indian Context*, London, D.L.T., 1984.
56. W. Owen Cole and Piara Singh Sambhi: *Sikhism and Christianity: A Comparative Study*, London, Macmillan, 1993.

The comparison of theologies of two differing faiths is a task fraught with difficulties as is evidenced by the cessation of such work in the 1970s in the CISS in Batala. There is the temptation to draw superficial parallels of belief, the problem of finding adequate English equivalents for Panjabi theological words, the need to find ways of remaining faithful to, and reflecting, the differing methods of theological reflection and the near impossibility of finding definitive statements about the faiths, since religious faith is essentially idiosyncratic in nature.

Cole and Sambhi attempted to overcome these problems as they dealt with such issues as the background from which the two faiths emerged; God; Jesus and the Gurus; Spiritual Liberation and Salvation; the Scriptures; Worship; Personal Devotion; Ceremonies; Authority; Ethics and, finally, Attitudes to Other Religions.

In doing so they make no attempt to establish the superiority or otherwise of one faith against the other, rather the book reflects an interfaith dialogue in which those who are involved explore not only the partner's faith but their own and in so doing deepen the theological search for understanding of the dealings of God and humanity. The authors were regular participants in the series of consultations of Sikhs and Christians organised by the United Reformed Church in the United Kingdom to which we shall later turn.

A Reflection

The writers and witnesses considered have all made distinctive and differing contributions to the encounter of Sikhs and Christians. Yet it must be recognised that there is an element of overlap, for all wish to testify and explain their faith, but their individual purposes and objectives dictate their methodology.

For the evangelical writers witness is essentially with one purpose in mind, that of conversion. There is, significantly and in contrast to the attitudes often taken towards Hinduism, an appreciation of the spiritual depths of Sikhism, yet as would be expected, they claim that faith to be inadequate. There is a tangible difference between the use made by Pillai, Khan and Ahmad-Shah of Sikh scriptures and terminology and that made by Massey. The former group read into Sikh concepts their own

Christian understandings. Often this becomes a matter of misappropriation which leads to inadequate understanding. Massey is more apt to use Panjabi concepts to illustrate Christian doctrines. He also attempts to re-engage his Christian readers with their own cultural background and in so doing break down possible seeds of alienation. In Massey and Godwin R. Singh one sees men who combine the role of both Presbyter and scholar, who combine knowledgeable objectivity, pastoral concern and faithful witness. It is regrettable that Massey's apologetic work is confined to a Panjabi milieu, not simply linguistically, but culturally also. Young Sikhs of the diaspora would remain estranged on two counts; first in terms of a language they rarely read and secondly in terms of cultural practices and expressions that remain foreign to their Western upbringing.

Both McMullen and Spencer reflect the scholarly approach characteristic of their association with academic institutions. To the former one must be grateful for his opening to the Western world the understanding of Sikhism from a village perspective, to the latter one is indebted for his encouragement of deeper inter-faith spiritual search, which he contributes from his essentially Sikh milieu, whilst Cole and Sambhi make their contribution from the perspective of the academic in the Sikh diaspora.

Thus far the history of the encounter has been in India. The venue changes to the United Kingdom where among others Cole and Sambhi were regular participants in the series of consultations organised by the United Reformed Church. That change of scene made for a different form of dialogue.

First, there was a genuine appreciation of contacts made. In 1984, when the U.R.C. consultations were started, Sikhs were in the unenviable position of being a minority under suspicion in India. That being so, any serious interest shown in Britain to them and their faith was responded to with warmth and hospitality. Secondly, there were common causes; the difficulty of the increasing erosion of spirituality, the effect of increasing secularisation and the alienation of young people from the faith. Thirdly, time was made to discuss spiritual matters. Whilst such daily dialogue as existed in India was generally concerned with matters of economic, social and business nature, in Britain the 'interior' dialogue of faith was possible.

How did dialogue in the Diaspora develop?

5

Bilateral Dialogue in the United Kingdom

Formal meetings for dialogue between Sikhs and Christians in India have been relatively few. The first such meeting after Indian independence was in 1963 and took place in Batala[1]. Thereafter meetings and seminars were organised by the Christian Institute of Sikh Studies during the 1970s and early 1980s. By 1984 and in the aftermath of Operation Bluestar such dialogue meetings became virtually impossible to organise.[2] It was at this time that the United Reformed Church in the United Kingdom decided to establish a series of consultations of Sikhs and Christians.

Since its inception in 1972, the United Reformed Church in the U.K. maintained a 'Mission and Other Faiths' Committee which has been responsible for the denomination's relations with people of other faith. Towards the end of the 1970's the committee established a series of consultations with the Jewish community in Britain one result of which was the production of a small book called *Christians and Jews in Britain*.

It was in the light of the success of these consultations that in 1983 the possibility of establishing similar conversations with the Sikh community was considered. Thanks to the support and encouragement of Dr. Owen Cole and the late Sardar Piara Singh Sambhi a weekend meeting in the Autumn of 1984 was held in which 36 people, women and men, of both faiths took part.[3] It was the first such bilateral meeting in

---

1. See above p. 62.
2. See: C.I.S.S. Director's Report, 1987/88, see above p. 66.
3. See: Southall Gazette of 24 Aug. 1984 & Church News Service, June 1985: 'The General Assembly of the United Reformed Church ... heard of a meeting which is probably unique as an official activity of one of the British churches. It was a weekend consultation between Sikhs and Christians.'

the United Kingdom and was characterised by a remarkable sense of the search for mutual understanding and trust.

Although the consultation was sponsored by the United Reformed Church, that denomination has never claimed exclusive participation and similarly the Sikh participants reflected a variety of Sikh opinion and background. 1984 was a time of considerable anxiety of the Sikhs who faced the censure from the Indian and other communities as a result of the assassination of Mrs Gandhi whose Government forces had 'invaded', or 'liberated', depending on one's political stance, the 'Golden Temple' in Amritsar the previous year. It was significant that Sikh participants were brought together whose political loyalties were on both sides of the Khalistan divide.[4]

Whereas in dialogue meetings with the Jewish community there had been some degree of suspicion and diffidence at the opening meeting, since Jews were more familiar with Christian persecution than dialogue, the openness of the Sikh community was readily apparent. Both communities were willing to trust their partners in dialogue. Many experiences within of spiritual development were recounted, often with the words, 'I've never said this to anyone before but...'

It was not until the consultation of the following year that scripture was read together.[5] Rather than start meetings with prayer as would be the case when many Christians meet together it was suggested that scripture study could be a suitable alternative which enabled people of both faiths to pursue the quest for common spirituality while recognizing but not betraying differences.

There arose a major difficulty. It is generally accepted that there is no really clear and accurate translation of the *Guru Granth Sahib* into modern English. Such translations as are available are not always able to

---

4   Present were Sikhs whose birthplace was East Africa, for many of whom the debate regarding Khalistan was not a particular priority together with participants such as Dr Sukhbir Singh Kapoor whose book *The Invasion of the Golden Temple*, London, 1984 was to demonstrate his very real concern. The graciousness which was characteristic of all participants was particularly noteworthy.

5.   The 'Lord's Prayer' and the *'Mul Mantra'* were reflected upon by Mrs Charanjit Ajit Singh and me, 31 August 1985.

reflect the subtlety of the text and, therefore, participants were thrown back to the original Sixteenth Century language and the need to translate passages to be studied. Usually two people would offer a draft translation which was then re-worded in the light of how the scripture study developed.

The corollary of this was that the Sikhs began to question the Christians about the nature of translations of the Bible into English. It had to be admitted that some translations were more interpretations than an accurate reflection of the language of the original texts.

The methodology for presentation was in terms of encouraging two people, one from either faith to consider such texts as were relevant to the theme, usually one from the *Guru Granth Sahib* and one from the Bible. If a Sikh text were to be considered the first person to lead the scripture study was a Christian and vice versa with regard to a Biblical passage. In this way it was felt that those who were involved would not be intimidated and reluctant to speak their minds in the mistaken belief that they might offend by not giving the 'right' interpretation. Such a method brought new insights into familiar texts.

One example of this was the discussion regarding grace. In North India, the monkey-hold doctrine of grace is commonly held. The analogy runs that just as when a tribe of monkeys faces danger a baby monkey runs and holds on to its mother for protection, so, Sikh colleagues claimed, human-beings must take the first step towards God in seeking 'his' grace. The Christians were far more inclined towards the cat-hold doctrine of grace whereby just as the mother-cat takes the initiative and lifts its kittens by the scruff of the neck, so God takes the first step in searching out 'his' people, deserving or undeserving. Irrespective of who takes the first step, in keeping with the faith of both Sikhs and Christians agreement was reached that without the grace of God none can find salvation/liberation.[6]

In an attempt to explore each others' spirituality texts which are often used in worship were considered. An obvious inclusion from the Christian perspective was the Lord's Prayer. The second word of the

---

6. J.S.Whale has previously recognised this insight in The Protestant Tradition, Cambridge, 1955, p. 150f. It was explored by Sikhs and Christians in the consultation of 1990.

prayer caused misgivings. Unlike Muslims this was not because Sikhs reject the concept of the Fatherhood of God, rather it was because of the inadequacy of such a means of address. God's role as Creator and Sustainer was readily understood and upheld, but the Sikhs were concerned that there is more to God's character than these essentially masculine roles would convey, for does not God operate as Mother, Friend, Relative, Guardian and so on? 'You are my Father, you are my Mother, you are my protector everywhere,' was a quotation often used.[7] However, the conversation did not stop there, since reference was made to the inadequacy of human language - 'the more you say about God,' said Guru Nanak, 'the more you need to say...' - and the fact that God is beyond gender epithets. God is both 'Father' and 'Mother' and neither of those terms.

Sikhs practise as a regular aspect of their spiritual life *nam simran*. Whilst it may mean 'the repetition of the name (of God)' perhaps it is more accurately understood as 'constantly holding God in mind'. Thus the 'hallowing of God's name' found a response in the Sikh because it is significant in the attempt to free oneself from the effects of self-centredness (*haumai*) inherent in all human-beings.

The inadequacy of English translations of the Greek *basilea* was brought out as Sikh participants indicated their misgivings with regard to the word 'kingdom'. If it were a prayer that God should be ruler of his own creation, this would be acceptable since they too would pray that God establishes his rule on earth. But how? Praying 'Thy will be done' would come naturally to the Sikh, for the line could 'have come straight from the Granth'. It was pointed out, however, that the will of God is not considered something that is arbitrary, the product of a vacillating mind, but that there is a constancy to God's will reflected in the term 'divine order.'

The prayer for 'daily bread' was something that some Sikhs found difficult to fathom, for why should one be concerned about such a matter when God is so generous, indeed over-generous? If the body and soul are God's gifts and his property, he, therefore, maintains them. This must be seen, however, in terms of the *langar*, the free-kitchen which is

---

7.   A.G. p. 103.

established in each *Gurdwara*. Money and food are offered by the Sikhs and in turn all who come to the *Gurdwara*, irrespective of race or religious faith or caste are fed. The gifts of God the Guru are mediated through his people in their service to human-kind. In an egalitarian society, the prayer for daily bread becomes unnecessary.

Praying for the forgiveness of sins from a merciful God found its parallels in Sikh prayers: 'O Lord, our sins are as many as the waters of the ocean, have mercy on us, show us your grace and lead us not into temptation.'

If one is attuned to God's will, it was said, then the words of Guru Arjan could be prayed:

> To you O Lord, my Master I pray,
> body and soul are your property.
> You are both Mother and Father,
> We are your children.
>
> Through your grace we have many blessings,
> yet we cannot comprehend you.
>
> You are the most supreme Lord
> All is held together by your divine will;
> all that takes place is under your divine command.
>
> We only know your will, Lord.
> Nanak, your servant is forever your sacrifice.[8]

Consultations tend to be the domain of those who are professionally engaged in religious studies, particularly amongst the Christians. In the West London town of Southall, a series of scripture studies amongst members of churches and *Gurdwaras* was begun. They were informal affairs which allowed all to contribute. Some came fearfully at first, not knowing what to expect or say. Out of politeness they feared they would be required to give assent to the beliefs of others. Perhaps even more difficult, was the possibility they would be expected to articulate their own faith. The atmosphere was not like that. People were allowed to be themselves, they said what they wanted, disagreed when necessary,

---

8.   A.G. p. 268 - trans: Mrs Charanjit Ajit Singh.

rejoiced in both similarities and differences and drank tea and ate vegetarian biscuits together. One year as Christmas drew near the Prologue of John's Gospel was read together. The theology of the Word was debated in which there was an element of mutual understanding of the qualities of the *logos/shabad*, based on the concepts outlined by Dr. Anand Spencer[9] of Panjabi University most of which found common acceptance with the exception of the Word as Divine Incarnation. The Sikhs quoted the *Guru Granth Sahib* where of God it is written: 'Immortal is his form, he is unborn and self-illuminated...' (A.G. p. 1); 'The unique Lord is the peerless immortal, unborn ...' (A.G. p. 838) At the heart of traditional Sikh theology is the doctrine of the unity of God echoed by the words of Guru Arjun: 'May the mouth burn by which it is said that the Lord becomes incarnate. He neither comes nor departs from this world.' (A.G. p. 1136)

Further matters were the subject of discussion:

If Jesus of Nazareth was not *the* Incarnation of God, who and what was he in Sikh eyes? For many he was a revered and respected human-being whose life and teachings are an example and model for all humanity. He was seen as someone through whom God powerfully made his will known and whose death was greatly respected as an example of the martyrdom that was to befall some of the human Sikh Gurus, the most important significance being that it was of a vicarious nature. Given the Sikh understanding of service for all humanity one recognises this logical appreciation.

Another challenge was in terms of: if God makes his will and being known through human-beings, why do Christians insist that it was only through the person of Jesus of Nazareth? Do Christians really believe they have a monopoly of the truth?

However, just as Christians argue theology so do Sikhs, reflecting in this case some of the attitudes outlined by McMullen's thesis,[10] for whilst some Sikhs were opposed to the Hindu concept of *avatar* and recognised

---

9. See above p. 79ff.
10. See above p. 90f.

the Guru's objection to such incarnations, the nature of the relationship of the human-being to God needed, for some, a clarification of the Sikh understanding of the *atma*, the 'soul' or 'principle of life' which can be described as 'a fraction of the Cosmic Soul, the *Paratma*.' Thus if the individual soul and the Cosmic Soul are one - 'he reckons the personal soul and Cosmic soul as one'(A.G. p. 661), - then, 'Why object to incarnation?,' was the question posed by Sikhs to Sikhs, since God is present within all.

A text central to the Gospel was explored: 'If any want to become my followers, let them deny themselves and take up their cross daily and follow me.' (Luke 9.23) Rejection of the Incarnation or no, Sikhs were impressed with the fact of Jesus' death. For them it was a reminder of the martyrdoms of two of their Gurus, Arjan and Tegh Bahadur, the latter of whom died for the sake of religious freedom, not that of his own followers but of Hindus. Thus the issue of a vicarious death is neither unknown nor rejected. For them the idea of denial is also of great importance particularly with regard to the need to overcome self-centredness.

Sikh scripture and theology abounds with the recognition that human beings are inherently dominated by *haumai* and thus are in need of liberation. Translated by both 'pride' or 'self-centredness' one may come to some understanding of the larger meaning of this word which in its literal sense is 'Me-I'. If a person is dominated by his or her self-centredness and will, then there is little likelihood of that person's being open to the promptings of the will of God and, therefore, little scope for liberation/salvation. Overcome *haumai* and the possibilities of a God-centred life become greater. Sikh partners in dialogue went on to explain that for them this was possible only through the grace of God and, though not through human agency, such liberation was reflected in a changed human life-style.

The idea of daily cross-bearing was also appreciated since it reflects the Sikhs' refusal to countenance a sacred-secular divide. If the whole of one's being is dedicated to God then one's daily life-style must reflect that.

It was at this point that a passage from the *Guru Granth Sahib* was mentioned which is worthy of examination: 'If you wish to play the game of love, come down my street. And if you set foot on this path, come with your head held in the palm of your hand and do not be afraid of public opinion.' (A.G. p. 1412)

Faith, Sikhs claimed, though a serious matter, also has to be expressed in light-heartedness and joy, reflected in the words 'the game of love', meaning devotion to God. 'He' is no stern authoritarian but one whose will is a delight to follow. However, the concept of 'game' must not be thought to be one in which there are winners and losers, but one which is embarked upon for the sheer joy of playing. Traditional churches were challenged to consider their sometimes dour worship and grey demeanour.

Though in mainstream Sikhism there is a rejection of the concept of an individual incarnation, nevertheless the presence of God amongst his people is readily accepted. Thus one finds God by going down 'his' 'street' or 'alley'. For the Punjabi the picture is a homely one reflecting as it does the narrow streets of Punjabi towns and cities. Here everyone seems to the Western eye to live on top of each other and may know each other's business. But this also implies that one is never alone either in joy or in grief. The new-born infant belongs not only to a particular family but to the street also. The grieving, bereaved family will be supported in their loss. So where human relationships are at their best, there is where you will find God, hence God's calling the street 'my' street.

Some element of human free-will comes into the picture with the word 'if... you set foot on this path.' Whereas all work under the will of the Lord, since the will of God is supreme, there is, nevertheless, some degree of freedom in terms of the actions done by an individual. Thus there is not a strict determinism. Guru Arjan, however, stresses that because of such freedom effort must be made to follow God's will: 'Live your life, always making an earnest effort ... meet the Lord by contemplation on Him, so that you are absolved of all anxieties.' (A.G. p. 522)

What is this 'path'? In Sikh theology it is a line of thought or a line of conduct which can bring about the eventual merger of the human soul with the Supreme soul. Yet such a path is not without its difficulties, for if one sets foot on that path one does so with one's 'head in the palm of one's hand.'

Setting foot on such a path requires sacrifice. Whilst both the Christian and Sikh faiths have their histories of martyrs for the faith two further issues emerged. One was in terms of the need for setting self aside, where 'head' can represent one's 'self'. However, within Sikhism the head also represents intellect since it is the seat of the brain. Here discussion turned to the recognition that at the end faith is precisely that - faith. Once one gets to the discussion about proofs for the existence of God then one passes beyond the realms of faith. That does not mean to say, it was agreed, that it was an area of sheer speculation, rather the imperfection of both human language and human intellect to fully understand the nature of God was acknowledged. Again, 'the more you say about God, the more you need to say about God'. Thus for the human being to approach God there is a need to set aside intellectual pretentiousness whilst at the same time acknowledging that the facilities of the head are gifts of God and should be used in his purposes.

'Do not be afraid of public opinion', was the final talking point. Sikhs are conspicuous by their dress-code. They were a persecuted minority during Mogul days and thus were targets for persecution. The very nature of the establishment of the *Khalsa* - the Sikh nation - by Guru Gobind Singh at *Baisakhi* in 1699 must have been such that it demanded a willingness to stand up and be counted. Witness to one's faith by the very nature of one's attire must have led to anxiety. Yet the Sikh is told not to fear public opinion.

For Christians there was the challenge to witness to faith in public, not so much in terms of street evangelism but more in terms of the demand for justice in life-styles. Were Christians willing to go against the tide of public opinion? Did Protestants still protest? The last journey of Jesus of Nazareth was recalled faced as he was with the antipathy of public opinion as he made his way to Golgotha.

From informal conversations regarding the scripture studies with members of the King's Hall Methodist Church in Southall it was apparent that the Christian participants were forced to consider a number of issues. Some schools of thought would bemoan the fact that no one was 'converted'. Yet all were converted. Just like the issue of who 'converted' whom in the story of Peter and Cornelius (Acts 10. 1-31) all the participants had to recognise that they were changed. For a number of Christian participants, particularly in the local scripture studies, there was the very central question of where do the Sikhs stand within the providence of God. Brought up in pietistic environment where Jesus was seen as the 'only way', suddenly they were confronted by a group of people whose spiritual searching often matched their own, whose value of the grace of God was similarly paramount, whose life-style reflected all those qualities sought by devout Christians, who had heard the Gospel story yet were not compelled to become Christians.

Some lived with these tensions, rejoicing in the further questions that dialogue brings. Others were more inclined to turn their backs on the dialogue since it had become too uncomfortable and undermined perceptions of 'the other' as spiritually alien. Some members of the local church were unnerved and thus in need to pastoral support and help, for did this not undermine all that time spent in supporting missions in 'lands afar?' If the 'heathen' could speak of God in this moving way what was the point of mission?

The Sikhs knew of these difficult questions, but for them the matter was more readily answered by the words of the Guru: 'O, Lord, save this burning world and do so by whatever means you can.'[11] Thus whatever path God chooses to use it is a valid one, for it is his path.

The dialogue, however, brought a number of insights:

- Scripture study is certainly enhanced by the use of the original languages. At a time when Christian theological education is being truncated it is often Biblical languages which suffer and thus deny the student access to greater understanding of the texts.

- One's own faith can be considerably enhanced by dialogue with people of other faith. This can happen in a number of ways. One is challenged to think about what one actually believes - not about what one is 'supposed' to believe. One is obliged to find ways of expressing that belief in a manner that the partner in dialogue will understand. New insights are gained because someone for whom a scripture text is new can bring fresh light into words which may almost have become stale through familiarity.

---

11. A.G. p. 853.

But there is a further challenge. As one talks with one's partners in dialogue one becomes increasingly aware of the depth of their spirituality, their reverence for the founder of their faith and, consequently, becomes moved by the figure of Guru Nanak.[12]

Such is the nature of the Sikh spirituality experienced in dialogue that one cannot but be aware of the Guru's having opened up to his followers a sense of the Holy Being whom many Christians would address as 'God' and Sikhs as Akal Purakh[13] and who encouraged his followers to recognise the spiritual nature of human beings. As with other 'Mediators', stories are told of Guru Nanak's birth which reflect the veneration of his followers. A pundit, in the manner of Simeon,[14] spoke of the young child's sitting under a canopy...

...both Hindus and Turks will reverence him; his name will become current on earth and in heaven. The ocean will give him the way, so will the earth and the skies. He will worship and acknowledge only the One Formless Lord and teach others to do so.[15]

There were early signs of his vocation in that he could sit in the posture of a yogi by the age of seven months and later learnt both Sanskrit and Arabic.[16]

The strong sense of the Guru's call is reflected in the story of his failing to come back from his ablutions one morning when he was aged about thirty. He was thought to be drowned but returned after three days, later to explain that he had been taken into the court of God, ushered into the divine presence, given a cup filled with *amrit*, nectar and told:

This is the cup of God's name. Drink it. I am with you. I bless you and raise you up. Whoever remembers you will enjoy my favour. Go,

---

12. What follows is the barest sketch of a Christian appreciation, on the part of the present writer, based on the figure of the Guru Nanak of the more popular faith of the partner in dialogue rather than the de-mythologised figure of modern scholarship. The schema used is mainly that developed by John Macquarrie in *The Mediators*, London S.C.M., 1995 to which are added details of the Guru's life as outlined in Cole and Sambhi: *The Sikhs: Their Religious Beliefs and Practices*, Brighton, Sussex Academic Press, 1995.
13. See: John Macquarrie (1995) p. 130.
14. Luke 2.22-35.
15. Cole and Sambhi (1995) p. 9 quoting the *Bala Janam Sakhi*.
16. Cole and Sambhi (1995) p. 9 quoting the *Miharban Janam Sakhi*.

rejoice in my name and teach others to do so. I have bestowed the gift of my name upon you. Let this be your calling.[17]

In a fashion similar to the prophets of the Hebrew Bible he recognised his own shortcomings: 'I was a worthless minstrel then the Divine One gave me work,'[18] but he was also the butt of ill-humoured persecution, as for instance when he was 'interviewed' by the spiritually arrogant Siddhs.[19]

His life-work resulted, like other 'mediators', in the founding of a community, in Guru Nanak's case, at Kartarpur, and the composition of 974[20] hymns which were later to become the basis of the *Guru Granth Sahib*. Those who have followed Guru Nanak have experienced that feeling of liberation which has not only motivated them to communicate it to others but involve themselves in the struggle to free others from ignorance, poverty, oppression and disease.[21]

Guru Nanak died like any other human-being, and prepared himself for death by establishing his successor.[22] The importance of this point is that in dying the Guru showed himself to be like any other human being and therefore a fitting mediator between God and humanity.

In terms of teaching, Macquarrie's pattern points out five essential areas.

First, Guru Nanak encouraged his followers to recognise the presence of the 'Absolute.' The Sikh scripture starts with such a recognition of the 'One Being.' Secondly, the Guru indicated that human beings are spiritual beings whose goal in life is communion with God, found through his grace. In the third instance, the created world is seen as something good, in which the divine dwells. Fourthly prayer and worship are deemed to be the basis of life, both religious and secular, since it is by *'nam simran,'* the repetition of God's name, his constant remembrance, that one is able to observe the fifth element of the Guru's teaching - ethical guidance which eventually gave rise to the *Rahit Marayada* (*Khalsa* code of discipline).

---

17. Cole and Sambhi (1995) p. 10f.
18. A.G. p. 150.
19. See: A.G. p. 938.
20. See: Bhai Gurdas: *Var* 1, Cole & Sambhi (1995) pp. 14 & 18.
21. See: Macquarrie (1995) p. 138.
22. Cole & Sambh (1995) p. 18.

It is the essence of Guru Nanak and his teaching, together with the nature of his sincere followers that has had an impact on many Christians who have come into contact over the years with the Sikhs' faith. It has enabled many of us to recognise all those qualities of a man of God. That impact will impinge on the life and thought of any individual involved in dialogue.

Dialogue in the United Kingdom was not confined to that organized on behalf of the United Reformed and Methodist Churches. Towards the close of the Twentieth Century Ruth Lambert was in contact with the Sikh communities in Leicester and Coventry. She wrote up her experiences in her M.Phil. thesis *What might Christians learn, theologically and spiritually, from Christian-Sikh encounter?*[23] She describes occasions when she has visited *Gurdwaras* and the variety of celebrations and forms of worship to be found and reflects on the generous hospitality of the Sikh communities. She further comments on the concept of *seva* (service) and challenges church congregations to consider more extensive use of church premises; improving links with educational organizations; greater active service within the community and the manner and methods by which these suggestions can be brought about. She further goes on to consider the place of scripture in Sikh worship and daily life. This leads her on to reflecting on the manner in which both Sikhs and Christians are challenged to clearer communication of their faith and the place of translations in the transmission of faith. She also considers the place of personal devotions.

Her experience with the Sikh community led her to challenge her fellow Christians in many ways: How does one communicate Christ's kingdom values in the world? How can Christians through their own *koinonia* expressed sacramentally and practically show Christ's love and acceptance? How do we overcome the stumbling block of disunity? She indicates that 'Church leaders are prompted by Sikh example to ask whether they are active communicators of the grace and gift of God received through Scripture. Preachers and teachers of the Bible are encouraged to ensure that their hearers appreciate the importance of Logos and understand its implications. Christians generally are reminded

---

23. Ruth Lambert (2001) Unpublished M.Phil. thesis, University of Nottingham.

of the importance of examining their attitudes towards the Bible ... and the implicit value of both the original languages and their role as mediating the word of God, whilst warning of the dangers of over-literalism.[24] In recognition that there is still so much to be explored jointly she finally suggests four areas for further exploration: "Incarnation and Christology; the nature of true discipleship and salvation; the identity of the people of God; the implications for the Church's mission."[25]

In the light of these various examples of dialogue we move on to a reflection on faith and the Church's expression of that faith. It is incomplete. It cannot be anything but incomplete for what is recorded here in terms of history is precisely that - history. The story will go on, the journey will continue and so will the travellers.

24. Ruth Lambert (2001) p. 52.
25. Ruth Lambert (2001) p. 53.

6

Christian Faith in the Light of the Encounter

Sikhism is an autonomous structure which does not need the Christian Church for the fulfilment of its salvific purposes. Therefore any understanding of the Christ figure or possible interpretation using Sikh concepts and values remains simply that - an interpretation. Nor from a Sikh perspective does an appreciation of the Christ figure by a Sikh imply that the Church may be an agent of liberation or salvation.

Whereas certain Christian critics of Sikhism will always point to the negative behaviour of individual Sikhs, sometimes overlooking the significant fall from grace of many Christians, the understanding and appreciation of Sikhs and Sikhism, from early days of the encounter between the two faiths, leads one to recognise the value of 'Peter's' dictum that one should always be ready to bear witness to one's faith and to do so with gentleness and reverence.[1] Sensitive Indian Christians have recognised this fact and Western mission enthusiasts will need to subscribe to the humility of Jesus' baptism by John[2] and his learning from the Samaritan woman, and the similarly despised, Syrophoenician woman. It is not necessarily the case that through dialogue with Sikhs the Church may learn anything spectacularly new. However, there are occasions when latent faith and understanding is rekindled or new insights are discovered.

---

1. 1 Peter 3.16.

2   See: Aloysius Pieris, 'Mission of the Local Church in Relation to Other Major Religious Traditions', *Sedos Bulletin* 82, 5 (Mar. 1982) quoted in Wessels: *Images of Jesus*, p. 166; John 4.7-30 and Mark 7.24-30.

Within the Sikh-Christian encounter of recent years[3] the nature of the Sikhs' rejection of the self-centredness of *haumai* may challenge Christians to reconsider the nature of personal salvation particularly if it is portrayed in an over-individualistic manner. Similarly Sikh nomenclature used in addressing God may be of value in the Christians' search for understanding of God's nature. It shows the value of addressing God as 'Mother' as well as 'Father' but also the inadequacy of using those terms since God is understood by Sikhs to be beyond gender bound epithets.

Throughout the history of the encounter of Sikhs and Christians there have been Sikhs who have manifested all those qualities of life and faithfulness which reflect the life-style advocated by Jesus of Nazareth. Indeed this has not only been demonstrated in the lives of individuals but in the life of the Sikh *panth*. That being so the discerning Christian is honour-bound to ask questions about the economy of the Holy Spirit which is demonstrated by the *koinonia* 'outside the gate' and the unity of God's purpose in the ultimate establishment of God's *raj*/kingdom.[4]

Given the Sikhs' very real emphasis on service, the Church role as a servant church and not as an end in itself needs to be highlighted. In the history of the Church in the Panjab, with its very rapid growth alongside the burgeoning *Singh Sabha* movement, it must have been viewed with concern and even alarm by Sikhs who would have been inclined to think that the real function of the Church was in terms of attracting larger numbers to itself and, therefore, that any element of service was with conversion in mind rather than service for its own sake.

---

3. e.g. during the consultations of Sikhs and Christians organised by the United Reformed Church.

4. Roger Hooker: *Uncharted Journey*, London, C.M.S., 1973, pp. 7, 9. See also Michael Amaladoss: 'The Pluralism of Religions and the Significance of Christ' in ed. R.S. Sugirtharajah: *Asian Faces of Jesus*, p. 91: 'Speaking of the primacy of God's action in salvation will also help us not to isolate God's action in Jesus, but to set it in the context of the totality of God's action in the world seeking to communicate Godself to human beings which embraces the whole process of history from creation through redemption to its ultimate consummation.' 'We would better respect the pluralism of religions in history and seek for their articulation into a unity according to the plan of the one God. A historical perspective would also make us see this unity not as a system that is already given, but as a unification that has to be achieved, built up, realized both by the Spirit and by us, precisely through dialogue and mission.'

At first sight Georges Khodr's essay on 'The Economy of the Holy Spirit' (in G.H.Anderson: *Faith meets Faith*, Mission Trends No. 5, New York, Paulist Press, 1981, pp. 36-49) seems helpful in demonstrating the work of the Holy Spirit outside the normally discerned patterns of 'salvation

This has implications for both the Church as a fellowship of faith and Christians as individuals who need to develop the nature of the Christian *jivan-mukta*: who has experiences of God's presence within his/her own life; approaches life in a Cross-bearing manner; demonstrates the selflessness of the Cross - which actually becomes self-affirming; and is '*seva*'-full.

Without practical expression dialogue and witness become meaningless. From a Sikh perspective the Church's servant role is best expressed through that form of Liberation Theology described by Bevans as 'The Praxis Model'. It is a model of reflective action, 'the central insight of which is that theology is done not simply by providing relevant expressions of Christian faith but also by commitment to Christian action. But even more than this, theology is understood as the product of continual dialogue of these two aspects of Christian life ... "truth is at the level of history, not in the realm of ideas."'[5]

Theology, therefore, may become something which is never a finished product, but an exploration of God's presence in each specific situation. For the Church, the consequence is one of a circle of constant action and reflection upon the activity of God through and amongst God's peoples.

'The role of mission is to make our own contribution to the realisation of the plan of God for the world. This requires listening to others, reading the signs of the times, building up community, promoting freedom, fellowship and justice and witnessing to the hope that is within us.'[6] Amaladoss from his Indian Catholic perspective here reflects the call to

---

history', but once again is in danger of confining the vehicle of salvation to Christian interpretations: 'There is a universal religious community which, if we are able to lay hold of what it offers, will enrich our Christian experience. What matters here is not so much that we should grasp the historical, literal, objective meaning of non-Christian scriptures, but that we should read these scriptures in the light of Christ. For just as the letter without the Holy Spirit can hide revelation from us in the case of the Old Testament scriptures, Christ being the only key to them, so is it possible for us to approach other religions and their scriptures either in a purely critical frame of mind and as objective students of history and sociology, or else in order to discern the truth in them according to the breath of the Holy Spirit.' (p. 47)

5.   Stephen B. Bevans: *Models of Contextual Theology*, Maryknoll, Orbis, 1992, p. 65, quoting: J. Miguez Bonino: *Doing Theology in Revolutionary Situation*, Philadelphia, Fortress Press, 1975, p. 72.

6.   Amaladoss (in Sugirtharajah (1993) p. 100.

co-operation made by the American Presbyterian missionary, C.H.Loehlin, from the perspective of the post-Partition encounter with Sikhism, but he effectively goes one step further in challenging the Church to ask, 'Who are our partners in mission?' One must, therefore, consider the possibility of a partnership in mission that transcends religious barriers and norms.[7]

If dialogue is to be a worthwhile learning experience then mutual understanding is of the essence. This calls for a careful, specific and non-polemical articulation of the Christian faith in a manner which can be understood by the Sikh partner in dialogue. The encounter thus far highlights certain aspects of the Christian faith which raise questions in the Sikh mind. These will include:

- the nature of the atonement and its relation to vicarious suffering. Any understanding of martyrdom that portrays the death of a passive victim will not find Sikh sympathy. Death must be for a purpose and to this extent the model of 'Christus Victor' may be worthy of exploration. The Cross cannot be portrayed as a mechanical transaction freeing the believer but that which enables the believer to go through the process of dying to self-centredness to find the power of God in self-renewal.

- an analysis of the nature of humanity and the consequent nature of enlightenment or redemption, since the Sikh will be more concerned about overcoming ignorance of humanity's inherent relationship with the divine rather than with what is seen as a Christian preoccupation with sin.

---

7. 'We often have an image of salvation history as the growth of the Church till the whole world becomes the Church. I do not know where this image comes from. The Bible rather speaks of the remnant, a community that is persecuted which looks forward in hope for the Lord's coming. I think that the image of the Church as the servant, proclaiming the mystery of the reign of God, ready to offer its life as witness, may be more authentic than the one of a triumphalistic army conquering all before it. Its service is precisely that of helping the unification of all humankind by promoting a human community of dialogue and collaboration. Its task is to proclaim Jesus and his mystery, more in action than in words, so that others too are challenged by him and turn to God - "converted." Some may be called to join the community of his disciples. Others may undergo real change while remaining in their own religions. The concrete way in which the transformation and unification will take place is a mystery that is known to God alone. All we can do is to be faithful witnesses in action, not only to the mystery of God's love, but to its self-sacrificing manifestation in Jesus.' Amaladoss (in Sugirtharajah (1993) p. 97.

- scrutiny of the nature of the Incarnation since Sikhs are inclined to recognise the presence of God among God's gathered people rather than an individual such as Jesus Christ. Of value in this respect would be an exploration of the meaning of the 'Body of Christ' especially in terms of self-giving service to humanity as the manifestation of God's nature and continuing sustaining concern.

- reflections on the research already done with regard to the understanding of the concept the Word as *shabad/logos* in both the faiths which would provide insight into the nature of God's continuing creativity.

- an enquiry into the nature of discipleship in terms of the continued search for a deeper understanding of faith; the nature of following the will of God and the consequent cost of discipleship.

- an examination of a spirituality which recognises the mystery of faith but is not divorced from the harsh realities of life since withdrawal from the world is an abrogation of the search for God's justice in creation.

- a recognition that at the heart of humanity's fulfilment is God's grace, which both faiths readily acknowledge but the initiative for which is disputed. Does humanity or God take the first step?

- consideration of what constitutes witness and identity. Unlike *Keshdhari* Sikhs who are easily identified by the carrying of the 5Ks, Christians are less readily distinctive. If service to the community is a manifestation of faithful living, how does one distinguish between the two faiths, or is such identification really necessary?

Preliminary Conclusions

The first major group Christian commentators on Sikhism were military officers who wrote because of the need to understand the men against whom they were fighting and later in the ranks over which they had control. Their work is already reviewed in such monographs as Darshan Singh's *Western Perspective on the Sikh Religion*[8] and, as such, does

---

8. Darshan Singh: *Western Perspective on the Sikh Religion*, New Delhi, Sehgal Publishers Service, 1991.

not need review or reference here except where, as in the case of William Keene, Cunningham's book provided an introduction to the missionary's understanding of Sikhism.

The missionaries, however, in the early days of their work in the Panjab gave the impression of not considering a deep knowledge of the faith of the indigenous peoples to be a priority since their express intention was that of conversion. When Keene asked if there was point in learning about other faiths, the response was in terms of 'only in one's leisure time'. The attitude towards Sikhism, indeed all faiths other than Christianity, was along the absolute lines of 'truth-falsehood' i.e. Christianity is true, all other faiths are false. Yet even in those early days there appears to have been an apparent respect for Sikhism if not for Sikhs.

The 1880s saw a major change in missionary work in the Panjab. This was in terms of the response to the unexpected 'mass movement' conversions of 'Dalits' to Christianity and the consequent concentration of work amongst the lower classes and, therefore, the lack of concern about relationships with the Sikh community. Sikhs also responded to the 'mass movement' by similar attempts to bring the lower classes into the Sikh fold.

Such a change in direction was not complete, however, and by the turn of the century scholars, including Trumpp, had worked on a study of Indian religions including Sikhism. This, together with the theological corollary of Darwin's *On the Origin of Species by means of Natural Selection*, established the 'Fulfilment' school, associated with J.N.Farquhar, which was embraced by the participants of Edinburgh 1910 and, in the case of this study, by Canon Guilford of Tarn Taran.

A second major change occurred with the arrival of Clinton Loehlin whose ability to befriend Sikhs and Sikh scholars established a firm rapport between leaders of both the Sikh and Christian communities. Thus there was a move from competition, to win the lower social groups, to cooperation. Largely as a result of this work the time was ripe for dialogue.

This must also be seen as an important post-Independence phenomenon when both these minority groups needed to establish their *bona fides* as Indians and not, especially in the case of Christians, as stooges of the ex-colonialist power. Hence cooperation in the business of nation-building was stressed.

Where there was trust, the scene was set for the establishment of dialogue and, therefore, the possibilities of mutual understanding, but the very attempt to create an understanding of Sikhism also brought with it that which was, in some cases, to undermine relationships, that is Western scholarship which was dominated, from the perspective of many Sikhs, by an unacceptable critical methodology both in terms of the analysis of Sikh history and the scriptures.

One hundred years after the first crisis of confidence caused by the influx of Christian missionaries, Western scholarship and the work of the *Arya Samaj*, a second major crisis of identity was developed in the 1980s by the political, social and religious upheaval of the Panjab. A consequence of this was to render the work of the Christian Institute of Sikh Studies all but impossible with the result that just as the major re-direction of effort on the part of the missionaries in the 1880s was towards the lower classes and away from the Sikhs, so there was a change in the emphasis of the Institution's work during the late 1980s towards greater support for the Dalit Christians of the Panjab.

That would almost leave the Sikh Diaspora as the venue for dialogue between Christians and Sikhs. This has been demonstrated by the depth of spiritual searching that has taken place in not only the consultations sponsored by the United Reformed Church but also the scripture studies which were part of the life of the King's Hall Methodist Church in Southall. Whilst not all of those who were involved in this latter style of dialogue were enthusiastic, others felt their faith really was challenged and deepened. The process of dialogue, often for the first time in their lives, demanded two procedures.

The first was to seriously consider what they actually believed. Years of sincere and devoted service within the church had not necessarily meant a life-time of reflection upon their faith. Suddenly people were confronted by the theological traditions of the church which they had often taken for granted and now had to ask themselves the question: 'Do I really believe that?' It was not an easy process, it brought the possibility both of doubt and of deepened faith. Dialogue is risk.

The second matter to confront those involved in dialogue was that of articulating the faith. It may be all very well to say one holds a certain belief. It is another matter to speak of that belief in a manner which is free of the jargon of closed religious systems. There was need to find words which actually described concepts and not to use words lightly. So, for instance, terms such as 'salvation' and 'liberation' were not interchangeable, nor, for that matter, the word 'God'.

The experience of Southall not only stimulated and provoked faith, but it demonstrated that we live in a pluralist society and that cannot be avoided. However, it can be of value in terms of recommitment to, and new understanding of, faith.

This is one side of the encounter. What of the Sikh perspective?

7

Suspicion and Concern

Thus far we have examined the early encounters of Sikhs and Christians from the latter's perspective. We are faced with the recognition that many of our resources come essentially from reports, letter and other documents written by missionaries themselves and that, therefore, they will put a particular gloss on their presentations since mission enthusiasts in home countries would have been looking for success. We move now to the other side of the coin, as it were. How did Sikhs respond to the incoming Christian missionaries? What were their expectations? This we shall explore from various documents and books, from newspaper articles of the time and from any other sources that may give us a sense of Sikh attitudes and understanding. By contrast to the albeit limited resources regarding the encounter of Sikhs and Christians from Christian perspectives, the material available from Sikh perspectives is even less and, apart from relatively short pieces written specifically on this matter, much must be garnered *en passant*. We will explore the issue in four areas:

The first is in terms of early Sikh responses to Christian presence in the Panjab, from the time of Bhai Gurdas, to the entry and establishment of Protestant missions in the Nineteenth Century. The second will be regarding the reinforcement of the Sikh religious base and will consider the establishment of the *Singh Sabhas* as a response to the challenge of both Hinduism and Christian missions to the Sikhs of the Panjab. We then move to see how popular notions of the work of the missionaries were considered in the Sikh press and tracts and finally consider how Sikhs responded to Western Orientalism.

Early Sikh Responses to Christian Presence in the Panjab

Bhai Gurdas (1558-1637) was Guru Arjan's amanuensis in the compilation of the *Adi Granth*. He was also the first Sikh theologian, a type of St Paul figure, who, in passing, commented upon the people of other faiths with whom he had contact.[1] Of them he writes:

> *Isai* (Christians) *Musai* (Jews)
> *Haumaim* (self-centred) Hairane (confused).[2]

This passage must be seen by way of a contrast to Hinduism and within its context, that of the qualities inherent in a true Sikh, especially such a person's being free from the practice of rituals because liberation is possible as a family member:

> Recitations, penances, mortifications, ascetic practices are acts of egoism;

> Fasts, rituals, pilgrimages, are done for personal ends...

> Many persons live and die for rituals, good deeds, fears and superstitions.

> Only the Guru-orientated get eternal happiness.

> They [are] ferr[ied] across the terrible world ocean aided by holy company and in the Guru's boat.[3]

Bhai Gurdas's criticisms are all the more significant in that whilst the Reformation was in process in Europe, he protests not only against

---

1. Ganda Singh in *The Khalsa* of 15 June, 1930 suggests that Bhai Gurdas met Akbar the Great at the Dharamshal of Babu Mang Parkash in Agra - no source is given. In his *Punjabi Duniya*, Patiala, Punjabi University, 1969, pp. 4f, Bhai Randhir Singh claims that Bhai Gurdas participated in such interfaith meetings - *Sarab Dharam Samelan*, organised by Abul Fazul, the Minister of Religious Affairs in Akbar's court. The suggestion is made that Bhai Gurdas attended an interfaith meeting of the *Deen Ilahi* of Akbar the Great at Fatehpur Sikri at which were also present Muslims, Hindus and Christians. Sourced from letters to the author from the Rev'd Dr Anand Spencer of Punjabi University, Patiala, dt. 16 December 1994 and from Dr Darshan Singh of the same university on 7 February 1995.

2. *Var* 38.11 quoted in James Massey: 'Christianity and Culture: Their Relationship in the 19th and 20th Centuries in Punjab' in *Bulletin of the Christian Institute of Sikh Studies (BCISS)* Vol. 17 No. 1, January 1988, p. 3, quoting S. Amar Singh Chaker: *Varan Gian Ratnavali Bhai Gurdas Ji*, Amritsar, Shiromani Gurdwara Parbandhak Committee, 1981, p. 409. See also, Macauliffe: *The Sikh Religion*, New Delhi, S. Chand & Company, 1983, Vol. IV, p. 271.

3. *Var* 38.12. in: Gobind Singh Mansukhani: *Hymns from Bhai Gurdas's Compositions*, Southall, Sikh Missionary Society, 1988, p. 85.

the self-centredness of the Christians but implicitly objects to Jesuit celibacy and contrasts the Sikhs' rejection of ritual with the ritual which would have comprised Roman Catholic worship. The phrase 'in the Guru's boat' indicates that liberation is possible only through the grace of God, a primary doctrine for both Sikh and Reformed theologians alike.

Sikhs may have seen themselves as targets, not simply of political and economic exploitation, but theological hostility too. 'The charter granted in 1600 by Queen Elizabeth of England to a colonising company spoke of "duties higher than those of Commerce."'[4] Colonial imperialism is thus seen as the first phase in religious imperialism by a present day Sikh historian - 'If merchants must buy and sell, they must also convert.'[5]

Even if most merchants did not see conversion as a major objective, the missionaries did and the consequence was anxiety, distrust and even hatred on the part of the Sikhs as is evidenced by the response of the families of Sikhs who had expressed some interest in Christianity. Mention has been made earlier of Keene's being met with a barrage of bricks on entering a village,[6] but such a physical response is trifling compared with the long term effects of conversion. Martin Clark reports the history and consequences of the Anglicans' first convert from Sikhism to Christianity. He was Kaiser Singh who later took on the name of Shamaun, on his baptism on 3 July 1853:

> The courage and faith of this first convert cannot be realised by Western standards, for it is impossible to understand by them how unutterly (sic) vile baptism would make him in the estimation of his co-religionists. He was at the time incumbent of a Sikh temple in a neighbouring village. Baptism involved his separation from an attached people. It meant an abandonment of the emoluments and high honours of priesthood, and the loss of position of perfect ease and happiness; above all, it meant the loss of caste; and a literal

---

4   Gurdarshan Singh Dhillon 'The Sikhs and the British' in ed. Jasbir Singh Mann & Kharak Singh: *Recent Researches in Sikhism*, Patiala, Publications Dep't, Punjabi University, 1992, p. 182. quoting Rene Maunier: *The Sociology of Colonies*, Vol. 1, London, 1949, p. 171.

5   Dhillon (1992) p. 182.

6   Annual letter to C.M.S. 24 January 1858 C I 1 0/160/20.

becoming as the "off-scourings of all things." Thenceforth, mere contact with him would be defilement, his very shadow a pollution, his existence an insult and an outrage to the deepest feelings of his countrymen.'[7]

The response of the populace to the Christian message was more in social terms than theological. In a country which values clan solidarity and family unity, expressed here by Clark in terms of 'caste', any conversion would undermine harmony and cohesion, split village opinion and call into question, in Kaiser Singh's case, the integrity of one whose function in the gurdwara had been probably respected and trusted. It is no wonder that faced with such ostracism, families objected vociferously. Thus the Sikhs' response to Christianity in this case was not so much in terms of a theological critique but in terms of concern about likely social instability.

This notwithstanding, on a more positive note, as far as the missionaries were concerned, many Indians, including Sikhs, were clamouring for the Western style education that the missions provided since it was considered to provide a opportunity for possible Government service. For the Sikh, however, it brought potential danger since such education would challenge accepted norms and philosophies of life. In schools and market places missionaries denounced the scriptures of the Muslims, Hindus and Sikhs as 'heathen' and condemned religious leaders as 'false guides'[8] 'Many Sikh students studying in missionary schools began to despise the religion of their forefathers. Some of them cut their hair and beards.'[9]

Indigenous Christians fared no better than foreign missionaries in forging a good reception of the gospel, perhaps because they were considered to have sold the pass. In the early days of Christian missions in the Panjab, after Lowrie had found himself unable to accept Maharaja Ranjit Singh's request to establish a school in Lahore, an Indian preacher,

---

7. H.M.Clark: *Robert Clark of the Panjab - Pioneer and Missionary Statesman*, London, Andrew Melrose, 1907, p. 67f.

8. J.C.Archer: *The Sikhs in Relation to Hindus, Muslims, Christians and Ahmadiyyas*. Princeton U.P., 1946, p. 266.

9. Gurdarshan Singh Dhillon, 1992, p. 182 quoting Government of India, Census of India, 1921, Vol. I, p. 117. with regard to despising their forebears' religion.

Goloknath by name, was sent to Phillaur to test the Maharaja's 'closed door' policy. 'The first apostle to the Sikhs stopped near the fort and began to preach the gospel. He was at once arrested and thrown on his back and a millstone placed on his chest.' He was later sent back to Ludhiana and warned not to return.[10]

The American Presbyterians, as has been noted already had come into contact with Hakim Singh of Rampur, who had had previous knowledge of 'the sinless incarnation' 'foretold in Hindu books and the Tenth Granth'[11] and believed by him to have been fulfilled in Jesus Christ. He had a considerable following of Sikhs, some of whom believed him to be himself the 'sinless incarnation'. Both Newton and Wherry noted that Hakim Singh 'did not wish to cut loose from the Indian community, although he uniformly treated the Christians with deference (and) ... encouraged his followers to observe worship on the Lord's day ... a simple reading of the gospel, all sitting in a circle ... and after meditation all prostrated themselves with their hands extended, palms upward ... to signify their expectation that they would receive the blessings they asked in prayer.'[12]

Whilst the missionaries considered such faith to be 'imperfect' they, nevertheless, acknowledged its significance. Here was an early, Panjabi indigenisation of the Gospel which reflected the practices of some Sikhs in terms of the centrality of scripture, meditation and intercessory prayer. Two further points demand mention, their faith in the figure of Jesus Christ and their desire to be freed from the constraints of 'normative', formal Christianity.

It is no surprise that such a distinction should be made since formal Christianity was associated in Sikh minds with the British Raj even though Queen Victoria revealed her policy: 'Firmly relying ourselves on the truth of Christianity and acknowledging with gratitude the solace of religion we disclaim alike the right and desire of imposing our conviction on any of our subjects.' To this the Begum of Oudh, who witnessed the techniques of the missionaries responded: 'To destroy Hindu and Mussalman temples on pretence of making roads - to send clergymen

---

10. Loehlin: 'The History of Christianity in the Punjab.' in *The Panjab Past and Present*, Vol. VII, No. I, April 1973, p. 183 quoting Lowrie: *Two Years in Upper India*, p. 144.
11. Loehlin (1973) p. 187.
12. Loehlin (1973) p. 188.

into the streets and alleys to preach the Christian religion ... with all this how can we people believe that religion will not be interfered with?'[13] The implied anger here would have been in no way lessened by the arrogance, as Indians saw it, of the British. The missionaries were considered to be no exception. C.F. Andrews, in his *Handbook of English Church Expansion in North India*, is quoted describing advice given to missionaries which gave rise to the attitude of many of his colleagues:

> Never under any circumstances give way to the native or let him regard himself as your superior. Though you are a missionary you must not forget that you are an Englishman first and must not forget that you are a *Saheb*. You may do incalculable mischief if you lower the dignity of Englishmen by allowing natives to treat you familiarly or take liberties with you. They are an inferior race and we hold them by the sword.[14]

The arrogance of the Westerners' desire to be called '*sahib*' is all the more striking when one considers its meaning of 'Master' or 'Lord' and its use by Indian mystics as a description of God.

Thus the Christian missionaries would have had a hard task to overcome the image they projected, however unwittingly: that of arrogant exclusivists whose religion was seen as a forerunner and support to colonial exploitation and as a potential for community and social disharmony.

The Reinforcement of the Sikh Religious Base

The period after the annexation of the Panjab by the British in 1849 to the rise of the Singh Sabha[15] in the 1870s was one of confusion, trauma and distress. Gone was the Sikh champion, Maharaja Ranjit Singh and his family, other leaders were under British influence or had been converted to Christianity, the Sikh *Gurdwaras* were in the hands of unscrupulous Hindu *mahants* and those who had become Sikhs during the reign of Ranjit Singh were backsliding. It was in this context that

---

13. N.K.Sinha: 'Historical data from Missionary Writings' - Second Sita Ram Kohli Memorial Lecture, 1964, Patiala, Pub. Dep't of Historical Studies, Punjabi University, 1966 p. 18.

14. N.K.Sinha (1966) p. 20. No page reference is given by Sinha. The quotation is included here, as with that of the Begum of Oudh, to indicate Indian anger, disbelief and perceptions of arrogance.

15. lit. 'Singh Society' - a movement dedicated to the reform of Sikhism, local groups were established in various parts of the Panjab.

the Singh Sabha was founded to promote the search for Sikh identity and self-assertion. Concerned Sikhs began to reconsider the nature of Sikhism and sought to expunge what had become effete, decrepit and contrary to the teaching of the Gurus.

The Khalsa Advocate, an English language newspaper, was later to describe the situation: 'False Gurus grew up in great numbers, whose only business was to fleece their flock and pamper their own self-aggrandisement. Properly speaking, there was no Sikhism. Belief in Gurus was gone. The idea of brotherhood in Panth was discarded ... Sikhs grovelled in superstition and idolatry ... It (Sikhism) has thus lost all that was good and life-giving in the faith.'[16] Sikh historians of the Singh Sabha tradition see this breakdown in Sikh practice actually to have been started during the reign of Maharaja Ranjit Singh when large numbers of Hindus adopted the outward forms of Sikhism with a view to material advantage and gain. Their understanding of, and allegiance to, the faith was considered to be merely tentative.[17] The fall in the numbers of Sikhs continued as was reflected in the Punjab Administration Report for 1855-56:

(T)he Sikh tribe is losing its number rapidly. Modern Sikhism was little more than a political association (formed exclusively from among Hindus), which men would join or quit according to the circumstances of the day. A person is not born a Sikh, as he might be born a Muhammadan or born a Hindu; but he must be specially initiated into Sikhism. Now that the Sikh commonwealth is broken up, people cease to be initiated into Sikhism and revert to Hinduism. Such is the undoubted explanation of a statistical fact, which might otherwise appear to be hardly credible.[18]

---

16. *The Khalsa Advocate* 15 December 1904, quoted in Harbans Singh: *The Heritage of the Sikhs*, New Delhi, Manohar, 1985, p. 227 and G.S.Dhillon (1992) p. 188.

17. Harbans Singh (1985) p. 228. A major debate exists amongst Sikhs at present as to the nature of Sikhism at that time. Some Sikh historians understand Sikhism to be less monolithic and homogeneous in nature than is often portrayed. See Harjot Oberoi: *The Construction of Religious Boundaries*, Delhi, O.U.P., 1994.

18. Harbans Singh (1985) p. 232. No other reference given. In a conversation with Mandeep Kaur of the Department of Punjab Historical Studies in April 1994 I was told that this fall in numbers was of greater concern to Sikhs than issues of establishing a Sikh theological critique of Christianity. The Sikhs being a practical people this is probably true and would explain the lack of material from a Sikh perspective regarding the theological encounter.

The analysis of the author of the Administration's Report betrays a superficial and mistaken understanding of the nature of the faith of the Guru's disciples, but may well reflect the nature of the popular Sikhism of the day.

A further matter to undermine Sikh morale was the conversion of Maharaja Duleep Singh, the son of Maharaja Ranjit Singh. He was the last Sikh ruler of the Panjab and since he was not yet come of age was placed under British tutelage with the result that at the age of fourteen he was baptized a Christian - 'the first instance of the accession of an Indian prince to the communication of the Church'[19] - on 8 March 1853. A similar occurrence took place in the 1860s when the nephew of the Raja of Kapurthala, Kanwar Harnam Singh, became a Christian. Many feared the consequences with this loss to Christianity of Sikh leadership. Christian self-assurance grew to the extent that the Gospel was preached in the neighbourhood of the Golden Temple in Amritsar. One of the pilgrim's *bungas* (rest houses) was rented for the purpose.[20]

The catalyst for the formation of the Singh Sabha was the declaration early in 1873 by a group of young Sikh students from the Mission High School in Amritsar that they would renounce their faith in favour of Christianity. Aya Singh, Attar Singh, Sadhu Singh and Santokh Singh shocked their co-religionists.[21] 'There were protest meetings all over the province and prominent Sikh leaders persuaded the boys not to abandon their faith. But the incident served as an eye opener to the Sikhs.

---

19. ed. Harbans Singh: *The Encyclopaedia of Sikhism*, Patiala, Punjabi University, 1992, art. 'Duleep Singh, Maharaja', p. 600.

20. Harbans Singh (1985) p. 232.

21. Harbans Singh (1985) p. 233; G.S.Dhillon (1992) p. 191, quoting the Report of the Singh Sabha, Patiala, 1880, pp. 5-6.

See also: Ganda Singh: 'Bhai Vir Singh and His Times' in G.S. Talib & Attar Singh: *Bhai Vir Singh, Life, Times and Work*, Chandigarh, Punjab University, 1973, p. 22: 'The Christian faith was new to the land, alien in its origin, and belonged to the Ferangis who had robbed them of their freedom and reduced them to political serfs. Moreover, the Christian scriptures were written in a language not known to the people, and their too literal translation in unfamiliar dictum and idiom would not appeal to their minds fed on simple and homely Punjabi.'

The intention of some Sikh students - Attar Singh, Sadhu Singh, Aya Singh - all of the Church Mission School, Amritsar, in 1873 to embrace Christianity alerted the loyal Sikhs in time and they were able to persuade them to continue in their loyalty to their ancestral faith. It, however, awakened the Sikh leaders in their duty and responsibility to the youth of the community and to intensify their own missionary work through (the) press and (the) platform of the Singh Sabhas.'

Sikhism, at this time, came under severe attack. In this state of affairs the traditional Sikh ethos was to react.'[22]

The boys' declaration coincided with a series of derogatory lectures about Guru Nanak given in the Jallianwala Bagh in Amritsar by a leading Hindu Pandit, Sharda Ram Phillauri. He was considered to be an agent of the British who had been asked by them to write a book about the Sikh faith, *Sikhan De Raj Di Vithya*, wherein were such slanted misinterpretations of Sikhism that the prestige of the Sikh community was considered to be undermined. In Sikh eyes an act of appalling indiscretion added further insult when under British patronage the book was prescribed for study at the Oriental College in Lahore.[23]

In the light of these various attacks on the Sikhs and their faith a number of prominent Sikhs convened a meeting in Amritsar and on July 28, 1873 the association known as the Sri Guru Singh Sabha, Amritsar was formed.[24] Two issues formed the essential role of the movement, the eradication of un-Sikh practices and social evils and the encouragement of Western education. To this end theirs was a fivefold undertaking to:

- restore Sikhism to its pristine purity;

- edit and publish historical and religious books;

- propagate current knowledge, using Punjabi as the medium, and to start magazines and newspapers in Punjabi;

- reform and bring back into the Sikh fold the apostates (sic);

- interest highly placed Englishmen in, and ensure their association with, the educational programme of the Sikhs.[25]

Dhillon describes how the Amritsar Singh Sabha was drawn from members of the British supported Sikh elite who found it difficult to rid themselves of their prejudices against 'low-caste' Sikhs, thus finding no support from the masses. To counter this the Lahore Singh Sabha was

---

22. Dhillon (1992) p. 191.

23. G.S. Dhillon (1992) p. 190, quoting Ganda Singh: *A History of the Khalsa College, Amritsar*, Amritsar, 1949 p. 2; the *Khalsa Advocate*, Amritsar, 20 September 1903.

24. Thus G.S. Dhillon (1992) p. 191, Harbans Singh (1985) p. 233 dates the origin of the association as 1 October 1873.

25. Harbans Singh (1985) p. 233.

constituted in November 1879 and drew its membership from all strata of Sikh society. Preachers were sent to the whole of the Panjab and by 1882 such was the support they found that branches were established in fifteen towns and cities.[26]

The response of the Sikhs to Christian missions is not to be measured solely in terms of conversions. In fact the response was low with more people from both the Muslim and Hindu folds receiving baptism than from amongst the Sikhs.[27] Influence may also be seen in the way in which Christian mission methodology was emulated by the Sikhs as they attempted to regain 'backsliders'. By the 1870s missionary ability to reach the masses was well established through conferences, regular meetings and reviews of their techniques. Similarly the propaganda machine was well established in terms of the writing of a Panjabi grammar and subsequent pamphlets and booklets; rooms rented for preaching; itinerant missionary speakers both foreign and indigenous; and the establishment of mission schools and medical work. These techniques became an example followed by the Sikhs, particularly in terms of the essential adoption of the Panjabi medium 'because (a) the Sikh community was largely rural-based and their language was Panjabi, (b) the Sikh scriptures were largely in Gurmukhi script, (c) the love for Gurmukhi learning, especially of a religious nature, had taken strong roots in the minds of the Sikh village people and there was a universal desire of learning and teaching Gurmukhi books among Sikhs of all classes. Moreover, the Punjabi medium of instruction was itself a powerful factor to keep alive the religious faith of the Sikhs as Gurmukhi was thought to have originated from the Sikh Gurus.'[28]

---

26. This is not the place to rehearse the subsequent history of the Singh Sabha. It is well documented in the works, amongst others, of G.S.Dhillon and Harbans Singh already quoted and in two further works by Dhillon: 'Origin and Development of the Singh Sabha Movement; Constitutional Aspects' in (ed) Ganda Singh: *The Singh Sabha and other Socio-Religious Movements in the Punjab 1850-1925, The Punjab Past and Present,* Vol. VII, Pt. I, April, 1973, Punjabi University, Patiala; 'Character and Impact of The Singh Sabha Movement on the History of the Punjab', Ph.D. thesis, Punjabi University, Patiala, 1973.

27. John C.B.Webster: *The Christian Community and Change in Nineteenth Century North India,* Delhi, Macmillan, 1976, p. 49.

28. Joginder Singh: 'The Founding of the Singh Sabha, 1873' in *BCISS,* Vol. 10, No. 1, January 1981, p. 13, quoting G.W.Leitner: *Indigenous Education in the Punjab since Annexation and in 1882,* Pt. IV, 2, pp. 29-30.

The Singh Sabha founders also recognised the benefit of boarding schools to train the coming generation of Sikh leaders, much in the same way that Baring Christian College had made a similar contribution to the Christian community.[29] As further support to Sikh education a Sikh Education Conference was founded in 1908 which then offered help to seven Khalsa Schools. By 1947 340 such Sikh schools had been established.[30]

With the foundation of the Singh Sabha the competition was now established for the hearts and minds of the Panjabi people of all classes.

Sikh perceptions of Christianity reflected in the Sikh Press and Tracts

The establishment of printing presses in the Panjab was due to the work of the early missionaries who used the printed word as a means of diffusing their message.[31] By 1897 Sikhs were following this method and after the establishment of the Singh Sabhas, many of the leaders of which were Western educated, the reformation of Sikh society was aided by a number of newspapers both in Panjabi and English. In the defence of Sikhism some of the newspapers recognised the need to learn from Christian mission methodology and, after analysis, to emulate these techniques.

The considerable growth of Christian influence within the Panjab both impressed and alarmed the Sikhs. The editor of the *Khalsa Akhbar*, Giani Ditt Singh, in an editorial wrote fearfully of the future:

An English newspaper writes that the Christian faith is making rapid progress and makes the prophecy that within the next twenty-five

---

29. Gurinder Singh Mann: 'Sikh Studies and the Sikh Educational Heritage' in J.S.Hawley and G.S.Mann: *Studying the Sikhs: Issues for North America*, Albany, State University of New York Press, 1993, p. 100.

30. Mann (1993) p. 101 quoting *Panjab Past and Present*, Vol. VII, No. 1, 1973, p. 68.

31. Harjot Oberoi: *The Construction of Religious Boundaries*, Delhi, O.U.P., 1993, p. 273, describes how the American Presbyterians John Newton and James Wilson were presented with an old wooden printing press, paper and ink by the Serampore Baptists. A trained Bengali compositor accompanied them to Ludhiana and there started the production of Christian literature and tracts.

years, one-third of the Majha area will be Christian. The Malwa will follow suit. Just as we do not see any Buddhists in the country except in images, in the same fashion the Sikhs, who are now, here and there, visible in turbans and their other religious forms like wrist-bangles and swords, will be seen only in pictures in museums. Their own sons and grandsons turning Christians and clad in coats and trousers and sporting toadstool-like caps will go to see them in museums and say in their pidgin Punjabi: 'Look, that is the picture of a Sikh - the tribe that inhabited this country once upon a time.' Efforts of those who wish to resist the onslaught of Christianity are feeble and will prove abortive like a leper without hands and feet trying to save a boy falling off a rooftop.[32]

By the latter part of the century the mass movement of lower castes to Christianity was taking place and their conversion was attributed to the Christians' profession of social equality.[33] A further method of gaining an increase in Christian numbers was said to be through marriage. Sikhs were warned to be careful in this respect since 'a nation can be built through the process of marriage.'[34] New converts were also criticised because of their commitment to the faith and their proselytising zeal. Thus one Avtar Singh was cited for his advocacy of freedom for conversion from Sikhism to other faiths. He was also seen as having the audacity to criticise the Singh Sabha in its zeal for preaching the message of the Sikh Gurus. Described as an 'agent' of the British he was also condemned for following Baba Sir Khem Singh Bedi in whom the British had found an influential ally.[35] In a characteristically evangelical manner newly converted Christians were also apt to stress the uniqueness of their faith, a doctrine which offended Sikh sensibilities.[36] It was not only preaching which was offensive. The *Khalsa Advocate*, an English language newspaper referred to the occupant of a *bunga* within the precincts of the *Gurdwara*

32. Harbans Singh (1985) p. 225, quoting *Khalsa Akhbar* 25 May 1894.
33. Khanna and Webster, p. 6. The basis for this section is Chander Mani Khanna and John C.B.Webster: 'Views of Christianity and Christians in the Sikh Press, 1897-1930', *BCISS*, Vol. 5, No. 1, January, 1976, pp. 5-12. Such newspapers as were available at Punjabi University Library were consulted with the aid of Dr Darshan Singh.
34. *Khalsa Akhbar*, 1 July 1898, '*Isai Kaum Nu Inan...*'
35. *Khalsa Akhbar*, 12 October 1900, '*Asi Sabh Ton Piche keium Rahe,*'
36. Khanna and Webster (1976) p. 6.

at Tarn Taran who, having become a Christian, placed a cross on one of thee walls, thus rendering it a Christian chapel.[37]

Not all criticism was condemnatory since favourable reports were given of schools, colleges, hospitals, homes for widows, leper hospitals, orphanages and various training institutes, the use of tracts and the willingness of Christians to give financial support.[38] Sikhs were encouraged to emulate these activities which were presented to the public as worthy of emulation.[39] It is noteworthy that when a Hindu preaching organisation warned the Sikhs about a new secret Christian missionary group, the Sikh response was a vociferous condemnation of the Hindu call to Sikhs to return to the 'true' Hindu fold rather than a denunciation of the Christians' activity.[40]

After the First World War the dominant movement among the Sikhs was the Akali movement with its demand that *Gurdwaras* be brought under Sikh jurisdiction rather than within the control of the Hindu *mahants*. By this time Christians were more greatly considered to be a threat, the age of encouraging imitation was over. The editor of *Mauji*, a short lived Panjabi medium paper published in Amritsar from 1927 until 1929, expressed concern about the decreasing number of Sikhs through the 'competitive war of conversions.'[41] As with the earlier period Christians were considered to be zealous in their faith, to reject caste, to support various social institutions, to support Sunday School work and to deal with social problems.[42] The threat against the Sikhs inherent in Christian missionary work was illustrated in various ways. A woman missionary's adoption of a Sikh orphan was condemned as was the depiction of a clean-shaven ex-Sikh on the cover of a mission society report. The potentially dangerous loss of leadership was condemned in a 'dangerous report from Jind District' which told of the Maharaja cutting

---

37. Harbans Singh (1985) p. 226 quoting the *Kalsa Advocate* for 22 April, 1905. No indication of this has been found in Guilford's writing though the venue of this occurrence indicates it is probably the result of C.M.S. work in that town.
38. Harbans Singh (1985) p. 226.
39. Harbans Singh (1985) p. 226.
40. *Khalsa Akhbar*, 5 August, 1898 '*Sat Dharam Parcharak, Jullundur...*'
41. *Mauji*, 2 July 1928.
42. Khanna & Webster (1976) p. 8.

the hair of his own son. What was this Sikh state to do since no Sikh state could exist without the protection of Sikhs by Sikh leaders? The Maharaja was reported to have been reading Christian books and wearing a cross. Demands were made that Sikhs should raise their voices against this development since they had a right to a Sikh head of state.[43] A similar denunciation was made in two letters published on 27 February 1928 which condemned the conversion of the chiefs of two Sikh states.[44] Equally distressing was the account given of a woman who protested that her husband beat her and put pressure on her to convert to his new found faith in Christianity. He had migrated to the United States of America and now demanded that she renounce her Sikh faith. She asked what she might do and from whom she might gain support and protection.[45]

Khanna and Webster point out that the concerns of Sikh owned and sponsored newspapers of the time were more to do with practical issues: decreasing numbers, non-Sikh practices in worship, the hold over *Gurdwaras* by Hindu *mahants* and less with regard to Christian theology. This had been the case since the First World War when nationalism was a preoccupation and the future of a hoped-for independent India seen as being a far more important issue for a popular readership.

Newspapers were not the only means of printed communication used by the Singh Sabha movement or the Akalis. A year before the Singh Sabha movement was founded, Bhai Vir Singh was born in Amritsar. He has been hailed as one of the greatest literary figures in the Panjab,[46] who established the first printing press in Amritsar at the age of 20 in 1892. All his life was devoted to the support of the Singh Sabha movement and his novels were written to that effect. Three of his novels, *Sundari, Bijai Singh* and *Satwant Kaur* started life as tracts published by his Khalsa Tract Society started in 1894. His other work, *Baba Naudh Singh*, appeared later in 1921 and was similarly made up of a number of tracts which had had been published during the previous twenty years. The eponymous hero was created as one through whom Bhai Vir Singh could

---

43. *Mauji*, '*Jind dian daraumian repotan*', 25 June 1928.
44. *Mauji*, 27 February 1928.
45. *Mauji*, 13 May 1929.
46. See: J.S.Guleria: *Bhai Vir Singh: A Literary Portrait*, Delhi, National Bookshop, 1985.

make his criticisms of those religious sects and movements with which Sikhism had come into contact. 'The governing idea was to bring out and establish by argument and narration the spiritual superiority of the Sikhs in comparison with the Sanatanists, Aryasamajists, Muslims and Christians.'[47] In the main the tracts dealt with the attempt by Sikhs to distinguish themselves as a distinctive religious community from the Hindus. However, one tract, *Iswi Prabodh*, was written in 1906 to deal with the relative merits of Christianity and Sikhism and describes a conversation between a Sikh and a recent convert from Sikhism to Christianity. Its major thrust was to dissuade Sikhs from converting rather than to persuade Christians to become Sikhs. The Sikh is portrayed as indicating that since the new Christian was ignorant of Gurmukhi it is likely that he did not know or understand fully his erstwhile faith and had he done so it was hardly likely that he would have become a Christian. Two criteria for judging the merits of a religion were then set up by the Sikh; first was the high character of a religion's founders and leaders, some of whom within the Bible and in the later history of Christianity, from an ethical stance, were considered to be wanting, including Jesus Christ. Secondly, the fact that Christians did not live up to what was indicated in the Bible, for example, with regard to miracle working, showed that Christianity and the Bible made false promises and could not be true or respected. Thus, Christianity failed on both counts.[48]

Some literature published in India was equally if not more critical and consequently banned. Thus Surya Narayan Singh's *Injil Se Baithalla Bazi Yani Kutiniti Ka Kam*, published in Mirzapur in 1944, is described as attacking both Christianity and the Bible, the latter of which Singh claims, was altered through the centuries to support various political ideas and regimes.[49]

---

47. Gurbachan Singh: 'Punjabi Tract Tradition and Bhai Vir Singh' in ed. G.S.Talib and Attar Singh: *Bhai Vir Singh - Life, Times and Works*, Chandigarh, Publication Bureau, Punjab University, 1973, p. 141.

48. John C.B.Webster (1976) p. 117f also points out that the major debate was between Christians and Hindus and Muslims rather than with Sikhs. Similarly the last group was more concerned to argue with Hindu and Muslim peers.

49 See: N. Gerald Barrier: *Banned, Controversial Literature and Political Control in British India, 1907-1947*, Delhi, Manohar, 1976. Of a similar nature is Sufi Amba Parshad's *Baghi Masih*, (Rebel Christ) which arises out of the interview of one Ajit Singh by the Deputy Commissioner of Lahore on 13 March 1908 who asked Singh whether he was Christ. Thus: 'Herod was

Sikh responses to Western Orientalism

Sikh perceptions of Christianity were not confined to articles in newspapers or novels. Sikh scholars responded to the writings of Christians. To this we must now turn, or rather, return, to the work of Trumpp and other orientalists.

Dr Trumpp has cruelly misrepresented our *Granth Sahib*, our holy Gurus, and our Religion which we so prize. He has spoken in very offensive terms of the language of our sacred volume and says that in proportion to its size it is perhaps the most shallow and "empty book that exists." We cannot conceal from Your Excellency that the obloquy thus attached to our religion is an object of the deepest concern to us and this result having been, though indirectly, obtained through governmental action, we now pray Your Excellency to have a correct translation of our Sacred Scriptures made into English which will be worthy of our religion and our race, and which will remove the stigma which Dr Trumpp sought to attach to us forever.[50]

In her introduction to the welcome address to the Viceroy, Madanjit Kaur describes Trumpp as a 'German missionary' who, as a professor of

frightened because he thought if among the Jews a leader has been born who will make the Jews a free nation, then the people are bound to follow him because during Herod's reign his officers were unjust tyrants. Heavy taxes were imposed and the subjects were not even consulted on their imposition. Officers of the Government were spending their time in debauchery ... We have shown ... that Christ was a political leader of his time and tried to free his nation from foreign rule under which they were heavily taxed and persecuted in many ways ... Against Christ (people) were clamouring for his crucification (*sic*). Against Ajit Singh too the flatterers (of the British) are expressing desires to have him hanged.' Ajit Singh, together with his brother Swaran Singh and father Sardar Arjan Singh were well known revolutionaries at the turn of the century. He had been employed by a number of Europeans to teach them Urdu and Panjabi. His name implies a Sikh identity though his father, also bearing a Sikh name is described as being a member of the Arya Samaj. Here may be an example of the lack of distinction made by many between Sikhism and Hinduism with some people managing to retain a foothold in both camps, particularly, if in the struggle for independence, it was expedient to do so. For the purpose of this thesis the most noteworthy theme is that of the use made of the person of Jesus Christ, portrayed here as a born freedom fighter whose context was portrayed as the despotic rule of an imperialist *raj*. See: ed. Ganda Singh, Devinder Kumar Verma, Parm Bakshish Singh: *Seditious Literature in the Panjab*, Patiala, Punjabi University, 1988, pp. xii, 12ff.

50. Madanjit Kaur: 'A Documentary Evidence of the Sikh Reaction at Trumpp's Translation of the *Adi Granth*' in *The Panjab Past and Present*, Vol. XIV, No. 1, April 1980, p. 162f, quoting from the Welcome Address of the contemporary representative body of the Sikhs, the *Khalsa Diwan*, to Lord Curzon, Viceroy and Governor General of India, on his visit to Lahore on 5 April 1899.

Oriental languages in the University of Tübingen, was invited to translate the *Adi Granth*. Besides the matter of the almost limitless damage Trumpp did to both his reputation amongst Sikhs and the disparaging remarks he made which added insult to injury, two further notes must be made. One is that the professor is still described as a 'missionary,'[51] though it must be noted that he no longer worked for C.M.S. and when he did it was as a translator and not as an itinerant missionary and, secondly, the insult and stigma is considered to be deliberate. In the eyes of many Sikhs, even to this day, this is to be seen as a prime example of the way in which the church has sought to undermine Sikh values and self-confidence.

Gurbachan Singh Talib, an eminent Sikh scholar and translator of the *Guru Granth Sahib* into English seems less ready to easily dismiss Trumpp's scholarship but recognises the derogatory nature of his presentation. Whilst acknowledging the popular attitude towards Trumpp he places his work within the ethos of the 1870s when Sikh morale was at a low ebb because the faith was discriminated against and some among the educated leaders were embracing Christianity. He also points out the establishment of Baring College in the Sikh heartland and the evangelical enthusiasm of the new converts. 'It is in this background that the charge of deliberately distorting Sikhism brought against Trumpp got credibility and has to be examined. Incidentally, this charge is not true...' Distinguishing between Trumpp's role as a translator for C.M.S. and that of professor of oriental languages, Talib notes the decline of Sikhism at the time and the fact that 'like the Indian Brahmin scholars, steeped in

---

51. This point is also stressed in Fauja Singh: *Historians and the Historiography of the Sikhs*, New Delhi, Oriental Publishers and Distributers, 1978, p. 169: Adopting an aloof attitude that reflected missionary background and rigorous linguistic training, Trumpp egotistically felt he knew more about the real meaning of the Adi Granth, at least linguistically, than those revered for their ancient knowledge of the holy book but who "had lost all learning." This quotation is from Trumpp's letter to the Secretary of State for India, 13 January, 1873 (Foreign General July 1873, 34-7A). The point is also made, as earlier, of the story that within minutes of his arrival at the Golden Temple to seek help in translation work, Trumpp lit up a cigar and blew cigar smoke over the sacred scriptures thus immediately offending those who would have been useful associates in the project. See also Trilochan Singh: *Ernest Trumpp and W.H.McLeod as Scholars of Sikh History and Religion and Culture*, Chandigarh, International Centre of Sikh Studies, 1995. Of Trumpp he writes: 'With his ingrained Christian missionary bias, the mental confusion and fog created by his Brahmin advisers, made him purblind to the truth of Sikhs and Sikhism....' p. 60.

classical learning and the ancient religious systems of India, Sikhism to him (Trumpp) appeared to be no more than a popular Hindu sect, without much learning or philosophy of its own.' Talib goes on to paint a distressing picture ... 'There was no one in that period of Sikh decline ... who could explain to him the differentiating features of Sikhism or put him wise about its character as a liberating and revolutionary force. The *Gyanis* he met, were conservative scholars with traditional learning unlearned in English, perhaps awed by the whiteman from the East (sic), and so the prejudice in his mind began to grow, without anyone presenting to him the contrary view point.'[52]

Talib may well spell out the context and the limited Sikh scholarship at that time, but it does not provide an excuse for impatience and arrogance on Trumpp's part. That, too, must be seen in the context of Christian missionaries who by that time had not come even to an understanding of Sikhism as a *preparatio evangelica* and whose forebears had thought of the faiths of India as being those of 'Satan's land.'

Talib points out two further deficiencies in Trumpp's make-up. First is his inability to interpret Sikhism other than in the light of classical Hinduism. The second is his lack of any mystical sense, so that his interpretation of *Gurbani* was very literal. Add to this his having 'no sense of evaluating history, but (taking) seriously all accounts, however spurious.'[53]

Whilst Talib acknowledges Trumpp's linguistic ability and the many misconceptions and inadequacies of his work, Talib sums up both the state of the Sikhism of the day and the attitudes of the missionaries: 'The man does not appear to be working from malice, but from the effect of the time-spirit when European imperialism was at its height and a Westerner could be arrogant about things oriental with impunity. Partly also the failings of the Sikh scholars of the time must take responsibility. With a scholar like Bhai Kahan Singh being available who along with learning had a knowledge of English, Trumpp's outlook would have changed.'[54]

---

52. Gurbachan Singh Talib: 'Ernest Trumpp's Translation of the *Adi Granth*' in *Studies in Sikhism and Comparative Religion*, Vol. III, No .2, October, 1984, Guru Nanak Foundation, Delhi. p. 65.

53. Talib (1984) p. 67.

54. Talib (1984) p. 68.

If Sikhism was not to find an accurate and just exponent in Trumpp, it was to find in a highly placed Irish civil servant in India a sympathetic ally who sought to champion the Sikh cause ... 'The British Government and all persons of discrimination set a high value on the Sikhs, but I thought that a knowledge throughout the world of the excellence of their religion would enhance even the present regard with which they are entertained. ...In my translation and in the lives of the Gurus which I propose to write, I hope to refute several statements made by European writers disparaging to the Gurus.'[55] Max Arthur Macauliffe (1837-1913) in so writing offered to Western readers a far more positive attitude to Sikhism than was Trumpp's. Added to this was the fact that his work was thoroughly examined, at his request, by leading Sikh scholars based in the Golden Temple. His effort was not without appreciation for they wrote:

> We ... have carefully perused the translation of the hymns of the Granth Sahib by Mr Macauliffe. The perusal cost us a month and a half of continuous labour. Wherever any of us found what seemed to be an error, we all met, discussed the passages, and either corrected it or allowed Mr Macauliffe's translation to stand. Wherefore we now state that Mr Macauliffe's translation has been fully revised by us, and is thoroughly correct. The greatest care has been taken in making the translation comfortable to the religious tenets of the Sikhs. The translation is quite literal, and done according to all grammatical and rhetorical rules.

> We now request the Rajas, Maharajas, Sardars, and the learned and accomplished of the Sikh faith to specially read or listen to this translation, if only for once. They will thus become acquainted with Mr Macauliffe's labours, and reap the advantage of the true instruction of their Gurus. They should also render all necessary aid to the translator, because he has resigned a high post under Government and spent untold wealth on this undertaking.[56]

---

55. See: Harnam Singh Shan: 'Macauliffe and his Contributions to Sikh Studies' in *Studies in Sikhism and Comparative Religion,* Vol. IX, No. 2, 1990, p. 96, actually in places, inaccurately quoting Macauliffe: *The Sikh Religion,* Delhi, S.Chand & Co., 1983², Vol. I, p. vii. The book was originally published by Oxford University Press in six volumes in 1909.

56. Macauliffe (1983²) p. x.

Equally positive was Macauliffe's lecture at the Quest Society's meeting at Kensington Town Hall on 12 May 1910 in which he concluded: 'To my mind, Sikhism offers fewer points of attack than any other theological system, and if patronised and cherished, as its religious and political importance deserves, by a powerful government, it might become one of the first religions on the planet.'[57] In his Preface, he is also quoted as saying, 'Now there is here presented a religion totally unaffected by Semitic or Christian influences. ...It would be difficult to point to a religion of greater originality or to a more comprehensive ethical system.'[58]

Thus even in the late Twentieth Century Macauliffe's work continues to be appreciated: 'Macauliffe's laudable and tremendous labour of love made suitable reparation to the Sikh faith for the injury and insult caused by Trumpp's work... It not only removed the great ignorance about the Sikhs but also earned for it and its adherents respect and reputation, goodwill and admiration all over.'[59] The reasons for such admiration are valuable pointers in the establishment of good relations between the two faiths:

- Macauliffe recognised the need for Sikhs to be self-defining. An important contribution was that here was an author who not only worked in conjunction with a group of the notable Sikhs of the time but also sent his work to be examined by Sikhs both in India and also in the USA.[60]

- He was well aware of the work of the Singh Sabha movement and its attempt to establish a more uniform and unified Sikhism. Thus there is a positive Sikh response to his assertion that Sikhism is an independent system.

- His assertion is that the faith has 'no mysteries' and 'presents the least difficulties of comprehension and the least anomalies or inconsistencies,'[61] together with being a monotheistic ethical system raises its status in the eyes of both Sikhs and others alike, thus helping in the restoration of self-confidence at a time of low self-esteem.

---

57. Harnam Singh Shan (1990) p. 99.
58. Harnam Singh Shan (1990) p. 100.
59. Harnam Singh Shan (1990) p. 100.
60. Harnam Singh Shan (1990) p. 97.
61. Harnam Singh Shan (1990) p. 99.

Macauliffe was not a missionary but his work features here because of its influence in the creation of a better climate of opinion amongst missionaries regarding the nature of Sikh faith. As Cunningham was to Keene, so Macauliffe was to Guilford. The positive attitude to their faith was valued by many Sikhs since Macauliffe's work was to be regarded as one of the few standard text-books on the faith even to the present day.

A brief consideration of the works of Professor Hew McLeod must find a place here, but his contribution will, no doubt, feature as a research topic in itself. His work is featured because at an early stage in his career he was a missionary of the Presbyterian Church of New Zealand based in Kharar and in Batala's Baring Christian College. Hence the Sikh response to Christianity is, at times, coloured by the response to McLeod's work. Having been trained for ordination into the Church's ministry his techniques for accessing the Sikh faith are to be found in his studies as a theologian, a historian and a historian of religions. When in the Panjab he had contact with a number of leading Sikhs. His *magnum opus* is *Guru Nanak and the Sikh Religion*,[62] a book which is a revision of his 1965 London University Ph.D. thesis and which deals with the life and teaching of Guru Nanak. His interpretations of Sikhism were his own 'in which he often differs from his Sikh friends.'[63] In short, his was a quest for the historical Nanak freed from hagiographical accretions. It was thus that offence was caused amongst many Sikhs who felt that their faith was being questioned and undermined in much the same way as many conservative Christians find Bultmann's demythologising programme unhelpful and unacceptable. The book also provided a study of the theology espoused by Guru Nanak, set out in a systematic manner, in which McLeod also considered some of the influences which may have played a part in the formation of the Guru's doctrine.[64] Sikhs were upset by the suggestion, as they saw it, that Guru Nanak made no new contribution to Indian religious thought and in this sense he could not be considered to be the founder of Sikhism as a new religion since it appeared to be simply a rehash of Nathism and Vaishnavism.

---

62. W.H.McLeod: Oxford, O.U.P., 1968, Delhi, 1976.
63. Darshan Singh: *Western Perspective on the Sikh Religion*, New Delhi, Sehgal, 1991, p. 52.
64. It is not a function of this thesis to enter into the substantial debate regarding the validity, veracity and justification or otherwise of McLeod's work and his critics' attitudes. The point at issue here is the response to his work by Sikhs and the manner in which some have seen it as being part of a conscious Christian attack on present-day Sikhism.

McLeod's work on Guru Nanak was followed up by numerous articles and other books: *The Evolution of the Sikh Community*, Oxford, O.U.P., 1976; *Textual Sources for the Study of Sikhism*, Manchester, Manchester U.P., 1984; *Who Is A Sikh*, Oxford, O.U.P., 1989; *The Sikhs: History, Religion and Society*, New York, Columbia U.P.,1989; *Sikhism*, Harmondsworth, Penguin, 1997; *Exploring Sikhism*, New Delhi, O.U.P., 2003 and *Sikhs of the Khalsa*, New Delhi, O.U.P., 2005

The Evolution of the Sikh Community had its genesis in four lectures presented at the University of Cambridge in 1970 and a paper read at the Panjab History Conference of 1969 dealing with the evolution of the Sikh community; the *Janam-sakhis* (life stories of Guru Nanak); Cohesive Ideals and Institutions in the History of the Sikh Panth; the Sikh Scriptures and Caste in the Sikh Panth. Whilst there was some criticism with regard to his comments on the presence of caste prejudice within a faith which espouses equality, and with regard to an apparent change in emphasis in the Sikh ethos as a result of the Jats joining the faith in large numbers, the major criticism was regard to his analysis of what Sikhs consider to be the original scripture, the *Kartarpuri Bir*, which he considers 'stands tampered with and (which) suffers from motivated deletions.'[65]

In response to the fact that there are few non-Sikhs in the world who read the Sikh scriptures in the original language Prof. McLeod's next published work - *Textual Sources for the Study of Sikhism* - was of great value in that it was a translation of portions of the Sikh scriptures together with suitable secondary material of value to students of Sikhism.

In *Who is A Sikh*? McLeod considered a controversial issue within the Sikh community. The book did not find favour with some reviewers[66] who condemned what was seen as a lack of references to the Sikh scriptures and a misrepresentation of Guru Nanak's doctrines together with an assertion that there was a change of emphasis in the central doctrines as expounded by Guru Nanak - the ideal of interiority - and those espoused by Guru Gobind Singh - the heroic ideal.

Sikhism was introduced to American audiences by Hew McLeod in a series of lectures which later made up *The Sikhs: History, Religion and*

---

65. Based on notes written by the late Dr Gobind Singh Mansukhani.
66. e.g. Daljeet Singh's review of *Who is A Sikh* in *Studies in Sikhism and Comparative Religion*, Vol. IX, No. 2, October 1990, p. 110ff.

Society. It was greeted with similar disdain by Daljeet Singh who indicated fundamental disagreement with McLeod[67] Yet within the same journal Surjit Hans suggests 'McLeod writes about the Sikhs with genuine respect, pained sympathy and critical generosity[68] and is himself pained by the hostility shown to McLeod[69] and finally writes 'not McLeod but Sikh scholarship is to be blamed.'[70]

Sikhism, is a basic introduction to the Sikhs and Sikh faith in both India and the diaspora. The final two books mentioned above are detailed in their presentation of elements of the Sikh faith and practice but do not deal directly with the issue of the encounter of Sikhs and Christians.

One final book from Hew McLeod needs a mention. That is, *Discovering the Sikhs, Autobiography of a Historian,* Delhi, Permanent Black, 2004. From the perspective of the review of the encounter of the two faiths it is important to understand that Hew McLeod indicates clearly ...' [f]or myself I am convinced that I never really believed in any religious system or held any firm belief in God, and that the awakening for me consisted of a simple recognition that this had never been the case.'[71]

One further matter must be added to this analysis. In 1994 Pashura Singh, a Panjabi Sikh now living in North America wrote his Ph.D.[72] which it is claimed questions the authenticity of the Sikh scriptures. The supervisor for this thesis was Prof. McLeod. Accordingly a committee of the Shiromani Gurdwara Parbandhak Committee forbade any further research on the Guru Granth Sahib since Pashura Singh's thesis was considered to be highly offensive, indeed blasphemous since it claims that Guru Arjan changed, theologically and linguistically the hymns of Guru Nanak. To this end concerned Sikhs produced a number of papers, now published in book form, condemning Pashura Singh's work.[73]

---

67. *Journal of Sikh Studies,* Vol. XIV, No. 2, 1987, p. 133ff.
68. *Journal of Sikh Studies,* Vol. XIV, No. 2, 1987, p. 129f.
69. *Journal of Sikh Studies,* Vol. XIV, No 2, 1987, p. 130.
70. *Journal of Sikh Studies,* Vol. XIV, No 2, 1987, p. 131.
71. Hew McLeod (2004): p. 47.
72. Pashura Singh: *The Text and Meaning of the Adi Granth,* unpublished Ph.D. thesis, University of Toronto, 1994. See McLeod (2004) for his presentation of the responses and debate as they developed.
73. ed. Bachittar Singh Giani: *Planned Attack on Aad Sri Guru Granth Sahib: Academics or Blasphemy,* Chandigarh, International Centre of Sikh Studies, 1994.

This matter is significant for the study of Sikh-Christian relations in that it highlights attitudes which previously have not been brought to the light of day in any conspicuous way within English medium Sikh studies. The scene is set in the book's *Preface*, the opening words of which are: 'Academic circles are aware that a group of scholars generally concerned with the Christian Mission in Punjab have been producing literature on Sikhism which is far from well-researched or even unbiased. But, it is now well known that Pashura Singh in his present work guided by the ex-missionary W.H.McLeod has evidently crossed all limits of propriety.'[74]   The context of McLeod's work is further explored in the *Introduction* to the book edited by B.S.Giani (see footnote 73 below) which describes the advent of Christian missions in the Panjab and then states: 'Almost since its inception, it has, apart from doing normal missionary activities, simultaneously been producing literature, subversive to the identity and growth of other religions, particularly Sikhism. It is well known that the reaction of the Singh Sabha was partly due to the activities of the Mission working under the wings of the British Administration.'[75]   The authors of the *Introduction* then indicate the nature of the Christian approach by quoting a speech of Metropolitan Paulo Mar Gregorios at a World Council of Churches meeting.[76]   The North American Churches are quoted as proposing that due to the dangers of secularism, Christian churches should seek the co-operation of people of other faith communities to counter a common danger. Whereas the Americans are portrayed as supporting such an alliance, the European theologians, 'particularly Barth, Brunner, and Kraemer, took a totally different view ... (and) ... maintained that secularisation, not secularism, is the primary process in which some of the values of the Christian faith have been put into a secular framework, bringing about a powerful force which is destroying all old ideas. Hence secularisation is an ally, because it will destroy Hinduism, Islam and other forms of what

---

74. B.S.Giani (1994) p. xiii.

75. B.S.Giani (1994) p. 2.

76. B.S. Giani (1994) p. 2. The quotation is unattributed but must have taken place at least one hundred years after the foundation of the work of the Presbyterian missions. It can, therefore, shed only a little light on the background to missionary work in the Panjab. In a letter (06 Mar. '95) to me the Rev'd Dr Wesley Ariarajah, then Director of the Dialogue Unit of the World Council of Churches, writes that the quotation from Mar Gregorios cannot be found in papers in W.C.C. archives.

they considered to be superstition. So we should ally ourselves with secularisation, and see if it is the work of God.'[77] The authors go on to describe 'a similar debate (which) took place in Madras in 1932 or 1933'[78] at which again 'the American point of view was totally defeated'. Quoting Brunner in *Either/Or*, who claimed 'the only remaining enemy was mysticism', Mar Gregorios was quoted as pointing out 'That is why at the World Council of Churches it was almost impossible to begin any kind of dialogue.'[79] Similarly Mar Gregorios is quoted as saying of the Nairobi Assembly that a resolution was passed 'saying that under no circumstances should multi-religious dialogue put Christianity at the same level as other religions...' In fairness to Mar Gregorios the authors also quote him as saying that he and others were trying to change this attitude. In summing up the attitude of Christians the authors write: 'We do not say that honest attempts at interfaith dialogue are not taking place, but the general approach governing missionary activities is quite clear.'

Thus dialogue with Christians may not come easily for some Sikhs who see their faith as having been undermined by Western academics at a time when it was also coming under attack from other forces in India, notably the staunchly Hindu R.S.S. Likewise the assault on the 'Golden Temple' together with further attacks on Sikhs and Sikh property following the assassination of Mrs Gandhi would have had the effect of lowering Sikh self-esteem and morale. In all, one hundred years after the events which resulted in the establishment of the Singh Sabhas one has a sense of *déjà vu* with many Sikhs understandably defending their ancestral faith, encouraging a recognition of the distinctive nature of Sikhism vis-à-vis Hinduism and being suspicious of those faiths, including Christianity, which sought to embrace Sikhs within their fold.[80]

---

77. B.S. Giani (1994) p. 2. This presumably is a précis of a speech made by Mar Gregorios in which he sums up the history of the W.C.C.'s involvement in dialogue.
78. Possibly the Tambaram Conference of 1938?
79. B.S. Giani (1994) p. 3.
80. See: Gurdarshan Singh Dhillon: 'The Sikhs and the British - 1849-1920' in *Punjab Past and Present*, Vol. XXIV, No. II, October, 1990, p. 454: 'As we have noted the British allowed, under the protection of their wings free play to the Christian missionaries to attack the identity and ideology of the Sikh religion, its history and institutions. These missions were located in the heart of Sikh areas like Batala. The purpose and work of these missions is well known. The journalistic work of McLeod, who has for long years been a functionary of the Batala Christian Centre can be taken to be typically representative and revealing of the aims and objectives of such centres.'

8

Sikh Reflections on Christian Theology

There is little material available on this issue from the pens of Sikh authors though the greater contact between the two faiths, due in part to the Sikh diaspora, has meant that a small number of Sikhs are beginning to take up this subject. In part, the previous lack of material from a Sikh perspective can be seen to be a result of the context in which the early contacts were made.

During the Nineteenth Century many Sikhs were inclined to make contact with Christians simply because through mission schools an opening had been established providing access to Western education and, therefore, potential posts with the British Government in India. Matters of theology were, therefore, of little importance. Furthermore, the numbers of missionaries interested in Sikhism were few with the result that there would have been little understanding of the Sikh faith and this, coupled with evangelical zeal, would have meant that many of the missionaries with whom Sikhs came into contact would have been disparaging about Sikhism. This would not have been a fertile ground for substantial intellectual critiques of Christian theology, let alone constructive, exploratory dialogue.

Sikhs were also faced with a further problem. In a Foreword to Wazir Singh's *Philosophy of Sikh Religion*, Prof. Pritam Singh of Guru Nanak Dev University, Amritsar, states that of the famous names in the field of Sikh Studies who were trained prior to the partition of India many 'had no regular training in philosophy or theology proper.'[1] With the creation

---

1. Wazir Singh (1981): *Philosophy of Sikh Religion*, Delhi, Ess Ess Publications, p. v. He names: Khazan Singh, Jodh Singh, Dr. Mohan Singh, Teja Singh, Sahib Singh, G.S.Talib, Natain Singh, Gopal Singh, Daljeet Singh. When Sher Singh returned to the Panjab after gaining his London University Ph.D. (published as *Philosophy of Sikhism*) he found no department of Philosophy in a Panjabi University in which to teach.

142

The Word of God is Not Bound

of Punjabi University, Patiala and Guru Nanak Dev University in Amritsar, opportunities arose for the likes of Dr. Wazir Singh to open up the area of Sikh Studies to students.

This matter is also influenced by the differing theological methodology of the two faiths. For the Sikh, dogma tends to be anathema consequently the experience of God in one's life is of far greater importance than systematic and dogmatic theology. Jasbir Singh Ahluwalia outlines why this is the case:

-   God is seen as possessing infinite attributes and aspects. From here, Sikhism, unlike Christianity and Islam, asserts that no religion can claim to be the full and final cognition of God, of reality. Such is the inexhaustibility of the Divine.

-   Guru Nanak says in his *Japji* that the glory of God is perceived and sung under such aspects as are relative to the endowments of the seeker. In other words, God reveals Himself to man in terms of the constitution and faculties of the human mind, and in accordance with the needs of the age. The relativity of the perceptual form and the historicity of the content of religious experience account for the validity of various approaches to the Divine and of different doors to salvation.[2]

This also leads to a further reason for such little interest being expressed in the creation of a critique of Christianity - if all faiths have the potential of leading to salvation there is little point in making such critiques. Such enterprises seem to be needed only by those whose views of their own faith's exclusivity demand proof of the salvific invalidity of other faiths.

In 1987 Prof. Hew McLeod suggested that, amongst Sikhs, in terms of the systematic expression of beliefs...' (t)heology is largely neglected'.[3] Few comparative studies of Sikhism and Christianity are to be found.

---

2. Jasbir Singh Ahluwalia (1983): *The Sovereignty of the Sikh Doctrine*, New Delhi, Bahri Publications, p. 128f.

3. Hew McLeod (1988): 'A Sikh Theology for Modern Times' in ed. O'Connell, Israel & Oxtoby: *Sikh History and Religion in the Twentieth Century*, University of Toronto, p. 32.

There are articles, but essentially the last book from the partnership of Owen Cole and Piara Singh Sambhi is the only substantial work on this issue.[4]

Thus one is left with gleaning references to Christianity which are made *en passant* in the books of various Sikh authors. In general such references are of a fairly positive nature since they are made by way of an attempt to enable the Western reader to understand Sikhism through the vocabulary of Christianity. This is not always successful. An example is in terms of the use of the term 'communion' for the distribution of *kara prasad*, the fudge-like preparation given to all members of the congregation after worship in the *Gurdwara*. Whilst parallel concepts of sharing, equality and fellowship may be readily apparent, the more subtle understanding of being caught up in the Body of Christ and the sacrificial events of Good Friday is absent.

References to Christianity *en passant*

Sher Singh in his *Philosophy of Sikhism*[5] indicates that although he is led to believe that Guru Nanak went to Arabia and Palestine, nevertheless he rejects the idea that Guru Nanak was deeply influenced by Christianity, e.g. when Barron Jean Pellenc suggests in his *India through French Eyes* (1936) that

it would not be too much to say that a good half of Nanak's work deals uniquely with the Gospel narrative.

Singh responds that this is

...an extremely exaggerated statement and shows utter ignorance ... about the contents of the Granth. But the idea that there is some Christian influence is suggestive and is shared by many scholars. This influence was about the inception of Sikhism. Its submission into the *Khalsa* has also been shown to have been a Christian example. Thus V.A. Smith says 'Guru Gobind Singh bound the Sikh fraternity together by instituting or adopting two sacraments, perhaps suggested by Christian example.' Fatherhood of God, brotherhood of

---

4. W.Owen Cole & P.S.Sambhi (1993): *Sikhism and Christianity*, London, Macmillan.

5. Sher Singh: *Philosophy of Sikhism*, New Delhi, Sterling Publications, n.d., p. 138f.

man, divine grace, righteousness and holiness, are some of the elements in Sikhism which suggest direct or indirect Christian influence. The teachings of Nanak cannot be analysed in such a way, that a particular element may be assigned to a particular source...'

Teja Singh, too, rejects such Christian influences. He recognises 'Sikhism as a new organic growth evolved from existing systems of thought to meet the needs of a newly evolving humanity...' and therefore to be '... a distinct system of thought.'[6] Teja Singh's vocabulary and style, however, indicates an awareness of Christian literature, for many Sikh scholars were influenced in this way, e.g. Prof. Harbans Singh's introduction to the practice of Sikh apologetics is due to his being asked when a student by Principal Sam Higginbottam to address his peers at the (Presbyterian) Agricultural Institute at Allahabad on the subject of Sikhism.[7]

Were anyone to embark on a Christian apologetic to Sikhs it is important to note passing references to the rejection of Christian beliefs, here 'original sin', and also to note that the style is not dismissive, but simply factual. Thus Trilochan Singh:

> The dogmatic Protestant Reformer, Calvin, asserted, "God is so wholly other than man that we learn about God not by interpreting our experience, but by turning away from it to God. It is not our values that reveal God, but we are driven to Him by our 'miserable ruin', our ignorance, vanity, poverty, infirmity, depravity, and corruption." The Sikh Gurus did not believe in such a purely supernatural God, who has created creatures doomed to such imperfections. The pearl of divine knowledge, the seed of godly perfection is placed by the Creator within the heart of man. He is deeply concerned with the destiny of the individual and the nations. His justice prevails over man's tyranny and despotism.[8]

---

6. Teja Singh (1938): *Sikhism*, Amritsar, Khalsa Brothers, p. 4.
7. J.S.Guleria (1988): 'Prof. Harbans Singh - A brief Life Sketch' in ed. Mohinder Singh: *Prof. Harbans Singh - Commemoration Volume*, New Delhi, Prof. Harbans Singh Commemoration Committee, p. xvii.
8. Trilochan Singh (1975): *Hymns of Guru Tegh Bahadur*, Delhi, Delhi Sikh Gurdwara Management Committee, p. 19.

Trilochan Singh also uses the concept of 'Saviour' to describe the work of Guru Tegh Bahadur. Here, however he implicitly contrasts the 'passive' crucifixion of Jesus with the martyrdom of the 'Saviour with the sword.'[9]

In his book, *The Sikh Vision*,[10] Wazir Singh makes a number of references to Christian theology:

- God's gracious gifts, he sees, are interpreted in terms of his 'relationship with nature, so that 'both history and creation stand under the providence of God.'[11] The points made here by Wazir Singh reflect Sikh ideas of panentheism, the lack of a sacred secular divide and the need to follow God's will.

- God's gracious work is reflected in his 'suffering in the sufferings of his people' Here he recognises the central message of Christianity, but also points out that the Sikh view 'accepts the fact of suffering and evil in the world as part of the divine scheme; a blessing in disguise, as it were. And, God in his grace knows how and when to redeem his people.'[12]

- In his section on the ecstasy of divine love he draws a parallel with the Christian mystics' symbol of the 'soul-bride participating in the divine-life, taking God as the Bridegroom'. This has a striking resemblance to the wife-husband-love-relationship employed by the Gurus.[13]

- The love of God reflected through the love of one's fellow human-beings is to be found in both faiths. In this regard Wazir Singh quotes Augustine that 'Through the Holy Spirit, God diffused a greater than human love in the hearts of the elect'.[14]

- He draws a parallel between Jesus Christ and the two martyred Gurus, Arjan and Tegh Bahadur, when he notes that faith must be reflected in the resignation to the will of God.[15]

---

9. Trilochan Singh (1975) p. 42.
10. Wazir Singh (1992): *The Sikh Vision*, Delhi, Ess Ess Publications.
11. Wazir Singh (1992) p. 14f.
12. Wazir Singh (1992) p. 15 & 101ff.
13. Wazir Singh (1992) p. 19.
14. Wazir Singh (1992) p. 22.
15. Wazir Singh (1992): p. 42.

- With approval he quotes the Indian theologian John B. Chethimattam
as summing up the quality of life of the *jivan-mukta* (someone who
has found liberation whilst in this life): 'Supernatural life according
to the Christian tradition is an elevation of man beyond the human
limits so that he is enabled to share in the life of God himself
without losing his human identity and personality.'[16]
- He refers to tithing to be found in both faiths.[17]

Wazir Singh's bibliography indicates reference to a number of works
by significant Christian authors and, therefore, he reflects a greater
understanding of Christianity than is possible for those who have
restricted access to Christian literature.

Of the latter group Bhagat Singh Hira's *Semitic Religious Thought
and Sikhism*[18] is a prime example. In his introduction to Christianity he
emphasises the Asian origin of the faith and mission as a central motive.
Much of the life of Christ is then portrayed through the quotation of
New Testament scripture. However, the period of Jesus' life from the age
of twelve until the age of thirty comes in for scrutiny with suggestions
being made that he could have:

- 'acquired theological knowledge from Egyptian theologians' or
- 'followed his ancestral occupation' or
- 'visited a Buddhist Nalanda University' or
- 'associated with Brahmins or Buddhist occulists (sic) to learn from
the secret of Occultism.'[19]

It is also suggested that Christ may have visited Kashmir. The author
then considers some of the central doctrines of Christianity which he
considers to be 'a great advance on Judaism'[20] but on which faith many
Christian doctrines were based. Thus God is recognised as loving, all-
sovereign and triune. However, the fact of evil is inadequately dealt with

---

16. Wazir Singh (1992) p. 92 quoting Chethimattam: *Journal of Dharma*, Bangalore, October-
December, 1987. No further details given.
17. Wazir Singh (1992) p. 112f.
18. Bhagat Singh Hira (1992) *Semitic Thought and Sikhism*, Delhi, National Book Shop.
19. Hira (1992) p. 111.
20. Hira (1992) p. 129.

according to Hira since Christianity espouses a 'two-power' theory. Angels, Cosmogony, Resurrection, Ethical teaching, Heaven and Hell (borrowed from Zoroastrianism) are dealt with, as is the concept of sacrifice about which he makes no reference to the nature of Christ's sacrifice but writes: 'The best sacrifice accepted by Christianity is the spiritual sacrifice, that is, the sacrifice of self-ego or complete surrender to the Divine Will.'[21] Baptism is described as 'a kind of pledge,'[22] and the Last Supper as 'annually celebrated.'[23] The Church's being the Body of Christ is portrayed but its exclusive nature is criticised.

In terms of the contrast of Sikhism to Christianity, the author rejects some Christians' exclusive claim regarding the Christ as 'Son of God.' Guru Gobind Singh, he says, was also called by that honoured title. The nature of Mary's pregnancy is described in terms of the 'Holy Spirit was conceived in a virgin.'[24] The Trinity is rejected, as is original sin. The ease with which Christians seem to find forgiveness is deplored and the portrayal of Jesus as 'sitting at God's right hand' dismissed as illogical in favour of a more logical merging of the soul with God.

From the perspective of well-resourced Western academia it is all too easy to severely criticise Hira's inadequate characterization of Christianity. However, herein lies one of the difficulties of the encounter. It is in terms of the lack of materials on Christianity available to Sikhs and, therefore, if any wish to make any assessment of that faith, let alone an adequate one, they are obliged to consult either very old books containing outdated ideas or newer material in terms of tracts of dubious provenance. Thus any Sikh misrepresentation of Christianity is less likely to be due to wilful pique than to woeful resources.

Daljeet Singh, whose major concern, of late, has been to counter Western methods of analysis of Sikhism, had previously written a study on mysticism entitled *Sikhism: A Comparative Study of its Theology and Mysticism.*[25] In Christ he sees one whose mysticism does not 'bifurcate

---

21. Hira (1992) p. 149.
22. Hira (1992) p. 153.
23. Hira (1992) p. 153.
24. Hira (1992) p. 176.
25. Daljeet Singh (1979) *Sikhism: A Comparative Study of its Theology and Mysticism*, New Delhi, Sterling.

the spiritual from the temporal,'[26] thus Christ's view in this matter is seen
to be in keeping with the Sikh ideal. Similarly appreciated is his
understanding of the reality of the world and the fact that he 'suffered
crucification (sic) not for his own salvation but for that of all men.'[27] As
he reviews the ideas of various Christian mystics, Daljeet Singh writes
with greater support for those mystics whose life-style is more towards
the 'active execution of God's will as was done by Christ'[28] rather than
in terms of mystic union with God. Such a 'quietist ideal of enjoyment
of the Beatific Vision, or of union with God...' seems to Daljeet Singh
to be contrary to Christ's life with its response of 'love to all men even
if they did him utmost harm.'[29] One detects the Sikh recognition that
liberation is possible in what is referred to by Hindus and Sikhs as the
'householder state', that is within ordinary, day-to-day life. There is a
consequent appreciation of active involvement in the affairs of state.
Thus of the injunction to 'Render to Caesar the things of Caesar' he
writes that the words:

> ...have, we believe, been often misunderstood. Those were spoken in
> a context where the objective was only to dispel an unwarranted
> charge. But, these have been misconstrued to exclude all socio-
> political activity from the mystic life. Christ's crucification (sic) by
> the Roman authorities, though not of his own seeking, could certainly
> have been avoided, if he had felt that the life of God had nothing to
> do with the path of moral confrontation with the authorities. It has
> been a misunderstanding of the issue that later led to the virtual
> division of life into the field of Church and that of the kings. That
> day, Satan must have gloated over his first major victory over the
> forces of religion, thereby securing the socio-political spheres as his
> special and exclusive presence.[30]

He finally considers most Christian mystics not to have fulfilled
their calling in that, unlike Christ who was actively involved in the love
and service of humanity, they 'have remained captivated and content

---

26. Daljeet Singh (1979) p. 117.
27. Daljeet Singh (1979) p. 117.
28. Daljeet Singh (1979) p. 121.
29. Daljeet Singh (1979) p. 122.
30. Daljeet Singh (1979) p. 128.

with the raptures and the ecstasies of the spiritual experiences, instead of returning to a life of active participation in the world.'[31]

Valuable for a consideration of a Christian apologetic to Sikhs is the passing reference to the differing understandings of the nature of God's gracious dealings with humanity to be found in Dharam Singh's *Sikh Theology of Liberation*.[32] For him '...the Sikh concept of grace is different from the Christian concept of grace. In the latter sense, the Divine grace is bestowed upon a human as a divine prerogative whereas in the Sikh metaphysical system man has to earn it through good and righteous deeds, implicitly suggesting that man could, while still living an active but righteous social life, earn divine grace and thereby realize God.'[(33)] As with other Sikh writers Dharam Singh also rejects the traditional Christian concept of 'original sin.'[34]

Kapur Singh was a graduate of both Panjab University in Lahore where he read Philosophy and Cambridge, where he studied Moral Sciences. His book *Parasaraprasna* arose out of discussions he had with his colleague Sri Sardari Lal Parasara, then, in 1950, a newly appointed Principal of the Government School of Arts in Shimla. Hence the title – *Parasara's Questions*. Naturally, the discussions of a Sikh with his Hindu friend did not have issues of the Christian faith as a prominent feature, but as with other books references to Christianity are made.

Kapur Singh takes up the issue of antinomianism and defines it in terms of 'the doctrine that the Christians are emancipated from the obligation to keep the moral law as formulated in the Old Testament Decalogue, faith alone being necessary, faith in Christ, the Holy Ghost and God.' He then goes on to write ... 'But in Sikhism such a doctrine or line of thought has been utterly and completely abandoned and repudiated, and the religious life has been altogether and absolutely identified with the moral life ...'[35]

---

31. Daljeet Singh (1979) p. 129.
32. Dharam Singh (1991): *Sikh Theology of Liberation*, New Delhi, Harman.
33. Dharam Singh (1991): p. 17.
34. Dharam Singh (1991): p. 45.
35. Kapur Singh (2001³) *Parasaraprasna*, Amritsar, Guru Nanak Dev University, p. 16.

It is regrettable that Kapur Singh's conversations did not include a Christian voice which could have challenged this misunderstanding of life guided by the Holy Spirit, which does not allow anything other than that which is moral, the more mainline Christian position being a critique of legalism.

Kapur Singh's ambivalence to Christianity is to be found later in his book. In a discussion regarding the increasing secularised nature of India, he questions the manner in which the then leaders of the country were enamoured of what was happening in the West and, as he sees it, the institution of government in the USA 'has freed itself from Christian Church authority and its obscurantism during the past three or four centuries, without destroying the fundamentals of Christianity, and has at the same time, established the right of the secular authority to regulate social inter-relationship and growth ...(and, therefore, the Indian leaders suggest) ... the same pattern may be followed by India with confidence and safety.' However, he counters that this is a tempting line of thought until one recognises

'that the transition from Church Christianity to the modern secular Christianity has involved compromises, the true nature of which is not apparent, but which are demonstrably tantamount to repudiation of certain quite fundamental doctrines of Christianity, of Biblical authority. Some of these fundamentals are involved in the suppression of Christ's turning his cheek to the smiter, Paul's belief in the approaching end of the World, and also adoption of new social ideals, unwarranted by the New Testament, such as the emancipation of women, sanction of matrimonial divorce and abolition of slavery. This transition was effected, not by the rule of the secular thumb, as some of our present leaders would, perhaps, like to think, but under the authority of a religious fiction which was given the name of "Christian Conscience," but which, in fact, is simply the will of the citizens of a state as expressed and enforced through the democratic process. This "Christian Conscience" usurped the throne of the Church of Christ at Rome as a consequence of the Lutheran revolt of Protestantism in the 16th century, while it took two hundred years for Christendom, two centuries of blood baths and spiritual agony, to accord a semblance of legitimacy to this "Christian Conscience", so that secular authority may employ it as its instrument of social reform.'[36]

Tempting as it is to take up these issues, one recognises how misunderstanding or misinformation can undermine a dialogue regarding the nature of New Testament doctrine, the place of women, the Protestant Reformation and the relationship of the Church to State. Here we seem to have an illustration of the dangers of the attempt to prove the superiority of one's own faith by demonstrating the inadequacy or erroneousness of another faith. In this particular regard one is at a loss to understand Kapur Singh's understanding of the nature of a reforming faith, since Guru Nanak and subsequent Gurus' critiques of Hinduism, and for that matter, Islam, with the call for liberation from the outward forms of religiosity, the equality of women and the recognition of the involvement of God in the secular world, all point to what one would have expected to have been a positive response to the Reformation and its consequences. At the time this book was originally published in the late 1950s, and subsequently, I find no Christian taking up the issues in published form.

Comparative articles by Sikh authors

In recent years three Sikhs have taken it upon themselves to offer comparative articles on Christianity and Sikhism, all three are resident outside India.

Piara Singh Sambhi:

The late Piara Singh Sambhi regularly attended the United Reformed Church's consultations of Sikhs and Christians and made a significant contribution to the understanding of Sikhism within the United Kingdom. In the light of his long experience with Christians he wrote a Sikh view the Christian Church for the *Expository Times*.[37]

---

36. Kapur Singh (2001) p. 273f.
37. Piara Singh Sambhi (1977): 'A Sikh looks at the Christian Church', *The Expository Times*, Vol. LXXXVIII No. 10, July 1977, pp. 292-295 & *Studies in Sikhism and Comparative Religion*, Vol. III, No. 2, October 1984.

In keeping with his character the article was typically appreciative of Christianity but was not without his criticisms of the practice of the faith and aspects of its theology for which he could find no logical justification. Thus he first demonstrated those elements of the two faiths where agreement could be found, notably monotheism; the concept of the Word/*Shabad*; the centrality of scripture; the need for fellowship and the presence of God's spirit among his gathered peoples. Regular worship and the ethical stance taken by Christians together with the spirit of service to the community were well received, though Christians were warned that for some Sikhs it seems as if Christians consider worship on one day of the week only to be adequate.

In terms of the Christian priesthood, Sambhi decried ordination since all humanity is able to come into a relationship with God without the aid of a priest. Similarly he questioned the secondary role given to women in many areas of church life and the concept of an unmarried clergy. For him 'the Quakers come nearest to the Sikh ideal...' for they '...have neither sacraments nor clergy.'[38]

The aspects of the teaching of the Christian church that Sambhi declares Sikhs cannot accept are related to the person and work of Jesus Christ. His uniqueness is questioned since there is a sense in which all humanity is divine. The concept of incarnation is rejected as is original sin, since for Sikhs ...'(m)an has both good and evil inclinations which are further strengthened by his environment and circumstances.'[39]

Sambhi also questioned the concept of final judgement and the possibility of eternal damnation since for him release (*mukti*) is inevitable. Rejecting the exclusive nature of the claims of many Christians based on the words of Jesus according to John's Gospel that 'no man comes to the Father but by me', he wondered why Christians cannot more readily accept the universalism implied by the doctrine of the *logos*.

Kispal Singh Gill:

In his article 'Unity of Religions - Similarity of True Worship in All Religions,'[40] Kirpal Singh Gill, the then President of the Inter-Faith

---

38. Piara Singh Sambhi (1977) p. 294.
39. Piara Singh Sambhi (1977) p. 295.
40. Kirpal Singh Gill (1987): 'Unity of Religions - Similarity of True Worship in All Religions' in *The Sikh Review*, November 1987, pp. 25-29.

Spiritual Fellowship of Malaysia, writes that self-surrender in prayer is vital to worship and to this end quotes Christian scriptures - Romans 12.1, Matthew 10.39 and Mark 10.15. For him the need to put away self-centredness is vital to true worship reflecting the Sikh's ideal of eradicating *haumai*. Worship too, he asserts must be joyful and this can only be attained through the power of the Holy Spirit and this may also lead to glossolalia. Thus he finishes: 'An appeal is made to all such Sikhs and Hindus who can understand the format of worship/meditation as spelt out above, to come out of their shells, to band together to propagate and actively practice this real and efficacious form of worship, already enshrined in the respective Scriptures for all time to come.'[41]

Santokh Singh Bains:

Santokh Singh Bains's review of Christianity and Sikhism[42] indicates once again the dearth of material available with regard to this study. He makes the claim that Guru Nanak may have met Christians though he quotes only surmises made by Sikh scholars rather than authenticated sources. His history of the early encounter includes much of the material arising from Roman Catholic sources and also deals with the vilification of the Sikh scriptures by Trumpp and the sympathetic work of Macauliffe. He claims that 'there were proposals even to buy the Golden Temple and convert it into a church,'[43] though no reference is given and none found.

Of similarities of the doctrines of both faiths he demonstrates the unicity of the creating and sustaining God; God's love and the need for people of faith to reflect that love in their lives. As does Piara Sambhi, Bains rejects the concept of incarnation in a single individual and the concept of the Trinity ... '(t)he Christian idea of God begetting a Son has no place in Sikhism except in a purely metaphorical sense in which the entire humanity consists of His children.'[44]

He is appreciative of the concept of the Kingdom of God especially where it involves 'Jesus Christ's inclination towards the poor.'[45] However,

---

41. Kirpal Singh Gill (1987) p. 29.
42. Santokh Singh Bains (1987): 'Christianity and Sikhism - A Comparative Study of Two Significant World Religions' in *The Sikh Review*, October 1987, pp. 23-43.
43. Santokh Singh Bains (1987) p. 30.
44. Santokh Singh Bains (1987) p. 32.
45. Santokh Singh Bains (1987) p. 33.

a super-natural second coming and the idea of a judgement which can result in the joys of heaven or banishment to hell are incompatible with his views on *mukti* and transmigration. Rejected, too, is original sin though that does not preclude the need for ethical conduct which reflects commonly held virtues of humility, forgiveness, charity and self-denial, all of which are possible only through the grace of God. The Christian search for reconciliation is likened to Guru Nanak's similar quest.

As were his predecessors during the latter half of the Nineteenth Century, Bains is impressed with the Christians' ability to propagate their faith and urges Sikhs to grasp the importance of using English for better communication of their faith ...'we vociferously claim Sikhism to be *Sarab Sanjha Dharm* (all embracing religion) but miserably fail to provide suitable literature for the English-knowing world which is desperately in need of the soothing message of Guru Nanak.'[46] His is a call to his fellow Sikhs to learn from the Christians' missionary techniques but also to involve themselves with Christians in the search for mutual understanding and cooperation for the common good.

Comparative research material from three Sikh students at Punjabi University, Patiala

The presence of Dr. Anand Spencer at Punjabi University, Patiala, gave Sikh Students an opportunity to make comparative studies of various aspects of Sikh and Christian theology. To this end three subjects have been considered:

In her thesis, 'The Concept of Fellowship in Christianity and Sikhism', **Harbhajan Kaur** notes the similarities between the faiths but she adds 'let us not for a moment imagine that the two systems or religions are identical ... the two remain distinct and independent systems and it would be vain and pretentious for either to claim to take the other's place.'[47]

---

46. Santokh Singh Bains (1987) p. 39.
47. Harbhajan Kaur (1981/2) 'The Concept of Fellowship in Christianity and Sikhism', unpublished Master's thesis, Punjabi University, Patiala, 1981/2, p. 91.

In the thought of both faiths where there is a true fellowship, a congregation of saints, there God is to be found. Equality is of the essence, whether it be of the sexes or of race, so that class is transcended by the love of the fellowship. In both cases a form of initiation is necessary, each uses water in a purificatory rite.

In **Joginder Singh's** work on creation[48] 'The Idea of Creation in the Guru Granth Sahib and the Bible' Joginder Singh indicates that in the 'pre-cosmic state only the creative *fiat* (wisdom, word, *hukum*) was there with God Himself'[49] which brought order out of chaos. He sees an evolutionary process in both faiths with humanity, the product of the dust or 'puppet of the soil' being the crown of creation.[50] In the Sikh scriptures one reads of 'many worlds' whereas the Bible speaks of the vastness of the universe, but for the Sikh there is a cyclical process of creation, destruction and recreation.[51] God, who is both immanent and transcendent, is seen by both faiths as beyond time and space but not one who abandons his creation since he is ever present with his creation.

'Missionary Journeys of St. Paul and Guru Nanak - A Comparative Study', written by **Kanwaljit Kaur**, concerns the missionary journeys of both Guru Nanak and St. Paul, both of whom she finds to be compelled in mission through the strength of inner convictions which they have experienced.[52] In both cases these pioneers encountered religious situations 'of popular beliefs in superstitions, blind faith, idol worship and polytheism, which they rejected and strongly condemned.'[53]

Sikh responses to Christianity - four conversations

Dialogue is not a matter of systems meeting systems but people of faith talking together. Four conversations are here reported because the points which arose are of value in a later consideration of a non-polemical Christian apologetic to Sikhs.

---

48. Joginder Singh (1981/2): 'The Idea of Creation in the Guru Granth Sahib and the Bible', unpublished Master's thesis, 1981-82.
49. Joginder Singh (1981/2) p. 143.
50. Joginder Singh (1981/2) p. 144.
51. Joginder Singh (1981/2) p. 144.
52. Kanwaljit Kaur (1986/7) 'Missionary Journeys of St. Paul and Guru Nanak - A Comparative Study', unpublished Master's thesis, Punjabi University, Patiala, 1986/7, p. 130.
53. Kanwaljit Kaur (1986/7) p. 130.

Dr. Shashi Bala is actually a Hindu whose Ph.D. thesis was with
regard to *The Concept of Monotheism*[54] and in particular a comparison of
Guru Nanak's concept of monotheism with that of other religious faiths.
On being asked what were the essential elements of difference between
Christianity and Sikhism she outlined five major points:

-   In an affirmation of the unicity of God Sikhs would be obliged to
    reject the concept of the Trinity.

-   Christians often portray Jesus as a Mediator. Since Sikhs would
    claim that all human beings have access to the Divine, the role of
    mediator is rendered unnecessary.

-   Suffering is better explained as an effect of *karma*.

-   The concept of 'original sin' is not acceptable to Sikhs. Sin is due
    to *avidya* - ignorance, and egocentricity.

-   Given that the elimination of self-centredness is central to the Sikh
    search for liberation a concept of individual salvation as is found in
    Christianity is unacceptable.

One of Dr. Bala's colleagues at G.N.D. University was *Dr. Ragubir
Singh Tak* whose task it was to teach Christianity. In conversation with
him[55] the difficulties of teaching about a faith other than one's own using
the concepts and vocabulary of one's own faith became apparent. Whilst
one may be able to inculcate some understanding of the presence of the
Holy Spirit within the Church as the Body of Christ by drawing a
parallel with the Sikh understanding of the presence of God amongst the
Gur Sangat, a major misunderstanding comes about with regard to
teaching about the Atonement. He likened the Atonement to the
forgiveness the truly repentant sinner feels when s/he has, with a clean
heart, performed the right rituals and asked the *sangat* for forgiveness
which has then been offered by the *sangat* together with re-baptism.
Whereas for the repentant sinner the feeling of forgiveness and renewal
may be not dissimilar, the nature of the work of Christ, essential to an
understanding of Christian atonement is omitted.

---

54. Shashi Bala (1993): *The Concept of Monotheism - A Comparative Study of Major Religious
    Scriptures*, Delhi, ABS Publications.   The conversation here reported took place at Guru Nanak
    Dev University, Amritsar on 26:iv:'94.
55. On 26:iv:'94.

At Punjabi University at Patiala *Dr. Darshan Singh* has been called upon to teach about Christianity. His is a sympathetic survey[56] appreciative of the dignity of language and the holiness of the Bible considered by him to be 'a supreme piece of literature.' He outlines the division of the Bible into various books, gives approximate dates of their writing and outlines their contents. He writes of the various Biblical translations before a sympathetic evaluation of the life of Jesus.

Of the Bible he says: 'Spiritually, morally and in terms of literature it is a superb document and we are proud of it, not only Sikhs but the whole world, because we receive moral and literary satisfaction from it.'

The doctrine of the divinity of Jesus was something he felt could be justified from a Sikh perspective in terms of the indwelling of God within all humanity. Thus, similarly, perhaps Sikhs could consider Guru Nanak as being a manifestation of elements of the Divine. He was also of the belief that Christians tend to be preoccupied with belief systems rather than spiritual life and the service of others.[57]

A similar sense of the appreciation of a Sikh for the figure of Jesus Christ was apparent in discussion with *Mr Justice Pritam Singh Safeer.*[58] Enthralled by Jesus he spoke movingly of his belief that 'once you are on the path He is always with you.' This was particularly so for him during a period of great suffering. In one of his poems[59] he describes the shadow-like half-creatures who torment the human frame bringing with them depression and fear yet from Palestine, two thousand years ago, comes the figure of Christ who takes on that same suffering.

In a second poem[60] he writes of a fleeting glance, like lightening, of Christ in Majesty, when his heart felt a burning, searing impact, which was to be his own crucifixion. Thereafter he was alone - 'the omnipresent, after manifesting himself, has become invisible. Someone visited me for a moment and has left me.'

---

56. Notes taken from a handouts in Panjabi regarding lectures on Christianity following a visit to Punjabi University, April, 1994. I am grateful to the Rev'd Rashid Choudhury for help in translation.
57. cf Sadhu Sundar Singh quoted in Heiler *The Gospel of Sadhu Sundar Singh*, Delhi, I.S.P.C.K., 1989, p. 133 'Religious truths cannot be perceived by the head, but by the heart.'
58. Conversation at his home in New Delhi on 31 March 1994.
59. 'These indistinguishable shadows ...' - a hand-written document.
60. 'Someone came for a moment'

Here is a man who seems to live with Christ, yet this Christ figure is as much his as he is the Church's. Here is the 'unbound'[61] Christ of a Sikh, universal in nature, adored.

Such a universal figure is also to be found in the work of *Dr. Gopal Singh* who was invited to address the Vancouver Assembly of the World Council of Churches. It was there that he reminded participants that Jesus is no stranger to the peoples of the East, whatever their faith.

'Will you be shocked,' he asked, 'if I told you that He was an eastern man, poor like the most of us here and a manual worker all His life? He neither had blonde hair, nor blue eyes as you have painted Him to be, and He spoke neither English, nor French, nor German, nor Spanish - the four official languages of the W.C.C. at this Holy Assembly. Perhaps, He was a black, but had the necessary I.Q. and the moral authority to shake the world through the centuries. We in the East recognised Him - three wise men of the East - at His very birth as the Son of God, along with a wonder-struck star that stood above Him in awakened silence and refused to move as He had seen a sight he had never seen before. You recognised Him not even after He was crucified, but only after He rose from the dead - and then, too, three centuries later when Rome accepted Christianity. But we in India accepted Him in 67 A.D. when St. Thomas, the Apostle, landed on the shores of Kerala in South India.[62]

Gopal Singh went on to acknowledge the very practical nature of the work of he Church in keeping with the mission of Jesus whose cross, he held, the church promises 'to carry wherever there's distress and poverty of the body or the soul.'[63] Having encouraged the Assembly to 'understand, even if not appreciate, the ethos and the spiritual viewpoints of other faiths,'[64] he finished with the words:

---

61. Here one may borrow a term from S.J.Samartha's *The Hindu Response to the Unbound Christ*, Madras, C.L.S., 1974.

62. Dr. Gopal Singh (1983): 'A Sikh Scholar Speaks to the World Church', in *The North India Churchman*, Vol. XII, No. II, November, 1983, p. 3.

63. Dr. Gopal Singh (1983) p. 4.

64. Dr. Gopal Singh (1983) p. 4.

So, kind Sirs, teach us something more positive and practical about the fullness of life - how to swim across (the river of life) and not how to argue and debate about the geography of the hereafter or the history and dogma of your divided Church.[65]

This speech to the Assembly of the World Council of Churches may be seen as an indicator of a response of Sikhs to the message of the Gospel. They distinguish between the medium and the message. The Church as medium is not seen in a good light since all too often it is seen as more interested in attracting numbers to itself than people to the person of Jesus Christ or as followers of God's will. Caught up in the Western desire for world dominance and thus seen as an associate of the British Government in India, the Church was understood as undermining the faith of the Sikhs by whatever means was possible, either through the bait of Western education or the scalpel of critical methods of scholarship.

Perhaps it was good that a distinction was made between the Church as medium and Christ's message, for in that way Sikhs may have overlooked the tarnish on his name caused by dubious missionary zeal. That notwithstanding, through the efforts and self-sacrifice of those who served on the mission field Sikhs have heard of Christ and many have acknowledged the universal, unbound Christ. He is not the Church's possession.

Sikh Responses - an overview

A short booklet may provide a basis for an overview of Sikh responses. *Sikha nu amar Sikha* (Eternal Verities for the Sikh), was published in 1912.[66] It takes the form of an imaginary dialogue between a Christian and a Sikh who claims that the Christian missionaries bring little that is new to the Sikhs' understanding of God's dealings with humanity. This the Christian denies and the conversation moves on to the Sikh's rejection of the incarnation to which the Christian suggests that with God all things are possible. Notwithstanding this, the imaginary Sikh

---

65. Dr. Gopal Singh (1983) p. 16.

66. Baba Amar Das Mukkhsari: *Sikha nu amar Sikha*, Walies Bros at the Ludhiana, Mission Steam Press, 1912. I am grateful to the Rev'd Rashid Choudhury, Principal of Baring College, Batala, for help in analysing this booklet.

goes on to question the Trinity only to be told that if the incarnation is possible then the Trinity is a logical outcome.

The Sikh interlocutor then questions missionary techniques, first their criticism of other religious faiths, for the Sikh considers this to be an improper method of sharing the Gospel and contrary to his belief that all faiths are of equal validity. The debate continues with the Sikh's expression of disagreement with the suggestion by some missionaries that those who do not believe in Jesus are sinful. He says that one can overcome sin by repentance and by having a good *karma*. To this the missionary suggests that whilst repentance is important it does not bring with it the assurance of forgiveness in Christ - grace, not works, is the answer.

The fact that this booklet was written at the time of the 'mass-movement' of Dalit conversions to Christianity is reflected by the next criticism made by the Sikh. He complains that the missionaries were more interested in addressing the figure of Christ to the Dalits than to upper-class Indians and thus attracts only rice Christians.

The document betrays its missionary source but, although short, demonstrates a significant approach in that even if in archaic language, it is balanced in presentation by the standards of the day, non-polemical in nature, and appeals for a better approach to the Sikh community, an approach which tries to establish mutual understanding.

The history of the encounter shows, at times, a lack of mutual understanding. This may not be due to wilful ignorance but may reflect the effects of the nature of the presentation of the Christian faith, its association with the colonial power and from an academic perspective the lack of readily available material on the Christian faith.[67]

In general six general observations may be made:

-   From early days responses were as much towards Christian life style as to Christian theology, e.g. Bhai Gurdas' rejoinder to the Jesuits, or the dislike of the 'sahib' mentality among missionaries and their close relationship with the colonial power.

---

67. This criticism works both ways, British university libraries cannot boast significant collections of books on Sikhism.

- There was a dichotomy of opinion with regard to conversion. On the one hand conversion may have led to social ostracism, and was something to be avoided to maintain family unity and dignity. Conversely, some seriously considered becoming Christian because it was thought to lead to preferment in employment in the British Government of India.

- Concern with regard to the considerable inroads which were being made in terms of the conversion of the oppressed communities and the possibility of the loss of some Sikh leading families to the Christian faith resulted in the founding of the Singh Sabha movement with its attempt to regain 'backsliders' to the Sikh faith. This, in itself, led to a reconsideration of the nature of the Sikh faith and a unifying movement within Sikhism.

- Sikhs have objected to what they have considered to be attacks on their faith, originating first in terms of the dismissal of the Sikh faith by those convinced of Christian superiority and secondly through what some Sikhs have seen as the undermining influences of Western Orientalism.

- Relations between the two faiths have not been helped by the relatively few publications which are available to scholars of either faith. Added to this is the fact of there having been comparatively few opportunities for meetings for dialogue until the developments of last decade.

- Yet, the picture is not all gloom. Of far greater importance than the Church itself is the figure of Jesus Christ. Appreciative of deep faith and commitment to the will of God, many Sikhs have recognised in Christ a teacher of great spiritual stature.

At the outset I suggested that dialogue is important in establishing mutual understanding and is an aid to the process of deepening one's faith. It is, therefore, necessary to move from the general to the specific to consider what may be learned from the encounter, particularly in terms of Sikh critiques of Christian doctrine and ecclesiastical practice.

9

Christ through the eyes of a Sikh Gopal Singh's *The Man Who Never Died* - a poem about Jesus Christ in a *bhakti* (devotional) style

Introduction

With one notable exception nothing has been written, in recent times, at any length about the figure of Jesus Christ by a Sikh. The one exception is Dr Gopal Singh's *The Man Who Never Died*.[1] The poem is self-evidently based on the life and death of Jesus Christ, yet running through it is a vein of Sikh thought, philosophy and theological perspective. Whilst many of the scenes portrayed, the teaching given, and the theological affirmations may remind the reader of the Biblical narrative of Christ, nevertheless there is a deeper meaning to be gleaned which is more in keeping with the faith and world view of the poem's author.

Even the very title can be off-putting for the Christian reader,[2] since the immediate perception one has is that the Crucifixion is denied. This is actually not the case as further reading of the poem would show. Rather, the title is in the light of the Sikh scripture which indicates that nothing that dies is worthy of worship.[3] A further illustration of the representation of the Christ figure via a Sikh framework is to be found

1. Gopal Singh: *The Man Who Never Died*, New Delhi, World Book Centre, 1987. The first edition was published by Macmillan, India, in 1969. A German edition is available and in the late 1980s French and Portuguese editions were being prepared. Hereafter the English edition is referred to as Singh, G. (1987)

2   I first found a copy of *The Man Who Never Died* on a remainder stand in Southall Broadway, but rejected the book on the discovery that it seemed to bear little or no resemblance to the figure of Jesus Christ as understood during my theological formation.

3. See A.G. p. 237.

in the depiction of the discussion Jesus has with the woman at the well in Samaria.[4] Here Gopal Singh cleverly recasts the story in Sikh terms by suggesting that the five husbands represent the five evil forces which, according to Sikh philosophy, constantly assail the human frame. Thus on denying she has a husband, Gopal Singh has Jesus say:

> ... you've had
> five husbands - Ego, Wrath, Envy, Infatuation
> and Greed....

Further he goes on to indicate that in accordance with Sikh theology she must escape the round of birth, death and rebirth and find her liberation:

> But now what you live with,
> - Time -
> is not your husband.[5]

Elements of the *bhakti* (devotional) tradition are to be found in the poem. *Bhakti* is shown not to be an end in itself. The crucially important ends of the Sikh faith, notably, ethical living and spiritual liberation are portrayed in the poem as the decreed purpose of the Christ figure:

> Every man has a judge, a jury and
> an executioner in his own being.'[6]
> 'I came...
> (to) open unto you the winged gates of eternity,
> within you....[7]

Gopal Singh makes use of the traditional nine forms of popular Hindu *bhakti* whilst at the same time incorporating a Sikh critique of the concept. These nine types of devotion are: listening (*srawan*); singing praise to God (*kirtan*); remembering (*simran*); worship/washing of the feet (*pad-sevan*), adoration (*archan*); praise (*vandan*), humility/service (*das-bhav*); friendship (*maitri bhav*); and sacrifice of self (*atman-nivedan*).[8] Each of these we shall now explore.

---

4 This theme will be explored at greater depth later.
5 John 4.7-26; Singh, G. (1987) p. 32.
6 Singh, G. (1987) p. 31.
7 Singh, G. (1987) p. 62f.
8 Surindar Singh Kohli: *Guru Granth Sahib: An Analytical Study*, Amritsar, Singh Bros., 1992, p. 360f. These forms are also outlined in ed. de Smet & Neuner: *Religious Hinduism*, Allahabad, St Paul Publications, 1968[3], p. 249f; Klaus K. Klostermaier: *A Survey of Hinduism*,

1. The first form of bhakti is listening. In Gopal Singh's work, the
   devotee is encouraged not to listen to a human teacher or simply to
   the praise given by God's people but to God:

   > listen to His SILENCE like the flower
   > opens its heart out to the mystery of the unknown stars.[9]

   Jesus is shown as one who attracts listeners who seek to understand
   more the nature of God:

   > As days passed and he talked more and more
   > of God, His Glory, His Grace, His kingdom everlasting,
   > Men asked Him more and more about God.[10]

2. The second step is to be seen in terms of *kirtan* - normally singing
   in praise of God. Here, however, the singer is not the devotee, but
   it is God who sings to awaken the spiritually dead:

   > 'The Dead tore their sepulchres,
   > awakened to the song of a living,
   > creative God.'[11]

3. Remembrance is the important third step, but the author is at pains
   to criticise the futility of false remembrance and worthless, spirit-less
   worship:

   > In the House of God he saw men with flowing
   > robes and pious beards,
   > who burn myrrh and frankincense at the altar
   > of God,
   > and told bead upon untold bead with a cat's eye
   > on the meat of the devout....[12]

State University of New York Press, New York, 1989, pp. 218ff. All three authors base their
discussion on the nine steps of *bhakti* found in the *Bhagavata Purana*. Klostermaier depicts line
drawings of the steps with particular reference to devotion to *Krishna* sometimes through the
use of a *murti* (image).

9. Singh, G. (1987) p. 36.
10. Singh, G. (1987) p. 40.
11. Singh, G. (1987) p. 14.
12. Singh, G. (1987) p. 26.

4. Fourthly, whilst it is normal for the devotee to worship God as his/ her beloved through the washing of feet, Jesus is shown to turn this practice on its head since it is he who washes the feet of the disciples:

    > ...He washed
    > with His gracious hands
    > the feet of His disciples...[13]

5. Within Hindu worship, adoration, the fifth step, can be considered to be in terms of making an offering to a *murti*. For the Sikh service is an inherent part of faith and is in the more practical terms of the devotee's service to the community, be it fellow worshippers or wider society. Within Gopal Singh's poem it is represented by generosity since the rich man of Matthew 19 is told,

    > Sell all what's not your feed, but
    > your overfeed, and,
    > give it away to those in penury and need, and then
    > you follow me.[14]

6. Worship is an outward manifestation of devotion to God. However, it can be sometimes merely mechanical and, consequently, valueless. In both the Gospels and in Gopal Singh's poem these forms of worship are questionable for some:

    > ... made endless prayers and yelled, 'Lord, Lord.'[15]
    > 'Men bow down with their bodies unto their God,
    > but their mind bows not down,
    > like the hunter,
    > who bows down twice as he aims at the deer!
    > But he preys, he does not pray.'[16]

7. In the traditional understanding of *bhakti*, obedience to, and the worship of, God as one's Master and Lord is very important, Gopal Singh, however, points to the dangers of wrong motivation:

---

13. Singh, G. (1987) p. 64.
14. Singh, G. (1987) p. 45.
15. Singh, G. (1987) p. 26.
16. Singh, G. (1987) p. 51.

We love God, not to glorify Him
but to sanctify ourselves.

Like an ass, when he has not
the burden of his master on his back
has to be tied to a tether,
so also the mind of man.

If it wouldn't yield to the yoke of God,
it will be crushed under the burden of
flesh and bones![17]

8. In *bhakti* stress is made of the personal nature of God and hence
    God's being approachable as friend and companion. God in Christ
    is portrayed as the one whose friendship is an offering of worship to
    God:

    For days on end, He fasted and prayed
    and then came eating and drinking
    with the publicans and sinners.

    And when they asked Him why, He said:-
    'I do both as an offering to my God.[18]

9. Self dedication is the final of the nine types of popular devotion. It
    is here portrayed as being willing to follow God and God's purposes:

    Men said to Him:-
         'How shall we live?'

    and He said:-
         'By dying to yourselves'

    When asked, 'How shall we die?'
    He said:- 'By being alive to
         what never dies within you![19]

---

17. Singh, G. (1987) p. 43.
18. Singh, G. (1987) p. 28.
19. Singh, G. (1987) p. 14.

Jesus is later shown to embody this dictum:

And then, he bowed down His head to His God,
saying - 'Father, I come! Let Thy Will be done.'

For the God-man loses with the world,
but wins with his God.

He loses the contingent, but
the everlasting he wins![20]

Whilst popular forms of *bhakti* are to be found, Gopal Singh opens up new and more Sikh-like understanding of the nature of *bhakti*. Outward show is condemned, false motivation denounced, mindless repetition censured and, on occasions, the one who normally would be the object of praise takes on the role of devotee, thus demonstrating divine graciousness and establishing a pattern for the person of faith. Yet a greater depth of devotion is needed: 'Fools worship and show themselves up, they constantly dance and jump and cause anguish. By dancing about one does not worship the Lord, rather the one who dies in the Word demonstrates true devotion....True worship is that by which one loses one's self'.[21] So writes Guru Amar Das in encouraging a deeper form of devotion known as *anuraga* (inward) as opposed to *laukika* (outward). In the *Narada Bhakti Sutras*[22] of Hinduism, higher forms of devotion are described with the suggestion that if only one type is to be found then devotion is perfected. Here grace plays the predominant role as it does in Sikhism. Gopal Singh's eclectic nature allows him to establish within his poem several examples of this form of higher devotional practice:

The **contemplation of God's attributes and greatness** are to be found in the worship given to God by the angels as they announce the birth of Christ:

....the whole universe reverberated
with the Song of the Angels of Light:-

---

20. Singh, G. (1987) p. 74f.
21. A.G. p. 159.
22. *vide* de Smet & Neuner, (1968 3) p. 250. Kohli, (1992), p. 39, makes no mention of the eleven types of higher *bhakti* which would have better supported the point he makes that the outward performance of rites, even devotional rites, are not highly regarded by the Gurus.

'Glory to God, on earth peace, goodwill
      towards men.

For, lo, our King has come to us as
      God and as man.[23]

The **contemplation of God's beauty as he is in himself** may be
reflected in the devotee's being rendered dumb by God's presence:

When God comes into you,
you lose yourselves,
and become mute
as when beauty passes by you.[24]

Love comes through adoration when the devotee's mind is fixed on
God such as when the poet writes that for the lover

time loses its timeliness....[25]

The **love of the servant for his/her Lord** has been explored earlier.
It is associated with humility and through serving God as the object of
devotion by means of service to one's fellow human beings. It also reflects
the concept of **friendship** which makes *bhakti* more intimate:

.... So he who seeketh peace with himself,
and his God, must look himself in the
mirror of his neighbour.

And he alone is our neighbour who is
the least of us all, and whom our God needs,
and man doesn't.[26]

Parental affection is a reflection of the loving relationship which
exists between devotee and God. Here it is reflected not so much in the
affection shown by Krishna's parents for the young Krishna as in Hinduism,
but the care of God as parent for God's children. Thus

---

23. Singh, G. (1987) p. 18.
24. Singh, G. (1987) p. 39.
25. Singh, G. (1987) p. 55.
26. Singh, G. (1987) p. 66.

> God never lets us alone ... just as
> ....the mother
> cannot leave (her child) to his fate.[27]

As in a number of faiths God is depicted as the **divine spouse of the devotee**. Sikhism is no exception with the result that in this poem God is referred to as

> ...the Beloved who is also the Lover
> (who) lies in wait for you to lift you up into
> the heavens...[28]

And as the Gurus depict themselves as 'bride' of God, so Jesus is made to say:

> Like a bride separated from the parents' home
> I enter into the threshold of my loved Spouse.[29]

The concept of **self-consecration**, that is, the complete **surrender** of the self to the beloved is to be found within the poem. In a teaching section the Christ figure indicates:

> It is the destiny of every flower
> to surrender, for nothing that keeps to itself
> ever grows.[30]

Without absorption into the being of God the soul finds no liberation. It is the goal of the devotee's desire and fulfils the potential of the *Brahman-Atman* synthesis.

Love in separation is the final of the types of devotion outlined by Narada but is not to be found in the poem here in question. The capacity to be a *jivan-mukta* (one liberated whilst in this body) is stressed by the faith that liberation is possible in the *grihasthya* (householder) state. The true *gurmukh* (one whose face is turned towards the Guru) is absorbed in the love of God and thus does not feel separated. 'The all-pervading Pure Light of the Lord is lit within him and visualised by him.'[31]

---

27. Singh, G. (1987) p. 42.
28. Singh, G. (1987) p. 37.
29. Singh, G. (1987) p. 61.
30. Singh, G. (1987) p. 31.
31. S.S.Kohli: *A Conceptual Encyclopaedia of Guru Granth Sahib,* New Delhi, Manohar, 1992, p. 126f cf. A.G. p. 1032: 'He who has love within, sees the vision (of God) .... and within his heart burns

Three further elements associated with *bhakti* should also be considered:

An element of **single-mindedness** is sometimes found, portrayed here in terms of praying like the

.......mute earth
that revolves ceaselessly round the sun,
saying 'Let Thy Will be done
on earth as it is in heaven.'[32]

There is sometimes **in love a lack of rational behaviour** shown in the poem in terms of the drinking of the water turned into wine since

......whosoever drank of it, delivered himself to His custody
in the madness of a discovery![33]

Similarly this is reflected in the phrase:

Prayer is a secret dialogue between lovers, where the mind
questions in doubt, and the heart answers
in faith.[34]

The *bhakta* (devotee) will also normally experience the **forgiveness of God**. This also is to be found in the poem, be it in terms of the adulteress,[35] the statements that God 'gives and forgives,'[36] or the need to forgive to find God's forgiveness.[37]

It is impossible to say if Gopal Singh consciously used these pre-existing models of *bhakti*. Whatever the case, they have two effects. First is in terms of demonstrating that the love of a person of faith for God is an essential part of religious response to God's prevenient love. Love is a theme which dominates both the poem and the teaching and life-

ever the immaculate light....' However, those who are not fully *jivanmuktas* will find themselves in the anguish of separation – See: McLeod, (1968), p. 157.
32. Singh, G. (1987) p. 34.
33. Singh, G. (1987) p. 19.
34. Singh, G. (1987) p. 36.
35. Singh, G. (1987) p. 22.
36. Singh, G. (1987) p. 41.
37. Singh, G. (1987) p. 66.

style of the figure of Jesus Christ as is portrayed by the Church. The second purpose is to be seen in terms of a reflection of Sikh misgivings with regard to, at least, popular forms of *bhakti* which, if confined to its outward Hindu manifestation with its use of *murtis* (images) is regarded as of little value in the search for liberation.

The poem reflects two further qualities vital to the Sikh way of life, for besides loving devotion the Sikh Gurus encouraged fearlessness and valour. Guru Gobind Singh demonstrated this by his choice for his followers of the 5 Ks, including the dagger and the bangle as a protection of the wrist in battle. Guru Arjan encouraged his Sikhs to 'overcome all fear by cherishing the fearless Lord.'[38] Jesus is also portrayed as fearless as he approached the Cross:

> He sought not to be saved from this hour.
> For it was for this crowning hour of the evensong
> that he had burnt the life-long day, like the sun.
>
> And he seemed to say unto those who knew:
> 'We possess life to be free, not to be bound.'
> And, as in life, so in death, I walk
> from one freedom to another![39]

There are echoes here, too, of the martyrdom of Guru Tegh Bahadur who gave his life, initially on behalf of Hindus rather than Sikhs, for freedom of religious practice.[40]

Hymns of a *bhakti* (devotional) nature are a common expression of human devotion throughout the Indian sub-continent. '*Bhakti yoga* (loving adoration of God) with *Karma yoga* (disinterested works) and *Gyan yoga* (discrimination through wisdom and renunciation) are considered to be integrated means of entering that super-consciousness (*Turiya*) needed to fulfil (the) human destiny of the transformation of the inner-being and thus absorption into the God-head.'[41] In writing in a *bhakti* style as he does, incorporating into the poem elements of both *karma* and *Gyan yoga*, Gopal Singh uses established Sikh formulae and standard methods of interpretation. In effect he is conventionally Sikh in his mode of approach.

---

38. A.G. p. 293.
39. Singh, G. (1987) p. 69.
40. See Cole and Sambhi: *The Sikhs: Their Religious Beliefs and Practices*, London, R.K.P. 1978, p. 34f. See also Guru Gobind Singh's tribute to his father in *Vichitar Natak*.
41. Gopal Singh: *The Religion of the Sikhs*, New Delhi, Allied Publishers, 1971, p. 32f.

The theology of 'The Man Who Never Died - A Sikh reworking of Christian Theology

At first sight the text of Gopal Singh's poem appears familiar yet it is subtly different. Woven into its nature is a Sikh theology which casts a different light not only onto the events of the life of 'his' Jesus Christ, but on the understanding of God, the human condition, the nature of liberation and of love, the Christ figure and the redeemed person - the *jivanmukta*.

a. God

1. The Nature of God

The poet recognises that God is essentially **ineffable**,
'whose voice you hear not, and whose face you cannot see.[42]

Consequently there is a tendency for each person to have his or her own theogony, illustrated here by the question: 'How is one to see God?' and the reply from Jesus:

Everyone has eyes to see,
but each one sees differently.[43]

Paradox is inescapable with regard to the being of God. Within the poem both the **transcendence** and the **immanence** of God are well illustrated:

How mysterious and distant is God in his vastness![44]

By contrast, within each individual there is 'the holy land within himself,'[45] that is the **presence of God within**. It is this same **God by whom creation is brought about** through the Word:

---

42. Gopal Singh: *op. cit.* p. 38. In his *The Religion of the Sikhs*, New Delhi, Allied Publishers, 1971, p. 31, Gopal Singh indicates that God lives in every heart but is nevertheless not apprehended: 'How shall I utter Thee, name Thee, who is comparable only to Himself, and is known only to His own Self?' cf. Namdev in A.G. p. 485 who says 'That One is manifest in innumerable forms. He alone is where I look. The alluring forms of *maya* perplex man's understanding - only rare souls realise this.'

43. Singh, G. (1987) p. 38.

44. Singh, G. (1987) p. 41.

45. Singh, G. (1987) p. 31.

When asked how the world was born,
He said:- 'Out of the Word.'

For even when the world was not,
the Word was.[46]

This same God is a God of **grace**, for

Like the star-lit space, we are surrounded on
all sides,
by Grace.
But we know it not.[47]

This also leads to human **participation in God's kingdom**, to use
Christian terminology, since
......mere effort
avails not with God, but
surrender of the mind and soul.[48]

God is also one who is **ever-fresh** - 'the eternal spring, that comes
to man, again and over again.'[49]

---

46. Singh, G. (1987) p. 20. Whilst the Rev'd Dr Anand Spencer has shown the similarities in the concepts of *shabad* and *logos*, Jasbir Singh Ahluwalia distinguishes between the Sikh and Christian concepts of creation, the latter he considers involves the idea of *continual* creation of material reality ... creation is taking place every moment. 'On the other hand in Sikh philosophy, there is the idea of creation having been instantaneously brought into being once for all by the Divine command in a Big-Bang manner. Says Guru Nanak: 'With His one Word, the whole expanse of reality came into existence.' (A.G. p. 3)' (Ahluwalia: *The Sovereignty of the Sikh Doctrine*, New Delhi, Bahri Publications, 1983, p. 26) He further contrasts the 'Christian notion of continued sustenance of the world by God' over against the Sikh view 'that the world has been made self-active, self-operative and self-developing by the Creator who imparted ... the principles of motion and activity, once for all, making the world autonomous as such.' (p. 27) By contrast Santokh Singh states in contradiction to Ahluwalia that '(t)he concept of creation is that God exists in totality and within His orbit the world exists. He at once remains manifested and unmanifested, transcendental and immanent in His creation. Nothing works outside His control or will.' (Santokh Singh: *Philosophical Foundations of the Sikh Value System*, New Delhi, Munshiram Manoharlal, 1982, p. 39) Differences of opinion are as likely to occur in Sikh theological circles as Christian!
47. Singh, G. (1987) p. 50. Within the poem Gopal Singh also indicates the very real difference between Sikhs and Christians in the understanding of the nature of grace. For the Sikh, the first step is taken by the human-being and not by God. This 'monkey-hold' doctrine of grace is illustrated in the poem in terms of: 'To *earn* (my italics) the Grace of God, one must live in the world, but not be of it...' Notwithstanding this the major role of God is shown in as much as 'Effort yields, if it may, only the seed. The rest is all Grace.' (p. 49)
48. Singh, G. (1987) p. 49.
49. Singh, G. (1987) p. 81. c.f. Gopal Singh: *The Religion of the Sikhs*, p. 82 in which he indicates that true faith enables one to 'discriminate between the contingent and the eternal. Once this is

174 The Word of God is Not Bound

2. God's dealings with humanity

In that God is involved with his peoples it then follows that a **personal relationship** with God is possible:

> Yea, it is your own God, but he's also
> the very own of those not your own.[50]

Humanity is often unaware of God's presence and does not respond. However, **God remains faithful and aware of human need**:
And,

> is there another like God who is ever
> at thy beck and call, the more
> when you need Him most and own Him least?

> How is one to see God, when
> he knocks constantly at the door, and
> we do not open?

> When
> He seeks us out at every cross-road
> and we always pass Him by![51]

Bounteous in nature,

> (m)y good God gives even to those who have
> nothing to give,
> as He gives to the lilies.[52]

---

known, one surrenders to the never-changing and ever-biding Real; then there is spring for one throughout the year...' c.f. the Christian's claim that God 'is not God of the dead, but of the living.' (Matt. 22.32)

50. Singh, G. (1987) p. 36.
51. Singh, G. (1987) p. 44, cf. Rev. 3.20. 'God never lets us alone,' the poet claims and once this is experienced there is no going back, 'for whosoever goes to Him goes not again to another.' (p. 42)
52. Singh, G. (1987) p. 26, cf. Matt. 6.28ff and *Rag Asa*: 'O Man, why do you worry yourself with a life of 'effort' when God above is always engaged in your care? The snow-white swallows travel thousands of miles, leaving their off-spring behind: do you know who feeds them and directs them to their food? (A.G. p. 495) In Gopal Singh's translation of this passage from the Sikh scriptures he adds a note with regard to 'effort' deploring that type of effort which is essentially self-centred rather than made through disinterested activity. 'The effort of the former kind leads to worry, care, sense of competition and even violence and frustration... the latter...results in man's fulfilment' (Gopal Singh: *Sri Guru Granth Sahib*, New Delhi, World Book Centre, 1989, Vol. 2, p. 488.)

God is also **forgiving** as can be seen both from Jesus' action in forgiving the woman caught in adultery -

Go woman, I forgive you. Sin no more.[53]
and his teaching with regard to God's forgiveness:

He gives and forgives.[54]

Such forgiveness is by way of contrast in the poet's eyes to the demands of those who unjustly uphold the Law:

Ye who've kept back the wages of the poor,
feasted when others fast,
condemned and put to death the just,
ye say ye keep the Law?

My God knows no rest, seeing the agony of man.
For He is **not a Judge but a Lover**.[55]

In keeping with the Sikhs' search for justice within society, it is hardly surprising that God is portrayed as **the supporter of the poor and marginalised**:

And he alone is our neighbour who is
least of us all, and whom our God needs,
and man doesn't.[56]

A corollary of this is the **sustaining nature of God** fulfilled in such a way that does not undermine humanity's self-confidence:

---

53. Singh, G. (1987) p. 22, cf. John 8.11

54. Singh, G. (1987) p. 41. Guru Nanak suggests that the devotee should cling to the forgiveness of the True Guru (A.G. p. 1030) and Kabir declares that where there is falsehood, there is sin and where there is forgiveness, there is God (A.G. p. 1372).

55. Singh, G. (1987) p. 30. (my emphasis) Justice and righteousness are here seen as inherent within the nature of God, but the overwhelming characteristic is God's love. Guru Arjan points out that in the Lord's court, the adjudication is based on Truth. (A.G. p. 621) Gopal Singh also contrasts the judgement of God and that of humanity: 'Judge not, lest ye be judged by man: forgive, that ye may be forgiven by God.' (*op. cit.* p. 66)

56. Singh, G. (1987) p. 66, cf. p. 47: 'The meek shall inherit the earth, as also the Kingdom of God. For, is it not the least on which the highest are raised?' This becomes more meaningful in that poverty is associated with humility and according to Guru Arjan: 'Blessed is poverty if one cherishes the Lord in the company of saints.' (A.G. p. 745)

> Great is the glory of God, for he knows
> our inmost thoughts, and gives, unasked, wounding not
> the pride or the sanctity of even our
> wildest dreams.[57]

Thus far Gopal Singh's portrayal of the nature of God and God's dealings with humanity have been considered. We now move to his portrayal of the nature of humanity.

b. The Nature of Humanity

As with Gopal Singh's portrayal of God, so with regard to his depiction of the nature of human-beings one finds the poem very much coloured by the Sikh analysis of the human condition. Thus one finds three distinctive elements within the poem: humanity is subjected to the round of birth, death and rebirth - *samsara*; human-beings are made in the image of God; they are subject to wayward impulses.

1. Humanity is subject to **samsara**.

An image which conveys the **fragility of humanity's physical existence** and the link with *samsara* is in terms of those 'who live ... in the glass-house of Time.'[58] The goal of humanity is to escape Time in favour of union with God. Thus Jesus tells the Samaritan woman at the well:

> So pray that you are released
> out of this illicit union (with time).[59]

'... (B)y and large, there is **no free-will** for an individual,' writes Gopal Singh in his *The Religion of the Sikhs*,[60] explaining that one is circumstanced by heredity, environment, training and motive ...'it is God who takes us on the right path and also strays us away from it.' (sic)[61]

---

57. Singh, G. (1987) p. 41, cf. A.G. p. 1021: 'He who creates, also keeps watch over what he creates.'
58. Singh, G. (1987) p. 22.
59. Singh, G. (1987) p. 33. Those who are engrossed in ephemeral matters are in fact engrossed in unreality and need to recognise that such matters are not the final goal. *vide.* Fauja Singh & Gurbachan Singh Talib: *Guru Tegh Bahadur: Martyr and Teacher*, Patiala, Punjabi University Press, 1975. p. 105.
60. Singh G. (1971): *The Religion of the Sikhs*, New Delhi, Allied Publishers, p. 84. See: A.G. p. 1021: 'And no one can erase the Writ that the True One writes.'
61. Singh G. (1971) p. 61.

'Man, if he abandons himself to himself (which he often does), is invariably driven to do things which, on mature judgement, he may denounce, but cannot overpower. Who says, then, that man is free?'[62] Within the poem it is illustrated thus:

> More often we do not what we wish to,
> but what we hate to, afraid of losing
> the secure, through trackless paths of
> the hills and dales within us.

> A king becomes a beggar in a dream, but
> when he wakes, no one blames him
> for what he went through in his sleep.[63]

The **believer is beyond death**:

> Then I shall come again to you like unto a cloud,
> upon the chariot of lightning and thunder,
> and destroy you all, save those
> that stand not by ME
> but by My Word.

> They shall see not
> Death.[64]

---

62. Singh, G. (1971) p. 86 . The Gurus suggest that human-brings in their essence are holy, spiritual, eternal and God-like and are destined not to identify themselves with that which is unholy and temporary. (*The Religion of the Sikhs*, p. 87.)

63. Singh, G. (1987) p. 24. In *The Religion of the Sikhs*, p. 93, Gopal Singh explains the reference to the king who became a beggar in a dream. It would seem that a king came to visit Guru Arjan and heard one of his hymns in which it is stated "O friend, the Writ thy God has written out for thee can be obliterated not," and thus became perplexed and anxious. The Guru explained that the Writ of God is based on one's own deeds and the disappointed king said, "If such be the case what is the need of the Guru's Grace or even of doing or being good, if what has to happen must come to pass?" The Guru said he would explain the following day, but that night the king dreamt that he was a sweeper ill-clothed and daily dealing with filth, in all, a miserable wretch. He woke up the following morning very disturbed and reported this to the Guru. The Guru replied: "O devotee, you slept as a King and in the dream became a poor wretch. Your dream-state was as valid at the time of your dreaming, as is your kingly state which you really possess. Such is the nature of the Guru's Grace that no matter what your past or present, you pass through, and are affected by it, only as one passes through a dream, till one's inself awakens to realise the essential kingly nature of one's soul.'

64. Singh, G. (1987) p. 64 cf. p. 71 'But he said to those who believe that nothing dies in the realm of God...' Note, too, the nature of the Word which here takes precedence over the figure of Jesus the teacher. See: A.G. p. 1010: O man, you can overcome Death only through the Word: otherwise to whom else can you turn?

The **goal of life is freedom**:

> We possess life to be free, not to be bound.
> And, as in life, so in death, I walk
> from one freedom to another![65]

The first freedom is that of the *jivanmukta*, i.e. one who, through God's grace, is liberated whilst in this life, forsaking ego and material attachment. Secondly, freedom will stand here for liberation from the constant round of *samsara*.

2.   *Humanity is made in the image of God and cannot exist without 'him'.*

At the heart of the philosophy of Gopal Singh's poem is the *Brahman-Atman* synthesis which implies that the **'soul' of each individual is intrinsically bound with the spirit which is divine.** The corollary of this is that the soul/spirit of each individual, be it the Christ figure or the devotee, never dies. In this way two affirmations are made by the poet: the claim that humanity is made in the image of God and that the divine rests within the individual:

> God has made us in his own image. So, he alone
> has faith in the divinity of God who believes
> in the divinity of man.[66]

Humanity cannot exist without God. One has to be 'alive to what never dies within you.'[67] That indicates the unity of the *jivatman* with the *paramatma*, the soul and the oversoul. The co-substantiality of the devotee and the Divine is expressed in the Sikh scriptures in terms of 'Thou art the fish and water too, there is no distinction between the two.'[68] Such is the nature of the personal relationship that exists between the devotee and God that to distinguish between the two becomes almost impossible.

---

65. Singh, G. (1987) p. 71.
66. Singh, G. (1987) p. 42, cf. p. 65: 'Man liveth not by bread alone, nor for himself, nor for Caesar alone but *for the glory of God within him.*' There are echoes here of the presence of God within humanity, here as much within the individual as the group, cf the *shekinah* (radiance, glory, presence of God), *vide.* Exodus 29. 45f, cf. *Rag Kanara* of Namdev: 'One sees one's Lord, who intimately knows all hearts as one sees one's countenance in a mirror. He lives within all hearts but has no blemish. He is free from the bondage (of samsara) ... As one sees one's face reflected in clear waters, so one sees the Lord.' (A.G. p. 1318)
67. Singh, G. (1987) p. 14.
68. A.G. p. 1278.

God is also to be found **within the 'temple of the body':**

The body of man
is the temple of God.
Shall we keep glass bangles in a box of gold?[69]

God is also **identified with all creation:**

.....Out of formlessness arise
all forms, and all melodies are wrung
out of the rhythms of Silence.[70]

In keeping with God's pleasure at seeing his creation[71] so Gopal Singh indicates that

God made everything good, like
the wise potter his vessels.[(72)]

However, humanity has the capacity to undermine the beauty and potential of creation:

....It is we
who pour wine into one and poison into the other.[73]

This reflects the Sikhs' concept of the *man*, which can be variously, but inadequately, translated as mind, thought, intelligence, understanding, heart, soul, psyche.[74] 'It is the faculty with which one thinks, decides,

---

69. Singh, G. (1987) p. 49. cf.1 Cor. 3.16 and cf. A.G. p. 1346 in which Guru Amar Das writes: 'See, by the Guru's grace, the Temple of God is within you, so search therein through the Guru's Word and enter his Temple cherishing the Lord's Name'. Glass bangles are cheap and nasty, easily broken, and therefore represent human weakness. By way of contrast gold represents the presence of God. Thus the poet shows the dichotomy which lies within human-nature, which can be open to the presence of God and/or to disastrous human frailty.

70. Singh, G. (1987) p. 73. S.S.Kohli: *A Conceptual Encyclopaedia of Guru Granth Sahib*: p. 68: 'The material of Creation, both souls and matter, was within Him ... When it was His Will, He created the world of name and form.' The divine is often referred to as formless, *nirguna*, without qualities.

71. Gen. 1.31.

72. Singh, G. (1987) p. 48.

73. Singh, G. (1987) p. 48. cf p. 40: 'Can a house be occupied by itself? No, it must house its Master. And, he who keeps it vacant, invites the ghosts to be his tenants.'

74. Christopher Shackle: *A Guru Nanak Glossary*, London, School of Oriental and African Studies, 1981, p. 235.

and feels, the source of all human good and evil, and that one indestructible attribute which must be released from the body and merged into the being of God.'[75] The *man* can be human-influenced with the possibility of the individual's becoming *manmukh* (self-willed) or God-influenced - *Gurmukh,* hence wine or poison can be poured into the vessel, or house, which is the *man.*

3. *Unregenerated humanity is inclined towards being manmukh - self-willed.*

   Sikhism rejects the concept of original sin, but recognises that humanity is inclined towards a self-centred lifestyle which can lead to preoccupation with the material world - 'God made everything good...'[76] - but the 'rich man' is also encouraged to recognise that whereas material possessions, whilst not evil in themselves, are not to be sought in excess:

> Someone brings his heart to bear
> the agony of receiving,
> that way we may have the fulfilment and the glory
> of giving.

> Since:
> It matters not what you have, but
> what you are.[77]

   Not only do many people crave for material wealth, but along with that goes grasping for power and the painful fear of the loss of such power:

> The tragedies of power are more heart-breaking
> than those of poverty.
> The mighty oak is afraid
> of each passing wind, but not so
> the meek grass...[78]

---

75. W.H.McLeod: *Guru Nanak and the Sikh Religion,* Delhi, Oxford University Press, 19782, p. 180.
76. Singh, G. (1987) p. 48.
77. Singh, G. (1987) p. 45. cf. A.G. p. 937: 'Man amasses gold and silver, but such wealth is like poison and dust. While gathering wealth he is happy to be called a banker but he is mistaken, as caught up in duality he stands humiliated.' See: Gurdev Singh Hansrao: *Ideology of the Sikh Gurus,* Dhode Majra (Ropar), Hansrao Publishers, 1990, p.109, in which he indicates that Sikhism does not condemn wealth *per se,* but does condemn acquisitiveness, greed and the accumulation of wealth by sinful means.
78. Singh, G. (1987) p. 47.

The Sikh Gurus lived at a time when many of the Mughal Emperors exercised considerable power over their subjects and feared the growing influence of the burgeoning Sikh community. By contrast the Sikh Gurus were of the opinion that the only one in whom power should reside should be God: '(He) alone has the power.'[79]

For the Sikh Gurus there had to be an alternative to such an unregenerate life-style. Liberation, they taught, was possible even in this world. Gopal Singh incorporates this into his poem.

c. The possibility of Liberation

1. The nature of Liberation.

It is this liberation that is the supreme purpose of Gopal Singh's Christ figure and it is closely associated with the synthesis of the *atman* of the individual with *Brahman*. Thus the Christ declares his purpose:

.....I have come
to make gods of you all. For
every man is greater than himself.[80]

But, how is this to be accomplished? Gopal Singh does not use the traditional Christian theories of the atonement, rather it is depicted in terms of the struggle against the powers which can attack the human-being. The Samaritan woman was encouraged away from her previous 'husbands', ego, wrath, envy, infatuation and greed[81] and would have to engage herself in the inner battle. 'Viewed from the point of view of man, it is a fight between the lower self of man as a natural being and the higher self of man as spiritual being, it is a fight between the egoistic self and the universal self.'[82]

The nature of the liberated life may be seen in a number of ways. It will involve forgiveness as was seen when the woman caught in adultery was forgiven by Christ[83] It is demonstrated in the dignity bestowed upon

79. A.G. p. 7.
80. Singh, G. (1987) p. 63.
81. See above p. 163.
82. Santosh Singh: 1983, p. 43.
83. Gopal Singh: *op.cit.* p. 22. Gopal Singh here conflates two Biblical texts here,, Luke 7.36ff regarding the woman who visited the Pharisee's house and John 8.3-11 regarding the 'trial' of the woman caught in adultery.

those normally rejected by society and shown by Jesus' 'eating and drinking with the publicans and sinners...[84] Likewise it is seen through the escape from *samsara* so that one may 'draw water of Timelessness from (one's) own well'[85] and the promise of new life:

> I came with a flame of fire to burn down the old,
> and out of its ashes build anew.
> So shall you.[86]

2. The Method of Liberation

Within the poem the followers of the Christ figure ask how they should find their liberation. Little value is placed on piety, the outward show of religion, 'endless prayers' and the 'yelling' of 'Lord, Lord'.[87] However, devotees are told of three ways in which they themselves can play a part. First, they should make a determined effort to change: 'If we want the vessels to be clean again, we should wash them from within, not without.'[88] The *man* (the mind/heart of the individual) must be fit to be *Gurmukh*, i.e. motivated by God. In his book *The Religion of the*

---

84. Namdeva is reputed to have indicated to God that it was all very well bringing salvation after death, but sinners need to know that they are redeemed. (Gopal Singh: *The Religion of the Sikhs*, p. 43) Within Sikhism, too, there is also the story of the time that Guru Nanak was offered lodging by the *thug*, Sajjan, whose habit it was to offer such hospitality but also cut the throats of his guests when they were asleep. On being discovered Sajjan begged forgiveness of Guru Nanak who established his first Gurdwara at Tulumba near Multan with the repentant Sajjan in charge. (*op. cit. p. 5f.*)

85. Singh, G. (1987) p. 32. The relative reality of relationships with one's fellow human-beings must not be confused with the authentic absolute reality of one's relationship with God.

86. Singh, G. (1987) p. 62. Herein is a different interpretation of the function of Christ in that the old is here thought to be destroyed rather than 'fulfilled' (cf. Luke 9.56). Note that Gopal Singh's interpretation is more in keeping with the traditional Indian belief in the periodic destruction and recreation of the whole universe.

87. Singh, G. (1987) p. 26, cf. Gopal Singh: *The Religion of the Sikhs* p. 64 in which he indicates the futility of chanting *mantras*, an activity considered to be 'spurious' by Bhai Gurdas whom he quotes: 'As by uttering 'sugar-sugar', one's mouth is sweetened not until one tasteth sugar ... as one becommeth not wise by imbibing not within but repeating 'wisdom-wisdom' with the tongue, so is one attuned not to the Guru-God till one mergeth in His Vision.' cf. A.G. p. 919: 'No one attains the Lord by babbling.'

88. Singh, G. (1987) p. 48. Note that the *man* must be fit to be *Gurmukh*, i.e. motivated by God. Gopal Singh: *The Religion of the Sikhs*, p. 65, points out that even the best ethical conduct, without self-surrender, does not attract the grace of God. Thus motivation, not simply outward behaviour is of the essence. It is not without consequence that he uses the phrase 'attract the grace of God' thus reflecting, by contrast with Christianity, the Sikh's monkey-hold doctrine of grace, i.e. humanity takes the first step. The vessel can also represent the human-body, hence the Temple of God.

Sikhs,[89] Gopal Singh points out that even the best ethical conduct, without self-surrender, does not attract the grace of God. Thus motivation, not simply outward behaviour is of the essence.

Secondly there is a need for the devotee to be engaged in prayer:

Pray unto your God
Which is in the heaven within you and
without.[90]

Thirdly the devotee is encouraged to
.... live
in the world but be not of it.[91]

However, the most important matter in terms of the method of liberation is in terms of dying to oneself or eliminating *haumai*. 'How shall we live?' Jesus is asked, 'By dying to yourselves!', came the reply.[92] Such preoccupation with the self is described as *haumai* in Sikh theology, a self-centredness that leads to self-willed disobedience to God. The result of such self-centredness is the erosion of the possibility of liberation. Only when one recognises the need to break out of egoism and to follow the will of God will one find the path to liberation.[93] However, none of this can be possible without the gracious activity of God.

---

89. Singh, G. (1971) p. 65.

90. Singh, G. (1987) p. 34. Sikhs will often read the *Ashtapadi* of *Sukhmani*, before beginning prayer to indicate their purpose and belief: 'I pray to you, O Lord, You are my Master. My body and soul are your gifts... In your grace are great comforts ... All your creation is bound by your laws ... Your servant Nanak is always a sacrifice to you. (A.G. p. 268.) Kohli, (1992), p. 241.

91. Singh, G. (1987) p. 49. Traditionally Sikhs recognise that liberation is possible within the *grihasthya* state, i.e. whilst a householder and maintaining one's normal life. However, it is the case that the Sikh is encouraged to participate in the *sadh sangat*, the holy congregation, illustrated by Bhai Gurdas in terms of the water which merges through the river into the ocean as being similar to the way in which one may lose oneself in the Guru by associating oneself with the *sangat*. (Bhai Gurdas: *Kabitt Swaiyyie*, 63 quoted in Dharam Singh: *Sikh Liberation Theology*, New Delhi, Harman, 1991, p. 61).

92. Singh, G. (1987) p. 14.

93. Thus: '(In *haumai*) he (humanity) fails to perceive the true nature of salvation. In *haumai* there is *maya* and its shadow (which is doubt). By acting in accordance with *haumai* he causes himself to be born again and again. If he understands his *haumai* he perceives the door (of salvation), but without understanding he argues and disputes. In accordance with the divine order (*hukum*) our *karma* is inscribed. He who discerns the nature of the divine order discerns his *haumai* also.' A.G. p. 466 in the translation of W.H.McLeod, (1968), p. 184.

3. *The Grace of God*

God is the one who is the 'Beloved who is also the Lover', who 'lies in wait for you to lift you up into the heavens...'[94]   A recognition of such grace comes in an instant for the one who is attuned to God's will:

> Darkness may have filled a cave
> for a whole age, but illumined,
> it is filled with light instantaneously,
> saying not, 'I'll take as long to depart.'[95]

As has been previously noted the grace of God is traditionally held to be earned even if it may come at the divine initiative: 'To earn the grace of God...'[96]

Liberation becomes possible through God's grace but not through any easy piety or effortless claims. In keeping with the nature of the Sikh experience Gopal Singh has the Christ figure claim:

---

94. Singh, G. (1987) p. 37. See: W.H. McLeod, (1968), p. 157. 'Within a man's soul God may, by grace, reveal Himself. The revelation comes, however, only to him who has prepared himself to receive it. The way of preparation is the path of love, a love addressed directly to the supreme Lord who is both transcendent and immanent, and a love which will inevitably involve long periods in the anguish of separation.'

The phrase 'lift you up into the heavens...' also has echoes of Christ as the 'life-saver' (Col. 2.12/ 13). See: Robin Boyd: *Krishtadvaita*, Madras, The Christian Literature Society, 1977, p. 202, in which he points out that in the *bhakti* tradition life is considered to be a journey in a frail boat across the stormy sea of life. God is addressed as the life-saver 'the one who causes to float' (*Tarnar* or *Taranahar*) cf. within the Sikh tradition, God as the ferryman who rows one across the ocean of life - A.G. p. 1147.

95. Singh, G. (1987) p. 52. cf. McLeod's description of Kabir's experiences: *ibid.* 'The point at which revelation occurs cannot be foreseen. It comes at the divine initiative and it comes with suddenness. God, the True Guru (*Satguru*), discharges the arrow of the Word (*Sabad*) and man is slain that in death he may find true life. This life is to be found in mystical union, an ineffable experience of dissolution in the divine.'

96. Singh, G. (1987) p. 49. There is some degree of ambiguity with regard to this point. G.S.Randhawa: *Guru Nanak's Japji*, Amritsar, Guru Nanak Dev University Press, 1990², p. 17 indicates that nothing can be done except through grace which, he writes, has an over-riding effect even above *karma*, thus 'Devotion and pious actions are basic essentials to merit his love, but they are not the final determinants, as beyond these, and overseeing these, is *nadar* or *bakhshish*. Even virtue may be imbibed, good deeds performed and devotion offered, only if the Divine Grace so facilitates.' 'Such alone are privileged to sing to thee, as thy good grace hath blessed, and deeply steeped in thy love ever abide.' (A.G. p. 6)

A new life has to be delivered through ME, and so,
like a mother,
I must suffer awhile.[97]

Salvation is possible only in a tragic world.[98]

This he writes is at the heart of the Cross through which in this poem comes the goal of faith, the immortality of humanity united with God:

God lives, for nothing dies in the
realm of God. For while man lives
in the past and present, God lives
with the ever-fresh splendour of
TOMORROW.[99]

But he said unto those that believe
that nothing dies in the realm of God -

neither seed nor drop, nor dust, nor man.

Only the past dies or the present,
but the future lives for ever.

And I'm the future of man.[100]

The question arises: Who is this Christ figure who claims to be the future of humankind?

---

97. Singh, G. (1987) p. 61.
98. Singh, G. (1987) p. 73. See below p. 203 regarding Sikh attitudes towards suffering.
99. Singh, G. (1987) p. 41.
100. Singh, G. (1987) p. 77.

10

The Person and Work of
Gopal Singh's Christ

a. The Humanity of the Christ Figure

Given the nature of the figure whom Gopal Singh wishes to portray it is not in his interest to depict one who is merely human. Yet the Christ figure's humanity must not be overlooked. It is shown in three ways. First in the inability of his apparent peers to recognise his being beyond human. Thus as one who gave offence by his attempt to undermine the norms of his day, he is referred to as 'this man'.

Secondly, the same sentence goes on to portray him as the:

> mere son of a poor Joseph and a Mary
> of whom we know all....[1]

The inclusion of Joseph and the implication of the questioning of the Christ's legitimacy may add to the author's attempt to show both the humanity of the Christ figure and his peers' failure to see beyond his humanity. Since the humanity of the Christ figure is beyond doubt, Gopal Singh does not indicate the need to make any claims for a virgin birth. Such a doctrine is not vital for the Sikh reader since if that of God is to be found in all human-beings, as Sikh theology would claim, a miraculous birth is not necessary to prove divinity.

In the third place Gopal Singh's suggests that the Christ figure is to be identified with humanity since his very birth in a manger depicts the poverty of his surroundings and was such that

---

1. Singh, G. (1987) p. 67.

.....He sought to establish
the identity of man with all life and no-life.[2]

Thus the *raison d'être* of the Christ figure is explained in the birth
narrative. Sikh piety uses a parallel description with regard to the birth
of Guru Tegh Bahadur and draws on Christian vocabulary to express this:
'It was Sunday, the 1st of April, 1621. In the early hours of the fragrant
dawn a great soul was born in the house of Guru Har Gobind Sahib.
Blessed was the child born in His spirit ... It seemed God sent this little
child *to bear the cross of humanity as a Saviour*.'[3]

b. The character of the Christ figure

1. Christ the Teacher

For the Sikh, God's nature is such that 'he' is beyond human
description and vocabulary. Gopal Singh brings out this difficulty in his
description of the method the Christ figure uses to teach. Rather than
picking up the Matthean suggestion that Jesus spoke in parables because
(Greek: *hoti*) people could then understand (Mt. 13.13) he turns to the
Markan suggestion that Jesus spoke in parables so that (Greek: *hina*) they
may not immediately see the point (Mk. 4.12). Thus Gopal Singh has
the Christ figure speak

---

2   Singh, G. (1987) p. 67 where the term 'no-life' may be used to represent that which is beyond
karma. It should be noted that Sikhs believe Guru Nanak's birth to be non-karmic and Singh
may portray the birth of Jesus to be of a similar nature -See: W. Owen Cole and Piara Singh
Sambhi: *Sikhism and Christianity*, Basingstoke, Macmillan, 1993, p. 63.
Note also the parallel here with Gopal Singh's statement at the W.C.C. Vancouver Assembly in
which he indicated the 'Asianness' of the historical Jesus of Nazareth with whom people of the
East could identify: 'He was an eastern man, poor like most of us here and a manual worker all
His life...' (see above p. 158). Hindu readers of Gopal Singh's work may well identify the birth
story of Christ with that of Krishna at Mathura, especially in terms of the disaster that would
be inherent in being born male and the persecution similar to that of the slaying of the innocents,
which would thus arise.

3. Ranbir Singh: *Guru Tegh Bahadur, Divine Poet, Saviour and Martyr*, Amritsar, Chief Khalsa
Diwan, 1975, p. 1. My italics. Note here Sikh inclusivity shown in the term *a* Saviour. In terms
of the purpose of the birth of significant individuals note, too, the sixth canto of Guru Gobind
Singh's *Bachitra Natak* (Wondrous Drama) in which he recounts his own birth story and
function. He tells of how his spirit had merged with the divine but the Almighty told him to
take birth in the world to demonstrate the path of truth, to eliminate superstition and worship
God alone. [See: ed. Harbans Singh: *The Encyclopaedia of Sikhism*, Patiala, Punjabi University,
1992, p. 244 & Gopal Singh: *Thus Spake the Tenth Master*, Patiala, Punjabi University, 1978,
p. 90f. for a translation of the text.]

.....in symbols
which seemed to say:- 'You all speak words,
but know not the Word, for it is hid
within the deeps of life-calm...[4]

Further, of the words used in communication

there is an inexplicable Void
within them.
Its name is silence.

Its content is the Spirit.

That is the Word.

He who knows it, and not the words,
alone knows how it works,
like the wind making music
upon the vacancy of the flute![5]

Singh instantly transforms Jesus' manner of teaching into the
methodology of Sikh spirituality in which there is need for the devotee
to find that illumination of God's Word that enables him/her to hear the
'eternal silence' of the 'unstruck Melody' and the 'words of wordlessness.'[6]

---

4   Singh, G. (1987) p. 20.

5. Singh, G. (1987) p. 20.

6. Gopal Singh: *The Religion of the Sikhs*, p. 52f. Kabir expresses it thus in the *Guru Granth Sahib*:
    'When the sunlight (of gnosis) illumines the lotus (of one's heart), the moonshine (of desire)
    comes not into the basket (of the mind). And the fragrance and the flavour of the soul in bloom
    that one tastes is unutterable, and even if one utters, who is there to understand? There one tastes
    the relish of tastelessness; a dozen suns blaze in the mind and, eternally, within, rings the Song of
    Bliss, unstruck, and one bathes in the pool of dispassion and non-sorrow.' (A.G. p. 340)
    The mystery of the close relationship with the being of God is also reflected in God's being
    beyond comprehension and expression, thus again Kabir: 'Through the fifty-two letters (of the
    alphabet), one can describe the three worlds and more; but these letters will be forgotten, yet He
    who will remain eternally cannot be described through them. Where there is speech there are
    words; and where there are no words the mind rests not on nothing. In words as in wordlessness
    abides He, the Lord. But as and what he is, no one can perceive, nor tell. Even if I knew the Lord,
    what shall I say of Him? Whatever I say of Him is of little avail.' (A.G. p. 340)
    Gopal Singh was also familiar with the works of Kahlil Gibran in whose book *The Prophet* one
    finds the claim: 'I cannot teach you how to pray in words. God listens not to your words save
    when He Himself utters them through your lips.' (Kahlil Gibran: *The Prophet*, London,
    Mandarin, 1993, p. 81.)

The teacher Christ is also the spiritual preceptor who
    made them See
        who couldn't See:
    and made them Blind
        who claimed that they saw all.[7]

In so describing the Christ figure, Gopal Singh not only brings out the Biblical accounts of Jesus' criticisms of the religious hierarchy of his day, but reflects, too, the censure of his peers expressed by Guru Nanak who, according to the *janam sakhis*, denounced the superstition and ineffectiveness of much that went for popular Hinduism in his day.[8]

The distinction between a traditional Christian view of Jesus Christ and the Sikh perspective of the Gurus is essentially that traditional Christian belief holds that Jesus Christ was the incarnate deity who reveals the nature of God; whereas Sikhs would hold that the Gurus convey the revelation about God but in themselves are not that revelation. Were one to consider incarnation from a Sikh perspective it would be in terms of the incarnation of God as Spirit (*Akal Purakh*) within the body corporate of Sikhs.[9] In the light of this one may understand the claim made by the poem's Christ figure that the message is more important than the messenger implied in the suggestion that at Christ's second coming many will be destroyed....
    save those that stand not by ME but My Word.[10]

Compare this with the Sikh belief that those who heard the Gurus speak heard also the voice of God,[11] but that did not imply a claim for divinity on the part of the Gurus: 'Recognise me as God's servant only: Have no doubt whatever of this. I am the slave of the Supreme Being... I tell the world what God told me...'[12]

7. Singh, G. (1987) p. 12.

8. See: W.Owen Cole: *Sikhism and its Indian Context 1469-1708*, London, Darton, Longman and Todd, 1984, p. 166ff.

9. See: W.Owen Cole and Piara Singh Sambhi: *Sikhism and Christianity*, Basingstoke, 1993, p. 63, with regard to the Christ and the Gurus and Jasbir Singh Ahluwalia: *Sikhism Today - The Crisis Within and Without*, p. 41, with regard to incarnation.

10. Singh, G. (1987) p. 64.

11. See: A.G. p. 946 variously translated as in Cole and Sambhi (1993) p. 63: 'The truth of revelation dawns upon whoever contemplates the celestial Word.'

12. M.A.Macauliffe: *The Sikh Religion*, New Delhi, Chand & Co. Ltd, 1983, Vol. V p. 300 quoting from Guru Gobind Singh's *Bachitra Natak*.

2. Christ, the religious rebel

The Christ of Gopal Singh's poem challenges the accepted norms of his day, as did Jesus of Nazareth. Within both the Hindu and Muslim societies of Guru Nanak's time the role of women would have been secondary, thus Guru Nanak's encouraging his followers to take a differing attitude towards women would have been as challenging as was Jesus' own response to many who would have been marginalised in his times. Thus the episode regarding Jesus' meeting the woman at the well in Samaria here not only provides a focus on his willingness to meet and talk to one who would normally be despised, but a platform for an exposition, albeit implicit, of Sikh theology.

The water which Jesus offers her must be a reminder to the Sikh reader of the *amrit* (nectar made of sugar crystals dissolved in water) which is given to the initiate during the ceremony which marks his or her acceptance into the *khalsa* (the Sikh community). For the Sikh it would be as life-enhancing as that described by the Christ of the poem in that those who drink it will

.... thirst no more.
And it will well up out of your
own deeps.[13]

The incident forms a platform for other elements of Sikh theology. On being asked to bring her husband to the Christ, the woman replies that she has no husband, at which Christ chastises her with the words,

.... you've had
five husbands - Ego, Wrath, Envy, Infatuation
and Greed.
    But now what you live with,
- Time -
is not your husband.[14]

The woman is portrayed as being embroiled in the search of ephemeral materialism which in effect means she is engrossed in the pursuit of

---

13. Singh, G. (1987) p. 32. The latter reference is to the presence of God within the depths of the individual's own being.
14. Singh, G. (1987) p. 32.

unreality. That is not a rejection of wealth or personal relationships on the part of the Gurus. These are not evil in themselves. However, it reflects the Gurus' recognition that if one gets entangled in them one forgets the priority of the search for, and unity with, absolute truth in God. Hence the encouragement by the Christ figure for the woman to seek 'Timelessness'.[15] The basis for Gopal Singh's interpretation is probably a passage[16] within the Sikh scriptures. In *Rag Gauri* the 'soul is depicted as a woman sitting in a bodily temple, erected by God and being ignorant of her true nature, (she) is entangled and betrothed by the five evils of the body.'[17]

In a similar seemingly unexpected mode the Christ figure causes upset as he cleanses the Temple of those self-important priests involved in false worship.[18] Yet this is not such an unexpected event since both Christ and Guru Nanak reflect their call to prophetic protest. This may not be the only influence on the poet, for the turn of the century saw in India the consolidation of the Singh Sabhas and later the founding of the Shiromani Gurdwara Parbandhak Committee which were formed not only as a response to Christian missionary activity but also because Gurdwaras had been under the control and mal-influence of Hindu priests rather than in Sikh hands.

A second incident reflects the humility of the Christ figure over against the arrogance of the spiritual elite. Jesus was willing to perform the menial task of washing the disciples' feet.[19] Here is to be found not only a reflection of Christian humility, but a recognition of the need, in Sikh terms, for service (*seva*) to the community. Such selfless service was the hall-mark of, and reason for, Guru Angad's being Guru Nanak's successor. Such activity as washing feet would have been regarded by the

---

15. Singh, G. (1987) p. 32. See also: Fauja Singh: 'Vision, Achievements and Impact' in (ed): Fauja Singh and Gurbachan Singh Talib: *Guru Tegh Bahadur: Martyr and Teacher*, Patiala, Punjabi University, 1975, p. 105f.

16. A.G. p. 155: 'The Lord created the temple of the body, within it sits the woman (soul). The woman seeks pleasure in life whilst the evil forces continue to rob her. Death demolishes the temple, robs it (of life) and captures the lone soul in its fatal grip.'

17. See Shashi Bala: *The Concept of Monotheism*, Jalandhar, ABS Publications, 1993, p. 76.

18. see above p. 164 & Singh, G. (1987) p. 26.

19. Singh, G. (1987) p. 64f.

orthodox religious of the day as being beneath their dignity. However,
to touch feet is a mark of respect and to wash the feet of a *murti* (image
of the deity) or the *murti* itself would be an act of devotion. Here the
Christ figure turns the act on its head and demonstrates the humility
which is real devotion.

Gopal Singh adds a further significant element. Having washed the
disciples' feet ...

..... He
entered into a reverie, and when He
opened His eyes upon the seeming silence
of the skies, the whole universe he heard
ringing with His deathless song...[20]

It is through selfless service that God is realised ... 'for all activity of
the God-conscious being grounded in God is self-effacing. "Joying the
joys of the earth one is redeemed, only if one meeteth with the True
Guru.'[21] For the Sikh such a selfless activity has a value far beyond
physical cleansing, it opens the soul to the presence of God:

And so it is that
poets, children and lovers can see God,
face to face, for,
they are poor in spirit, having
wholly abandoned themselves
to another.[22]

---

20. Singh, G. (1987) p. 65.
21. Singh, G. (1971) p. 33.
22. Singh, G. (1987) p. 38. In the Sikh faith the life style of the devotee is emphasised. Only those
who have expelled self-centredness from their mind are able to have a vision (*darshan*) of God -
See A.G. p. 767.

To the Western reader there is an apparent contradiction here since the 'ineffable' God gives a
vision of 'him'self. Normally that would be the case, but within Sikhism 'a devotee following the
discipline of the True Guru cannot only have a sight of the Lord, but can also merge in with
Him, just as a ray merges in the Sun'. (Kohli, *Real Sikhism*, New Delhi, Harman, 1995, p. 57.)
Kitamori attempts to overcome this apparent contradiction by claiming that 'God reveals his
glory by covering us with his own hand, allowing us to escape death. Although we cannot see his
glory directly, we are allowed to see his hand covering us. The pain of God reveals himself while
saving us. The glory of the cross reflects the radiance of his face ... thus ... it became possible ... to
have hope of seeing his glory face to face. "And we all, with unveiled face, beholding the glory of
the Lord, are being changed into his likeness from one degree of glory to another..." (2. Cor. 3:18)
(Kazoh Kitamori: Theology of the Pain of God, London, S.C.M., 1966, p. 146.

3. The one who performs miracles

There is an ambivalent attitude towards miracles on the part of Sikhs. In the *janam-sakhis* (life (lit. birth) - stories) of Guru Nanak there is a predilection to portray the Guru as a man of miracles.[23] The expectations of popular religion may have influenced this. However, according to Bhai Gurdas, Guru Nanak was not inclined to such practices. In response to a group of yogis he is said to have claimed: 'I have no miracles to exhibit except the miracle of the divine Name.'[24] That same ambivalence is to be found in the poem. Whilst reference is made to the healing of the blind,[25] it is as much with the healing of spiritual blindness in mind:

> And, lo, He made them See
> who couldn't See:
> and made them Blind
> who claimed they Saw all.[26]

The need for a spiritual preceptor is an inherent part of Sikh faith: 'By mere listening, how can a blind person find his path? He can reach his destination safely if the hand of another person is held by him.'[27] The poem further elaborates the theme of symbolic miracle with the pregnant phrase:

> Like the morning mist,
> He walked on the Sea ...

but then adds,

> .....of coming and going,
> without a boat or a raft.[28]

Not only does Gopal Singh hint at the event on the Sea of Galilee but he also alludes to a number of issues of Sikh theology. The phrase

---

23. See W. Owen Cole: *Sikhism and its Indian Context 1469-1708*, London, Darton, Longman and Todd, 1983, p. 193ff.

24. Bhai Gurdas: *Var* 1.43 quoted in Cole: *op. cit.* p. 283.

25. See Mt. 11.5 / Lu 7.22.

26. Singh, G. (1987) p. 12 cf. Mt. 23.13-15.

27. A.G. p. 267 cf. Guru Nanak's belief was that the false pursuit of materialism brings not benefit but anguish - see: A.G. p. 419.

28. Singh, G. (1987) p. 12.

'coming and going' represents the concept of *samsara*, the round of birth, death and rebirth. Thus the Christ figure is able to negotiate and indeed, conquer *samsara*. Further, unlike normal humanity and because of his divine nature he is able to do so without the aid of a boat or the oarsman, usually portrayed as God, e.g. 'Ferry me across the world ocean ...O my loved father' / 'O Govind, Ferry me across the sea of 'coming and going.'[29]

Another aspect of the Christ figure's miracle working is in terms of his ability to heal, but again this is also in terms of the symbolic:

> He healed the sick, bringing them back
> to themselves.[30]

Herein is a reference to the Sikh understanding that one must avoid separation from oneself, that is that one should recognise the essential unity of the human soul with the 'Oversoul' - one's essential essence: 'Dieth the individuated consciousness, dieth one's strife, one's pride of self, but dieth not the soul that seeth all.'[31] Thus when one finds the potential for the fulfilment of one's soul healing occurs: 'Now alone is thy time to see thy God and to meet thy self.'[32] Thus one may understand the opening words of this section of the poem:

> Men said to Him: -
> 'How shall we live?'
> and He said:-
> 'By dying to yourselves!'[33]

---

29. A.G. p.1196. (cf. A.G. 1147) The first translation is that of Manmohan Singh, the latter of Gopal Singh. Note the similarity of symbolism here from the perspective of the Hindu reader who may have in mind the raised left foot of Shiva in the *Shivanataraja* figure depicting his being outside the round of *samsara*. Surprisingly, Gopal Singh does not deal with the stilling of the storm which would have been a fitting reflection of A.G. p. 1087: 'The sea is tempestuous and no boat ferries me over, save the boat of truth ...' or A.G. p. 746: 'Impassable is the (sea of maya) and the winds cause us to drift where they will, I am terrified even as I hear that the Lord of justice is severe and stern.'

30. Singh, G. (1987) p. 14 The sickness is *haumai* - self-centredness - which must be overcome. This is not to say that the self must be eliminated. Guru Nanak once complained of people who thought he suffered from bodily illness and said: 'They have called a physician to feel my pulse. But the innocent one knows not that the pain is in my heart. O, physician, you are yourself wise if you first know the malady of my mind.' (A.G. p. 1297). He then suggested that the true medicament is the Name (of God) by which all maladies are cured and peace abides in one's body.

31. Singh, G. (1971) p. 75, quoting A.G. p. 152.

32. Singh, G. (1971) p. 76, quoting Gauri M5.

33. Singh, G. (1987) p. 14, cf. Mt. 10.39, 16.25ff.

4. The Divine Nature incarnated

The opening words of this poem tell of one who

.....came out of NOWHERE,
yet vaulted over us all.
And seemed like those who saw
      like the milky way,
reflecting in His overwhelming Void
the luminous hearts of a myriad stars
and making the heavens aflame
with a lover's dream.[34]

From the very beginning of the poem one has to recognise that the figure about whom Gopal Singh writes is no mere mortal. Herein are various references to divinity:

• 'Man' must not be confused with 'man.' The story is not simply that of a bygone figure but an amalgam of past, present and future as a continuum. The Christ figure is lifted above time and space in the same way that God is beyond time - *akal* - within Sikh theology.

• NOWHERE implies that this is no contingent being, dependent on another. Gopal Singh writes of that which is non-material and elsewhere uses the term 'noughtingness' in much the same way:

Lo, the tense atomic heart of the
primeval noughtingness was broken
and I saw a glorious God
bursting out of His Inner Dark ...[35]

Dr Gopal Singh Puri considers Gopal Singh to be describing the scene of the Resurrection of Christ in that there is a sudden burst of light which comes from nowhere as the *jivatma* of Jesus meets with the *paramatma*, the human soul merges with the 'oversoul', and in so doing

---

34. Singh, G. (1987) p. 11.
35. Gopal Singh: *The Unstruck Melody*, New Delhi, World Book Centre, 1989,[2] p. 74. cf: 'Like a Meteor, unwilling to be tied
to the ageless strings of stars, like
a dark cloud, baring its whole
crimson chest with a thunderous flash ...' Singh, G. (1987) p. 73.

produces a sudden burst of light.'[36] According to Guru Ram Das, the light of the soul ultimately merges in the light of the Lord'[37] and Kabir maintains that when the Tenth Door is opened (i.e. when one gains insight and illumination) then there are flashes of light and one recognises the presence of God.[38]

Gopal Singh's technique is similar to that of Dhanjibhai Fakirbhai who begins his *Khrista-Gita* with the *darshan* (view) given to the author of Revelation of Christ's appearance in glory.[39]

Yet the concept of incarnation in terms of a single individual is traditionally outside the orbit of Sikh theology. Thus, for the purposes of redemption God does not descend to the earth. He is *ajuni*[40] and, therefore, does not take birth. Guru Nanak makes it clear that 'they who meditate on the everlasting Reality become immortal, but they who worship those who died after being born are pursuing the falsest path.'[41] Thus one may understand Guru Arjan's denial of any divine status: 'Burnt be the mouth which says that the Lord enters into existences. He is not

---

36. Letter to the present writer, 14 April 1993.
37. A.G. p. 446.
38. A.G. p. 1162.
39. See: Robin Boyd's Foreword in Dhanjibhai Fakirbhai: *Khristopanishad*, Bangalore, Christian Institute for the Study of Religion and Society, 1965, p. x. Fakirbhai takes up a similar theme in his *Shri Khrist Gita*, Delhi, Unity Books, 19732, p. 1:
   1.1 'I heard behind me a loud voice like a trumpet
         Then I turned to see the voice that was speaking to me ...
   1.5 His eyes were like a flame of fire ...
   1.6 His face was like the sun,
         Shining in full strength.'
   As John Hick points out the appearance of a bright light is a not uncommon phenomenon with regard to the presence of the divine whether it be in terms of the bright light which appeared to Paul on the Damascus road or the experience of those who have been brought back from near-death circumstances who speak of 'a bright light or a bright, shining figure, from which there emanates a profound accepting love and peace.' - *The Metaphor of God Incarnate*, London, SCM Press, 1993, p. 24.
40. A.G. p. 1, *ajuni* = literally: does not pass through the womb.
41. A.G. p. 463. See: ed. Pritam Singh: *Sikh Concept of the Divine*, Amritsar, Guru Nanak Dev University Press, p. 103. Note the implication of this text for the title of Gopal Singh's work. Christ is described as the one who 'Never Died' not out of support for the Muslim view that he was not crucified but because one who dies is not worthy of worship. A further point may here be noted that in Sikh theology nothing can be considered to be equal with God, thus Dharam Singh: *Sikh Theology of Liberation*, New Delhi, Harman, 1991, p. 164: 'The attitude of being self-born and thus ever free from the cycle of birth and death means that He never incarnates Himself in human or any other form, thereby putting an end to any speculation that any being could be His equal.'

born, nor does he die. He does not come and he does not go.'[42] Notwithstanding this, the birth claims made by the tenth human Guru, Guru Gobind Singh, cast an interesting light on Sikh spirituality and the manner of God's revelation: In *Vichitar Natak* he 'tells of his previous life as one of a dedicated soul; meditating on God at *HemKunda*, where one is face to face with the seven Himalayan peaks. He says he was merged with God and had no desire to come to the earth but his Lord and God said: "I appoint thee as my son. Go thou and spread my religion. Others before thee have spread their own, not Mine.' For Gopal Singh this implies that 'like a Bodhisatva, the emancipated ones also come to the earth in order to emancipate others.'[43] It is in this manner that his Christ figure may be defined.

At one and the same time the Christ figure is beyond *samsara* and yet is involved with creation and imbued with divinity, seemingly to a degree beyond that of mere mortals.

It has been noted already that the Christ figure comes 'from NOWHERE', implying his being outside space and, as in the Sikh doctrine of God, *akal*, beyond time. It may be possible at this point to borrow the Christian term 'eternal' in describing this figure. It was from this eternal being that the world was created, thus,

> When asked how the world was born,
> He said:- 'Out of the Word.'
>
> For even when the world was not,
> the Word was.
>
> Like a melody, even if unsung,
> lies wrapped up in the waves of space.
>
> They knew not what the Word was.'[44]

In a matter of six lines Gopal Singh reflects not only the opening of the Prologue of John's Gospel but also the lack of recognition of the Christ figure.[45] As has been seen earlier[46] the concept of the *shabad* is

---

42. A.G. p. 1136.
43. Singh, G. (1971) p. 104n.
44. Singh, G. (1987) p. 20.
45. John 1:1-10.
46. see above p. 79.

close to the Guru's understanding of the nature of God's being and creative energy, thus Gopal Singh is as much reflecting a Sikh theological concept as a Christian one.

The concept of the known yet unknown Christ is to be found not only in terms of the world not recognising him but the disciples also:

> I have lived with you all these days,
> And you've followed ME, as if you've
> known ME not.[47]

This reflects the Sikh understanding that one has to be rid of self-centredness before one can fully understand the nature of God, follow his will and find liberation:

> He who loses his life like
> a drop in the ocean, becomes
> the ocean himself.[48]

Gopal Singh's Christ is also described as 'God-man' in a way which implies his being a fore-runner of new humanity:

> For the God-man loses with the world
> but wins with his God.[49]

In keeping with one who is considered to be an incarnation of the divine nature, the Christ figure is portrayed as having four noteworthy attributes: he is the light, the provider, the forgiver and the water of life.

As Light, the Christ is likened to the sun
'that gives sight to most',
but which paradoxically,
'also blinds those who see it face to face,'[50]
because they are sinful and unable to encounter the light.

The vision of the spiritual is only possible in Sikh thought through the Guru whose very title indicates the overcoming of darkness by the

---

47. Singh, G. (1987) p. 59.
48. Singh, G. (1987) p. 61.
49. Singh, G. (1987) p. 75.
50. Singh, G. (1987) p. 39.

light – In Panjabi, *Gu* = darkness, *ru* = light. The Guru is the effulgent, dazzling source of light upon whose face the devotee cannot look and who, therefore, turns his/her head downwards his adoration. Gazing upon God face-to-face, as it were has no part in Sikh thought.

The Christ figure is one who is provider of food, both spiritual and material,

> Quoth He:
> 'Of my flesh you'll eat
>   *the Bread of the Spirit,*
> And of my blood, you'll drink
>   *the Wine of Ecstasy.'*

> And lo,
> in whatever number men came unto Him,
> He provided them with enough
> out of what seemed no-THING
> to the naked eye.'[51]

The concept is very much seen by Sikhs as the role of the Guru from whose presence no one could leave hungry, hence the institution of the *langar* or free kitchen in which all, irrespective of case, creed or status could be fed. This may also be interpreted in spiritual terms as was seen expressed by Rai Balwand and Satta: in terms of the kitchen of Guru Angad's wife from which 'was distributed rich fare .... tasting like *amrita* elixir' and was such that 'the faces of the Master's disciples became radiant.'[52]

'I forgive you.' the Christ figure says to the woman caught in adultery.[53] Forgiveness is, however, a prerogative of God according to Sikh thought for it is impossible to hide one's sin from him because he is all-seeing but is also the source of mercy and forgiveness.[54] 'The Guru's servants are pleasing to the Lord. He forgives them and they no longer fear death's courier.'[55]

---

51. Singh, G. (1987) p. 13.
52. A.G. p. 967 Gurbachan Singh Talib's translation.
53. Singh, G. (1987) p. 22. Two stories are conflated here by Gopal Singh, that of the woman who visited the Pharisee's house (Luke 7.36ff) and the woman caught in adultery (John 8. 3-11).
54. Singh, G. (1971) p. 34.
55. A.G. p. 1190 (Cole and Sambhi's translation) cf Guru Arjan: 'All too sweet is the speech of my Master and Beloved: I have seen his care: bitter is never his word.' - quoted in Singh, G. (1987) p. 104 - no ref. given.

The Samaritan woman was privy to the source of the 'water-of-life' which is Christ himself.[56] However, Gopal Singh calls to mind not only the *amrit* of the Sikh baptismal ceremony but also the source of spiritual power being within the human being and, therefore, from the divine. Thus,

> I'd give you such water that you'll thirst no more.
> And it will well up out of your
> own deeps.[57]

It will follow that such a figure will be viewed as one who is the author of salvation:

> I have sown with blood
> that you may reap with honour
> ... a new life has to be delivered by ME,

he tells his disciples.[58] In so writing Gopal Singh reflects the lives not only of the Sikh Gurus Arjan and Tegh Bahadur who gave their lives as martyrs, but countless other Sikhs whose lives are celebrated in the history and worship of the Sikh nation.

5. The Death of the Christ figure

As has been indicated earlier in Sikh terms one who dies is not worthy of worship.[59] A title such as 'the death of the Christ figure' must, at first sight, seem contradictory and likely to undermine the Christ figure in Sikh eyes. Further investigation, however, leads to a clearer understanding of Gopal Singh's purposes. Of the physical death of the Christ of the poem there is no denial, it is the *atman* that lives on in a new and more glorious form, hence 'The Man Who Never Died'. In such a sense all humans would be immortal. The association of the Christ figure with humanity is thus maintained and consequently the potential for all humanity, through God's grace, is strengthened.

Gopal Singh portrays first the nature of humanity that seeks the death on a cross of the likes of Jesus Christ.

---

56. Singh, G. (1987) p. 32.
57. Singh, G. (1987) p. 32.
58. Singh, G. (1987) p. 61.
59. see above p. 196.

Men worshipped Him as God
as Spirit, as the Son of Man,
and scourged and smote and nailed Him to the Cross
for the same reason.

For men can suffer not a man
unlike unto them.[60]

In Sikh thought the challenge of a God of justice or indeed of the Living God's prophets is too much for humanity to bear given the 'thieves in their hearts'[61] - pride, anger, greed, avarice and lust - hence such peoples' response to the Christ figure. Yet even at this point of death the Christ figure is still in control:

---

60. Gopal Singh: *The Man Who Never Died*, p. 16 cf. Gopal Singh's *On the Cross* in *The Unstruck Melody*, New Delhi, World Book Centre, 19892, p. 56, in which many of the themes of *The Man Who Never Died* find succinct expression:

They nailed all they thought was him
to a handful of cross.
His innocent, lily-white dust,
yielded all the milk it had stored
in its blood,
in tears of pity, in pledges
of an eternal, resplendent
Tomorrow, to all men
who saw, and yet
did not believe!

They mocked him with a
crying crown of thorns, saying: "O king, thy father come?"
And he smiled at their blind spots and vacant fury,
        saying nothing,
for he loved the look of innocence
in their children yet to be born, and
had not heart to smite them with a curse that they meet
with the fate of
mere men!

With his each hushed breath of
cold-sweating tenderness, they saw
but a dying man sigh, like sheep
in vain pursuit of an unknown dream.

But, like the scare of life
to the universe of death,
he spoke to them through an awesome smile of Silence,
what was, what ever shall be.
And they saw it all, but could not see!

61. Gopal Singh Puri: undated letter to J.M.P 1994.

It is not you
who take away my life; it is I who abandon it, for
I can take it up again
like the lute its melody.[62]

The theme here is freedom - 'we possess life to be free' and 'as in life, so in death, (he walks) from one freedom to another'[63] - yet a freedom which is to be found within the will of God: 'Father, I come! Let Thy Will be done.'[64]

This can be accomplished through the second major point Gopal Singh makes. Whilst the Christ figure may be killed, he will not be destroyed. In a passage reminiscent of the opening of the Bhagavad Gita Christ explains his attitude towards death:

If someone kills my body,
there's nothing more he can do to it.[65]

Sikh theology recognises that the biological reality of death is the inevitable destiny of everyone. Says Guru Nanak: 'Death will inevitably strike.'[66] However, it is not something to be feared for 'death is the privilege of those who live life positively.'[67] Such a blessed state is to be found by eliminating one's *haumai* (self-centredness) and dying within the Holy Word - *sabda/sabad*, 'The one who ceases in *sabda* has a death which is blessed.'[68] More significantly, if death is through sacrifice then it finds the blessing of union with God, hence the requirement of the symbolic sacrifice on initiation into the *Khalsa* in which one joins 'the kindred spirits who served their Lord while they lived and kept him in mind while departing.'[69] This would also explain the attitude to death

---

62. Singh, G. (1987) p. 71.
63. Singh, G. (1987) p. 71.
64. Singh, G. (1987) p. 115.
65. Singh, G. (1987) p. 96. cf. Bhagavad Gita 2.11f in which Krishna as charioteer assures Arjuna that the spirit lives on: 'While speaking learned words, you are mourning for what is not worthy of grief. Those who are wise lament neither for the living nor for the dead. Never was there a time when I did not exist, nor you, nor all these kings; nor in the future shall any of us cease to be.'
66. A.G. p. 237.
67. A.G. p. 579.
68. A.G. p. 1067.
69. A.G. p. 1000.

of the martyred Sikh Gurus who met their deaths without fear.[70] Thus
Gopal Singh portrays the death of Jesus Christ in similar vein for:

> ... death is not the end, only
> the beginning of life:
> the bird of night out-flieth,
> but only from dawn to dawn.[71]

As one should greet death with joy,[72] there is also justification for the
Christ figure to ask for the forgiveness of his persecutors:

> And he prayed unto God:- 'Father,
> forgive them, for they know not that it is
> the destiny of every rose to blossom
> on the cross.[73]

Perhaps the most important point Gopal Singh makes here is that
only through pain and suffering may new life be found. Whilst Sikhism
is not a philosophy of suffering, the realities of death and suffering are
never far away. Thus the Gurus write of these matters to enable their
followers to recognise the goal of their lives. Such a 'vision keeps in focus
... regenerate man, transformed from the ordinary, existential plane of
living into a qualitatively higher order of being.'[74] Guru Arjan, who was
himself to be no stranger to martyrdom encouraged human-beings to give

---

70. e.g. See: Gobind Singh Mansukhani: *The Quintessence of Sikhism*, Amritsar, S.G.P.C., 1985, pp. 25
  & 35; Trilochan Singh also indicates the nature of martyrdom. With regard to the deaths of
  Gurus Arjan and Tegh Bahadur he writes: 'They did so (faced martyrdom) to show to the world
  their belief in the eternity of their spirit, and the fearlessness they acquired in the love of God.'
  'Theological Concepts of Sikhism' in ed. Fauja Singh: *Sikhism*, Patiala, Punjabi University, 1969,
  p. 50. See also Surjit Singh Chawla: *Martyrdom of Guru Tegh Bahadur*, Gurgaon, Harmony
  Publishing House, 1991, p. 114. of God it is said:
  When His saints suffer sorrow and pain,God feels their pangs of pain; then His saints feel
  joyous and happy, God is pleased and happy.
  The Lord feels everyone's suffering,
  Our inmost feelings are known to Him.
  [Guru Gobind Singh: *Benti Chaupai* 12 quoted in Trilochan Singh, in Fauja Singh (1969). p. 50]
71. Singh, G. (1987) p. 96.
72. cf. A.G. p. 418, 'Why do you cry? The soul is and will be.'
73. Singh, G. (1987) p. 71.
74. See: Wazir Singh: *The Sikh Perspective on Death and Suffering, Journal of Sikh Studies*, Vol. IX,
  No. II, August 1982, p. 31 cf. A.G. p. 470: 'Pain is the cure, pleasure the malady, for where there
  is pleasure, there Thou art not.'

up all expectation of 'the good life'[75] to become of service to their fellow human-beings and to God: 'Let my mind bank upon the support of that Lord through whose contemplation joy descends and sufferings vanish.'[76]

The fourth point Gopal Singh makes in terms of the death of the Christ figure is of his being the author of 'new life.'

> For my God is not the God of the dead, but
> of the living.
> He who loses his life like
> a drop into the ocean, becomes
> the ocean himself.
> But whosoever saves his life from the sea
> shall lose it in the dust.
>
> A new life has to be delivered through ME....[77]

Whilst there are many passing references to Biblical themes in this passage, Sikh readers would recognise themes which arise out of their own tradition.

As was noted above one who dies is not worthy of worship. It follows, then, that for the Sikhs God is a Living God, but for them this also implies one who is not confined to measurable time. Further since the *atma*, much less the *paramatma*, is not subject to death, it follows that that which is divine cannot be anything but 'living'.

---

75. A.G. p. 517 cf. Guru Nanak who encouraged his followers to give up their expectations of an easy life: 'Vain is our desire, Nanak, to ask for pleasure and to shun pain. For pain, and pleasure are the clothes one gets to wear at the Lord's Gate. Where of no avail is our wailing, wise it is to keep one's silence there.' (A.G. p. 149)

76. A.G. p. 517. Both Guru Tegh Bahadur and Guru Arjan, his grandfather, died martyrs' deaths, thus creating a basis for the Sikh theology of martyrdom. 'All sorrow is transmuted and transcended in devotion to God, and His sight is revealed to the seeker, annulling all suffering.' Guru Tegh Bahadur reflects this in the Guru Granth Sahib:
In this hour I lodged the name of God in my heart -
God's name that is supreme over all,
Whose meditation annuls all suffering,
And favours the devoted with a sight of the Divine Face.
(A.G. p. 1429, quoted by Gurbachan Singh Talib: *The Concept and Tradition of Martyrdom in Sikhism*, in *Guru Tegh Bahadur - Background and Supreme Sacrifice*, Patiala, Punjabi University, 1976, p.199, who points out that 'not a bitter word or hint of desperation or frustration is in these words, the noblest testament of a great soul departing this life with the vision of a mission being fulfilled through his sacrifice.')

77. Singh, G. (1987) p. 61.

The theme of the 'drop in the ocean' is of traditional Indian philosophical origin and would thus be familiar with Sikh or Hindu readers, but is here woven into the dictum of Jesus of Nazareth, that whoever would 'save their life will lose it, and those who lose their life for my sake will find it.'[78] In that the drop may represent the soul of the human-being, its loss in the ocean implies merging into the divine, the goal of human life.

The above quotation continues with the words

> I've given you much, and so,
> much shall be required of you.[79]

It is a call to witness to faith, 'much being required of you' being often manifested in martyrdoms of the Sikh history, a theme which finds distinct parallels with the Christian concept of witness/*martus*.

A distinction must be drawn here between a traditional Christian understanding of the once-for-all sacrifice of Christ as that which brings about atonement and the Sikh view that atonement through the agency of another being is impossible: 'But no one purges me of my evil, my sins,' says Guru Nanak.[80] Whilst within Sikh theology Christ is redundant, within the poem Gopal Singh depicts him as one who paves the way for humanity to imitate. Each individual must follow the will of God and not rely on the saving nature of Christ's work. It is for each individual to find liberation through his/her effort in conjunction with God's prevenient grace:

> .... to whomsoever God comes, He
> comes in the strangest of ways -
> through PAIN ....[81]

---

78. Matt. 16.25.
79. Singh, G. (1987) p. 61.
80. A.G. p. 1021
81. Singh, G. (1987) p. 72. Wazir Singh quotes Kierkegaard with approval on this point: 'The suffering which restores man to awareness of sin is also a means to reconciliation, only, however, if one dutifully accepts the suffering and turns it to good purpose.' (Arbaugh: *Kierkegaard's Authorship*, London, Allen and Unwin, 1968, p. 176.)

The word 'whomsoever' here implies the individual believer as much as the Christ figure. Pain not piety is of the essence: 'He whom ritual bathing, fasting, charity fill with arrogance - all his pious acts, says Guru Ram Das, are of little worth as is the elephant's bath ....' i.e. the elephant pumps dust all over itself after washing itself.[82]

Atonement also is dependent on the elimination of *haumai*, the self-centredness that causes arrogance and prevents the individual from following the will of God. As author of salvation the Christ figure is to be viewed not as the one who initiates, for example, a transaction on behalf of humanity with God, but one who is a forerunner opening up the possibility of new life for all humanity, provided they, too, are willing to undergo the suffering inherent in the process.[83] Death is not the end of the story. Thus Gopal Singh writes of the resurrection and beyond.

6. Christ beyond the Cross

i. *The 'Resurrection'*

This poem begins with a vision of the resurrected Christ coming 'out of NOWHERE'[84] to guide humanity to its final goal of unity with the divine. There is a sense here of a second advent in that this is a post-crucifixion event, but it is also a reminder of a transcendent divine status also previously held. From a Sikh perspective one could claim that regeneration into the divine is not unusual, indeed to be expected. It is a natural development in the passage of the *atman* as reflected in the words of Guru Arjan:

> He (Brahman) does not die, I (Atman) have no fear. He does not perish, I have no worry. He is not poor; I am not hungry. He is without sorrow; I am without grief ... He has no ties; I am not bound ... He is not impure, I am not tainted. He is blissful. I am always ecstatic. He has no worry, I have no anxiety. He is uninfluenced, I

---

82 A.G. p. 367.

83. This understanding of the function of Christ was to be reflected in a conversation with Mr. Justice Pritam Singh Safeer (New Delhi, 29:iii:'94) in which he spoke of his experience of the pain of his own suffering which he likened in one of his poems to being nailed to the Cross. Like Gopal Singh he spoke not in terms of the Cross as a once-for-all event, but an experience which may well be replicated in one's own life.

84. Singh, G. (1987) p. 11.

am without any effect. He is not hungry, I am not thirsty. He is pure, I am deemed holy. On meeting the Guru illusion has been removed. He and I have become one, imbued with the same hue.[85]

More in keeping with the traditional Christian story of the Crucifixion, Gopal Singh captures some sense of the devastation expected by the disciples and the utter surprise at the outcome, one reads:

> And so, when men thought,
>   all was over with Him,
>   He rose from the dead ...[86]

The expression is Christian through and through for the Sikh would think more in terms of liberation from *samsara* rather than rising from the dead be it either in physical or spiritual terms.[87]

ii. The Christ figure is able to take up new life

'Nothing dies in the realm of God,'[88] is how Gopal Singh describes the outcome of the resurrection both for the Christ figure and the believer. Again this reflects Sikh rather than Christian theology with its basis in the words of Kabir that the soul 'cannot be erased like ink from paper.'[89] Gopal Singh also expressed this general understanding in his poem with the words:

> .... life grows not only the flowers of death,
>   but also the seed of life.[90]

The ability to take up new life is also held out to humanity for the Christ figure claims:

> .... I am the eternal spring, that comes to man,
>   again and over again....[91]

---

85. A.G. p. 391.

86. Singh, G. (1987) p. 77.

87. See below, p. 220 regarding Michael Goulder's discussion of Petrine Theology.

88. Singh, G. (1987) p. 77.

89. A.G. p. 871.

90. Singh, G. (1987) p. 61.

91. Singh, G. (1987) p. 61 cf. the affirmation of new life made by Ravidas: 'The dawn of a new day is the herald of a sunset. Earth is not your permanent home.' A.G. 793.

Such an affirmation of new life and regeneration by Gopal Singh is unusual for a Sikh who was later to be responsible for a translation of the works of Guru Gobind Singh who wrote:

> As many were the prophets and seers,
> Them all the All-time subdued but they subdued not Him.

> And as many were the Ramas, Krishnas and Vishnus,
> They all could not but surrender to it: they could prevail
> not over Death.

> All Indras, beauteous like the moon,
> Are subject to Death:
> Yea, no Muslim oracle, no prophet, no sage,
> Can either escape the ravages of Time.

> Great emperors like Mandhata
> Were also driven away by the Angel of Death.
> And He alone was redeemed who uttered God's Name,
> Yea, Death is the deserts of those who seek not His
> Refuge.[92]

iii. The Christ figure is to be found amongst humanity

The implication of Christ's being the 'eternal spring, that comes to man' also implies the presence of Christ amongst humanity much as in the same way the Guru is amongst the Sikh congregation who follow the will of God both as unseen spiritual presence and through the Holy Book.

iv. Christ is remembered in body and blood

> Quoth He:
> 'Of my Flesh you'll eat
> the Bread of the Spirit.
> And of my Blood, you'll drink
> the Wine of Ecstasy.[93]

Christian readers will bring to mind the elements of the Lord's Supper but further interpretations are seen from a Sikh perspective. It is

---

92. Gopal Singh: *Thus Spoke the Tenth Master*, Patiala, Punjabi University, 1978, p. 73.
93. Singh, G. (1987) p. 13.

a commonly held belief among Sikhs that no one should leave the Guru's presence hungry. Thus in every Gurdwara there will be found a *langar* (free-kitchen) where all may eat. The *langar*, as both kitchen and shared meal has as much spiritual significance as the place of worship or, indeed, worship itself, for it represents the fellowship of the Sikh congregation and the continuing presence of the spirit of the Guru. 'The bread of the Spirit' is as much the chapatti of the langar as the wafer of Eucharist. Similarly when the Christ figure speaks of his followers drinking the blood which is 'the wine of Ecstasy' Sikh readers will be minded of the ceremony of Sikh baptism rather than the Christian communion service. '[T]he wine of ecstasy' may be a simile of the *amrit* (elixir) drunk at Sikh initiation. The outcome of such initiation is in itself a form of 'new life'. Known as *Amrit Chakna* (the drinking of the nectar of immortality) the initiation confers on the Sikh the privilege of new dignity and opportunity to partake in the path of liberation, the ecstasy of recognition of God's presence.

7. Christ the *Jivanmukta*

In his book *Sikh Theology of Liberation*, Dharam Singh describes the nature of the *jivanmukta*, that is, the one who is spiritually liberated whilst alive.[94] He goes on to define such a person as 'one who has, through loving devotion to God, attained "a state of entire bliss, entire light, complete merging of man's own will with the Supreme Will of God."'[95]

Gopal Singh's Christ figure reflects many of the qualities of the *jivanmukta* who is liberated whilst still in the body. It is a characteristic of such a person that they not only attain their own release but help others to become liberated.[96] The beginning of Gopal Singh's poem demonstrates both the rebirth and the return of Christ in a blaze of light 'from NOWHERE' and 'making the heaven's aflame with a lover's dream.'[97]

---

94. Dharam Singh: *Sikh Theology of Liberation*, New Delhi, Harman Publishing House, 1991.
95. *op. cit.* p. 80, quoting Ishar Singh: Ishar Singh: *The Philosophy of Guru Nanak: A Comparative Study*, New Delhi, Ranjit Publishing House, 1969, p. 162.
96. Dharam Singh (1991) p. 81.
97. Singh, G. (1987) p. 10.

His express purpose was 'to establish the identity of humanity with all life and no-life.'[98] Characteristically Gopal Singh combines something of both Sikh and Christian theologies in his presentation, for he indicates the importance of the physical death of Christ but combines this with the Sikh understanding of the immortality of the soul. Thus:

> .....as in life, so in death, I walk
> from one freedom to another....

but note, too, the implication of liberation here, especially given the proceeding line:

> We possess life to be free, not to be bound.[99]

A second characteristic of those who are *jivanmukta* is that they recognise the presence of God in each being and place, but do not live a life of ritual orthodoxy.[100] Both these issues are reflected in the behaviour of Gopal Singh's Christ in that:

> When an adulteress wept before Him
> and wiped her tears from His feet
> with her black, lustrous hair.
>   and begged forgiveness for her sins
>
> committed because she was helpless
> and alone in the fury of life,
>
> He said simply:-
> 'Go woman, I forgive you, sin no more.'

---

98. Singh, G. (1987) p. 18. The interpretation of this line is difficult and reflects Gopal Singh's subtle use of language. 'Life' can mean that of a human-being but probably is better interpreted as the liberated life of the *jivanmukta*. However, is 'no-life' to imply life beyond death when it could equally well apply to the inadequacy of human life? The express purpose of Christ is more clearly expressed elsewhere where he says: 'I have come to make gods of you all' (p. 63), a much more explicit indicator of the *Brahman-Atman* synthesis.

99. Singh, G. (1987) p. 71 cf the search for freedom, both political and spiritual which is the nature of the true Sikh: 'He has an ardent love of freedom and if so required he willingly gives up his life in the defence of freedom.' See: Lt Col J.S.Guleria 'The Martial Traditions of the Sikhs' in *The Spokesman Weekly* (Baisakhi Number), 13 April 1992, p. 9.

100. Dharam Singh (1991) p. 81.

And when men raised their hands to
stone her to death
- for, such was the law -
He warned:- 'He alone can cast a stone at her,
who lives not in the glass-house of Time.'[101]

This reflects the rejection on the part of the Christ figure, as Guru
Nanak, of the religiosity of his day with its inefficacious formalism.[102]

The consequence of such religiosity is that 'You see God not in the
temple of God'[103] but should look for 'him' in the temple which is 'your
own body.'[104] That same religiosity is depicted as the cause for the death
of Christ and his behaviour as an indicator of his radical values:

And men, inflamed with rage turned their
back upon Him.
Yea, even those that He claimed
as His very own.

'This man is too much for us,' they yelled,
'If He lives more, He'll destroy
all the ancient values of man.
'And the kings shall lose their glory,
and the courtiers their honour.
'The poor shall lose their misery and the harlots
their ill-repute.
'And the sinners shall proclaim their inner virtues,
'And the virtuous their halo,
'And the prisons their keepers,
'And the hallowed temples, with their age-old treasures,
their custom and their call.'[105]

---

101. Singh, G. (1987) p. 22.

102. See: Cole and Sambhi (1993), p. 11f.

103. Singh, G. (1987) p. 42.

104. cf. A.G. p. 695 and 1 Cor. 3.16.

105. Singh, G. (1987) p. 67. Whilst this is the consequence in practical terms of the religiosity of
Christ's persecutors, their words also indicate their hypocrisy:
'You all speak in words but, know not the Word... (and) ...
"protect" a holy idea like the barbed wire!' (p. 20f)

This awareness on the part of the Christ figure of the plight of the marginalised of society also shows another aspect of the life of the *jivanmukta*, that is that such a person has an active participation in social life and in seeking an improvement in society is engaged in the creation of paradise on earth.

> The meek shall inherit the earth, as also
> the Kingdom of God. For, is it not the least
> on which the highest are raised?
> God's rain
> falls upon one and all, but it's assembled
> by the lowest and the least.
>
> The tragedies of power are more heart-breaking
> than those of poverty.
> The mighty oak is afraid
> of each passing wind, but not so
> the meek grass that lies low in its way, and
> laughs in grateful silence
> at its impotent fury![106]

Such an attitude on the part of the Christ figure is in keeping with the concept of *swarga*, an environment of justice which is not beyond this world but reflects the Sikh understanding that 'heaven is there (on this very earth) where the holy congregation meets to remember the Creator Lord.' Moreover, 'it is for the *jivanmukta* to transform the entire earth into a *swarga* ...' giving rise to '..., the values of ethnic and social equality, love, universal brotherhood, justice, altruism, etc., thereby causing cessation of the evils like ethnic and social inequality, injustice, exploitation, oppression, etc.'[107]

Those who are *jivanmukta* are also aware of the transcendent God, the love of whom, though remote, is expressed through the love of the nearest. Thus Gopal Singh claims,

---

106. Singh, G. (1987) p. 47.
107. Dharam Singh (1991) p. 81f. The Sikh works for '*sarbat da bhala*, i.e. the welfare and liberation of all because all human beings are constituents of the universal brotherhood.' (p. 86) It is interesting to compare the vision of the City of No-Sorrows seen by Ravidas (A.G. p. 345) and John's vision of the New Jerusalem in *Revelation*.

How mysterious and distant is God in His
vastness! And, yet,
how seeable, tastable and knowable
in His deeds![108]

Just as the lotus lies on the surface of filthy water, so the *jivanmukta*
and the Christ figure are in this world but not of this world.[109] '... one
must live in the world, but be not of it,' writes Gopal Singh,

.....like
the fish lives ever in water, but moves
always against its current.[110]

In keeping with both the Sikh understanding of the *jivanmukta* and
the Christian's affirmation of the efficacy of the death of Christ, Gopal
Singh writes of the approach to God being made through 'PAIN'[111]

In the final lines of Gopal Singh's poem one discovers the ultimate
claim made by the Christ figure. Proceeding the affirmation made regarding
the *Brahman-Atman* synthesis,[112]

To me, being and non-being were always one,
I always was and never was!,

is what may be considered to be the ultimate interpretation of Jesus
Christ in Sikh terms -

And, I'm the future of man.[113]

---

108. Singh, G. (1987) p. 41, cf. Dharam Singh (1991) p. 84.

109. cf. Bhai Gurdas (Varan 6.15). There is no compulsion to become an ascetic to gain liberation, in
Sikh theology, rather as a householder one is able to find liberation for 'the *jivan-mukta* lives the
life of a householder in this world but he does not let himself be of the world.' [Dharam Singh
(1991) p. 87.] This will also imply that the *jivanmukta* 'is fully aware of the empirical world as
well as his relationship with this reality and the Ultimate Reality.' The world is also regarded
as being relatively true or real - relative in that it is created by the True One but does not exist
for ever unlike the Creator – See: Dharam Singh (1991). p. 90.

110. Singh, G. (1987) p. 49.

111. Singh, G. (1987) p. 72. See also: Dharam Singh (1991) p. 93: 'The *jivanmukta's* love of God is
not only selfless but is also so intense that he is prepared to undergo any amount of suffering or
pain for his faith unflinchingly. Love demands sacrifice and the *jivanmukta* is prepared 'to tread
the path of love with his head on his palm'. (A.G. p. 1412)

112. A.G. pp. 846, 391.

113. Singh, G. (1987) p. 77.

214 The Word of God is Not Bound

Gopal Singh portrays the Christ as a type of proto-*jivanmukta* whose loving devotion to God, care for God's peoples and sacrificial work made the possibility of liberation a reality.

So how may we start an appreciation of Gopal Singh's Christ figure? Perhaps it is *a 'Turbaned' Christ...*

The various writers of the New Testament attempted to portray Jesus Christ in a manner which appealed to their readers, be it in terms, for instance, of the Fourth Gospel writer's use of the concepts of *logos* or *sophia*, or Matthew's portrayal of one who is the fulfilment of Jewish hopes. The issue now becomes one of attempting to interpret the Christ figure in the light of the Christian-Sikh encounter. What, then, are the insights into the nature of Christ which may arise as a result of that encounter? What would appeal to the Sikh searcher into the many ways in which God has dealt with human-kind? How would God's action through Jesus be viewed and portrayed by a Sikh? What can the Church learn from a Sikh understanding of Jesus Christ?

It must be recognised first that much of what follows must be seen as the present writer's construct, since, with the exception of Gopal Singh's work, little has been written about the Christ figure.

Secondly, this must not be seen as an attempt to impose the Christ figure on the Sikh faith. Like Hinduism, Sikhism will want to stress that 'theologically and doctrinally other religions do not depend on Jesus for their existence or pine for fulfilment in him.[114]

From a Christian perspective, however, it must be recognised that the fullness of Christ has always to be discovered. It is an on-going process to which reflection arising out of the encounter of Sikhs and Christians may contribute.[115] So what issues does the encounter reveal?

The humanity of Christ is of vital importance. Sikhs are always desirous to point out that God, although outside time, works through 'his' witnesses, such as the Gurus. As with the recognition of their historicity, Sikhs may recognize the historicity of Jesus of Nazareth and

114. R.S. Sugirtharajah: 'An Interpretative Foreword' in *Asian Faces of Jesus*, London, S.C.M., 1993, p. 4.
115. See: A. Wessels (1990) p. 174f: 'We do not fully know who Christ was and who he will be'; p. 155/6: Greek Christology does not enable us to understand Christ exhaustively.

the fact that he was born an Asian like them. But more than that, there may be an appreciation of one who was dedicated to a life-style of unselfish service to humanity, expressed in his manifesto at Nazareth[116] and through his sacrificial death. If one minimises the humanity of Christ then it will diminish support for the continuation of the human struggle against the very injustice which was the object of Jesus' Nazareth manifesto and the cause of the Sikh Gurus' martyrdom.

Like the Sikh Gurus who taught as much by their life-style as by their words or poetry, the Christ figure is respected as one who is a teacher and enlightener. The whole of Gopal Singh's epic poem is indicative of this.

The Death of Christ must be portrayed as something beyond passive acceptance of Jewish and Roman authority. The Sikh struggle for justice and the consequent historical martyrdom of not only Gurus Arjan and Tegh Bahadur but thousands of Sikh soldiers as well lends itself to a better understanding of the analogy of the Cross as a struggle between good and evil, and the eventual overcoming of evil by that which is good. The spiritual and the temporal are not seen to be estranged but are in keeping with the Sikh ideal.[117]

Thus both the death of Christ, and his followers who take up their own crosses, cannot be seen as a regrettable event or viewed as punishment, but must be greeted as that which opens the possibility of future life. Thus any atonement theory which includes an element of punishment will not find a ready accord.

That having been said, it is as well to recall the use of analogy in Sikh theological presentation. Thus with regard to the presentation of atonement theories there must be an element of continuity with the ministry of Jesus and a suggestion that the outcome of the Cross met the demands of justice or established a decisive victory.

The Christ figure, however, seems to transcend humanity and take on a cosmic nature in the Christology of Gopal Singh's poem. No longer bound by space and time, since that is the nature of the soul united with God, the 'Sikh Christ' is the Cosmic Christ of a universal

116. Luke 4.18ff.

117. See: Daljeet Singh: *Sikhism: A Comparative Study of its Theology and Mysticism*, New Delhi, Sterling, 1979, p. 117.

faith. Here, however, 'universal' must be used not in terms of a faith that has universal application, but a faith that is beyond religious boundaries. In that way one could escape from the domestication of other faiths by the Church as a jealous 'guardian', as if this were needed, of the Christ figure. In this way **the encounter with Sikhism has brought into focus again the 'unbound' Christ**[118] of, here, Indian, rather than narrowly Hindu, spirituality. This means that he becomes no one's proud possession.[119]

A theocentric theology is needed rather than a Christocentric theology. A Sikh understanding of Christ's position would be more inclined towards his being considered a God-inspired and imbued messenger and pattern for humanity, rather than a possible end in himself. The establishment of the Kingdom would be considered his major purpose, much as in the same way Sikhs would pray and strive for God's rule through the *Khalsa*.

This raises questions regarding the **nature of conversion - to the Church, to Christ, or to God?** For the Sikh any thought of 'horizontal' conversion, from religious faith to religious faith would be unacceptable. Thus conversion to the Church would be given little consideration. To think in terms of conversion to Christ may elicit the reply that faith must be placed in the ultimate being rather than a messenger. The suggestion that one convert to Christ's way, may bring the response that true Sikhs already pursue a life of self-giving service to humanity within the context of worship given to God. To suggest that Sikhs should be converted to faith in God may result in the rejoinder that Sikhs believe in God already, so if both faiths think in terms of one God, as they do, then the concept of 'conversion to God' is patently nonsense, unless it be thought of in terms of conversion to God's will - in which case all, Sikhs and Christians alike, need to seek conversion.

Christ the proto-*Jivan-mukta* is the implication of Gopal Singh's poem. It is not, however, a generally held Sikh concept of Christ but is worthy of further exploration in terms of added significance to the Christ

---

118. See: S.J.Samartha: *The Hindu Response to the Unbound Christ*, Madras, C.L.S., 1974.

119. Samartha is right from the perspective of Christian commitment to use the phrase 'our hope, not our possession' (p.200), but within the context of interfaith dialogue one could not impose the word 'hope' since it would, once again, potentially imply a Christian theological 'take-over'.

figure. Given two elements of Sikh theology, that is, the recognition that the divine is within all humanity and, secondly, the involvement of the individual within the *Khalsa* in which God dwells, then from a Sikh perspective it is possible to think in terms of the Christ figure being present in each of those who follow his way. Christ is come alive in each and every generation. Each person becomes a Christ in microcosm. Indeed in terms of Gopal Singh's poem, Christ becomes the potential for all humanity.

What has been written may be seen as the beginning of an apologetic. The question is: 'Whose apologetic to whom?' It could be argued that it is part of a Christian apologetic to Sikhs - a portrayal of Christ in terms conducive to a Sikh understanding of him. The argument can be turned on its head. For is it not just as accurate to say that this is a Sikh apologetic to Christians? Is it not an attempt to break the Christian mould and initiate the more universal faith which Guru Nanak sought?

A reflection on Gopal Singh's Christ

Whilst Gopal Singh's work is the first full-length treatment of the Christ figure written by a Sikh, it must be put into the context of the author's own faith commitment, his eclectic nature, and Indian religious philosophy in general. From a Sikh perspective such a poem about the Christ figure may be novel, though not in a pejorative sense, it is certainly, from a wider Indian perspective, not a new departure.

Gopal Singh has been found to reflect certain traditional *bhakti* formulas, as has been demonstrated on pages 162–171. Whether this was a conscious usage or not is impossible to say, the author does not give any indication of this in a foreword or in other material. Singh does not lie outside the Sikh tradition in terms of his style of writing, nor outside the wider Indian tradition of respect, indeed reverence, for the person of Jesus Christ. The novelty of his work is in terms of the considerable Sikh theological influence in his analysis and presentation of the person and work of the Christ figure. He brings similar baggage, but it is packed in new luggage.

For over a century Hindu writers have addressed the matter of the nature of Jesus Christ.[120] One may find in Gopal Singh's work echoes of

---

120. See: Samuel Rayan 'Hindu Perceptions of Christ in the Nineteenth Century' in ed. Boff and Elizondo: *Any Room For Christ in Asia*, London, S.C.M./Concilium, 1993/2.

their perceptions of the Christ figure. Thus, in line with Rammohan Roy one finds Gopal Singh's affirmation of the pre-existence of Christ, but in contrast Roy rejects incarnation. With K.C. Sen, Gopal Singh stresses the Asianness of Christ, his divine humanity, the link with the universal *logos*, the Cross as a symbol of self-sacrifice and the *kenosis* of Christ. Along with Vivekananda there are echoes of the plurality of divine incarnation, since all humanity will find its true identity in God. Though whilst Vivekananda writes of the 'disembodied, unfettered, unbound spirit'[121] which was his understanding of Christ, Gopal Singh stresses his humanity. With Mozoomdar one finds an Eastern Christ, 'the incarnation of unbounded love and grace'[122] - a theme taken by Gopal Singh. Thus Gopal Singh was one amongst many who sought to re-shape Christ for India, contributing to what Keshub called 'the Greater Christ.'[123]

Gopal Singh was also engaged, in the late 1960s, in what became known as extratextual hermeneutics such as were developed by Asian Christian Theologians in the 1980s. That is that the inherited concepts which were expounded and elucidated were not those of the Western theologians, but in Singh's case those of the Sikh faith. Singh started where he was, and many of his readers were, discovering new theological truth for both themselves and for the Christian readers who were 'looking over his shoulder'. The texts of scripture which gave new insights to the Christ figure were not from the Bible but from the *Guru Granth Sahib*. He made his own Sikh addition to 'a (later) distinctive Asian contribution to theological methodology (which) seeks to transcend the textual, historical, and religious boundaries of Christian tradition and cultivate a deeper contact with the mysterious ways in which people of all religious persuasions have defined and appropriated humanity and divinity.'[124]

But one might suppose that although such a methodology was not alien to India and the author's own Sikh faith, that aspects of his theology/philosophy and hermeneutical approach may be alien to some, if not all, of his Christian readers. This is not the case.

121. See: M.M.Thomas: *The Acknowledged Christ of the Indian Renaissance*, London, S.C.M., 1969, p. 122.
122. Rayan (1993) p. 17.
123. Rayan (1993) p. 22.
124. ed. R.S. Sugirtharajah: *Frontiers in Asian Christian Theology - Emerging Trends*, Maryknoll, Orbis, 1994, p. 3.

Let four themes be taken for consideration. The first is with regard divinity; next, the nature of resurrection; humanity's relationship with the divine and last, the use of allegory in illuminating scripture.

As has been seen earlier[125] Gopal Singh writes of the Christ figure in terms of his divinity. Here the author is at odds with orthodox Sikh belief, although not necessarily popular belief. The concept, however, would not be foreign to some potential Christian readers. Whilst Cullman, for example,[126] is guarded in his treatment of the use of the term *theos* for Jesus Christ in the New Testament, other Christian writers have no hesitation: 'When, therefore, the Bible proclaims Jesus as the Son of God, the statement is normally seen as an assertion of His distinct personal deity. The Christmas message rests on the staggering faith that the child in the manger was - *God*.'[127]

With regard to Gopal Singh's presentation of the resurrection he writes that 'nothing dies in the realm of God'[128] yet he also writes that 'He (i.e. Christ) rose from the dead.'[129] To the Western reader there is a logical *non sequitur* here. The latter phrase seems to imply a physical resurrection akin to some aspects of Pauline theology. The former phrase implies the continuing nature of the immortal soul/*atman*. What does Gopal Singh mean by the latter phrase? Is it compatible with the former phrase? Is that compatible with Christian belief? Let Michael Goulder's *A Tale of Two Missions* lend possible understanding. He differentiates between the resurrection of the body and the immortality of the soul, pointing out the influence of the Greek understanding of the latter which led Socrates to claim that whilst his body might die, his soul would live on. Paul, however, consistently held that Jesus had risen physically from the dead in keeping with the (later) traditional Jewish line. However, Goulder claims, a second interpretation of the resurrection was being taught, that is, by the followers of the apostle Peter and was in terms of

---

125. see above p. 195f 'The Divine Nature Incarnated' It is not proposed to argue the case here regarding the Christian belief, or that of Gopal Singh, about the nature of Jesus Christ, but merely to point out how Gopal Singh portrays the Christ figure.

126. Oscar Cullmann: *The Christology of the New Testament*, London S.C.M. 19632, pp. 306-314.

127. J.I.Packer: *Knowing God*, London, Hodder and Stoughton, 1973, p. 58 - his italics.

128. Gopal Singh: *The Man Who Never Died*, p. 41.

129. Singh, G. (1987) p. 77.

a *spiritual* resurrection.[130] Now if this was the case, Gopal Singh's interpretation may well be close to a *very* early Christian view of Christ's resurrection: 'The Jerusalem Christians thought that Christ had left the human Jesus on the cross, and that Christ, as an angelic power, was spiritual; Jesus had risen from the dead and had gone to heaven, the realm of spiritual beings - so his resurrection was non-physical.'[131] Gopal Singh's presentation in terms of the above-mentioned phrases may not be logically out of sequence and, in addition, it may not be totally alien to Christian belief after all.

Apotheosis is at the heart of Gopal Singh's poem and is the goal of the Sikh religious quest. It closely, but not completely, echoes the Patristic Church, notably Origen[132] whose understanding of this issue is described: 'The pre-existing soul of Jesus was, in distinction to the souls of other men, completely surrendered to the Logos and thus united with it already before they were bound together in one body. In this sense a universal unification of the human with the divine begins with Jesus: through faith in the historically comprehensible man Jesus, each Christian becomes drawn upward through everything bodily into the pure spirituality of the Logos to which Jesus was completely dedicated.'[133]

The fourth point for consideration is the poet's use of allegory. This has been particularly illustrated by the passage regarding Jesus and the woman at the well in Samaria,[134] where, it may be recalled, Gopal Singh allegorises the five 'husbands' as those forces which, according to Sikh

---

130. Michael Goulder: *A Tale of Two Missions*, London, S.C.M., 1994, pp. 166-180.

131. Goulder (1994). p. 178.

132. Origen: *De princ.* II, 6, 3. quoted by Wolfhart Pannenberg: *Jesus: God and Man*, London, S.C.M. 1968, p. 41.

133. Pannenberg (1968) p. 41. Note the similarity here with the thought of Maximus the Confessor (580-662): 'The human being too has his *logos*, and its fulfilment points him to God and a life in God, which Maximus, following the custom of the Eastern theologians, calls 'deification'. The human being is also considered to be a microcosmos, summing up the several levels of creation. The first man, Adam, was created so that he might unite himself in the whole creation and, fulfilling the goal set by his *logos*, led the whole creation to God in a kind of cosmic deification. The purpose was frustrated by the fall, and now we see the role of Christ in this scheme. In Christ is the divine Logos which integrates all the *logoi* of the created realm.' John Macquarrie: *Jesus Christ in Modern Thought*, London, S.C.M. 1990, p. 167.

134. See above p. 190.

belief, constantly assail the human-being - pride, anger, lust, avarice and greed. Allegorical interpretation is nothing new within Christian circles, however. Augustine interpreted the five 'husbands' to mean the five books of Moses.[135] In a similar manner Origen suggests that the woman represents the soul which should be wed to the Christ figure, 'the word of truth which was to rise from the dead, and never again to die.'[136] The New Testament writers were not averse to using allegory having been influenced by Greek literature, itself under the influence of the Oracles which 'spoke in an obscure way' so that there needed to be an 'unpacking of the riddles.'[137]

Gopal Singh is being true both to his own faith and to that of early Christian interpretative principles. Thus within the *Guru Granth Sahib* the individual is presented as the journey-man whose destination is *Begam Pura* (the city of bliss) or *Sac Khand* (the region of truth) or *Amara Puri* (the eternal habitation). The path leading to such places is always hazardous and the traveller, who is blind, carries a burden of sins and has to cross desolate and thorny hills and dales.[138] As with the Sikh recognition of the limitations of human ability to understand the full nature of God and God's dealings with humanity and similar impediments with regard to language, so Origen felt justified in the use of allegory on the grounds that 'if the Bible is the Word of God, its truths are not limited or defined by the human language which is its inevitable vehicle; if the Bible bears witness to God's revelation, that revelation is not contained solely within the 'events' behind the narrative, any more than the text itself.'[139] Origen further claimed that the use of allegory was controlled by scripture's unity and that the use of text to interpret text builds up meaning. Gopal Singh was unimpeded by such constraints and his eclectic nature allowed him to utilise the Sikh faith's scriptures and traditions to unfurl new meaning and understanding to Christian texts and theology.

Gopal Singh's Christ, however, has been criticised on two counts. First, 'He is certainly not the Jesus worshipped by Christians', and secondly

---

135. Augustine: lib. lxxxiii. Quaest. qu. 64.
136. Origen: tom xiii. c. 8.
137. See: Frances Young: *The Art of Performance*, London, DLT, 1990, p. 75.
138. A.G. p. 729, *vide*: S.S. Kohli: *A Conceptual Encyclopaedia of Guru Granth Sahib*, Delhi, Manohar, 1992, p. 10.
139. Frances Young (1990) p. 85.

'He suffers but not vicariously.'[140] This latter objection holds good only if one is inclined towards an objective view of the Atonement. In fact, Gopal Singh's overall portrayal of one who suffers, who is martyred by evil people, who is victor, who gives of himself, who has eliminated self-centredness, comes near to the 'classic' view of the atonement outlined by Gustaf Aulen in his *Christus Victor*.

Gopal Singh's treatment of the crucifixion, particularly in terms of its being something to be imitated by Christ's followers reflects an insight of John Macquarrie: '...the work of Christ, finished on the cross, while in one sense a "once-for all" event of history, is at the same time an event for all times, an eschatological event that continues in the community of faith.'[141] The question becomes, 'What constitutes the 'community of faith'?' Are Christians in danger of restricting that community of faith?

The statement that the Christ of Gopal Singh's poem is not the Christ worshipped by the majority of Christians may well indeed be true. It reflects, however, an inadequacy on the part of Christians to recognise the smallness of their Christ figure and their inability to let go of him who is only apparently their possession.

Gopal Singh starts his poem with the 're-entry' of the Cosmic Christ. In so doing he seems to widen the concept of the Cosmic Christ, opening up the nature of the unified community which is the Church. Does the Church need to look beyond itself...'to the measure of the stature of the fullness (*pleroma*) of Christ'?[142] If this is not done, is the Cosmic Christ not limited, not fully cosmic, not 'all in all'?

There is a parallel here with Samartha's treatment of the Mystery, the Truth of the Truth (*Satyasya Satyam*), 'the transcendent Centre that remains always beyond and greater than apprehensions of it or even the sum total of those apprehensions. It is beyond cognitive knowledge (*tarka*) but it is open to vision (*dristi*) and intuition (*anubhava*).'[143]

---

140. Cole and Sambhi: *Sikhism and Christianity*, p. 59.

141. John Macquarrie: *Principles of Christian Theology*, London, S.C.M. 1966, p. 293.

142. Ephesians 4.13. Does this not include the 'larger "unstructured stream" of *koinonia*-in-Christ ... in human history which is spiritually continuous and discontinuous with it'? See M.M.Thomas: *Risking Christ for Christ's Sake*, Geneva, WCC, 1987, p. 114.

143. Stanley J. Samartha: 'The Cross and the Rainbow' in ed. R.S. Sugirtharajah: *Asian Faces of Jesus*, London, S.C.M. 1993, p. 111.

Likewise, Wessels and Klostermaier affirm that Greek Christology has not exhausted the mystery of Christ, though it has helped the church to see certain aspects of Christ more clearly.' Equally important is the following sentence: 'Indian wisdom will not exhaust the mystery of Christ either. But it will help the church of India to understand Christ better...'[144] Why stop at India? The Church throughout the world can learn more about Christ, but the quest will never end:

The Lord hath yet more light and truth

to break forth from his Word.[145]

---

144. Wessels: *Images of Jesus*, London, S.C.M. 1990, p. 147, quoting K. Klostermaier:*Christ und Hindu in Vrindaban*, Cologne, Hegner, 1968, pp. 155-6. Klostermaier actually continues with the words 'and to make him really understood'. This claim is excessive. The important point here is in terms of the need to break out from the confines of European thought forms.

145. George Rawson: 'We limit not the truth of God to our poor reach of mind...' 230 in ed. K.L. Parry: *Congregational Praise*, London, 1951.

11

The Encounter of Sikhs and Christians at the turn of the Millennium

We turn to a period of nearly twenty years from the early 1990s onward to discover the development of the encounter between the people of the two faiths both in India and the United Kingdom. This is a period of mixed responses with regard to dialogue *per se*. In India Sikhs were more concerned with issues surrounding the debate as to who is a Sikh and a safeguarding of the nature and expression of the faith. Christians in the Panjab concerned themselves with the matter of support for the marginalised classes. In the United Kingdom the rise of militant Islam was the dominant matter of interfaith relationships. Interest was further undermined by the fact that there were comparatively few who were actively engaged in Sikh studies, even amongst the Sikh community, let alone amongst Christians. However, that is not to say that nothing happened and to such that did we must now turn.

The early years of the final decade of the Twentieth Century saw the publication of Owen Cole and Piara Sambhi's last joint contribution: *Sikhism and Christianity: A Comparative Study*.[1] Sadly Piara Sambhi did not live to see its publication, but it will serve to be a fitting tribute to one who made such a remarkable contribution to mutual understanding. The task before the authors was fraught with difficulties such as the temptation to draw superficial parallels of belief; the problem of finding adequate English equivalents for Panjabi theological words; the need to remain faithful to the differing methods of theological reflection; the need for a modern translation of the Sikh Scriptures into English and, not least, the near impossibility of definitive statements about the faiths

---

1. Cole and Sambhi (1993), Basingstoke, Macmillan.

since religious faith is often so idiosyncratic in nature. The response of the authors is logical and deals with essential issues in an informative and reflective manner. It opens with a survey of the religions in the context of which the two faiths arose: Hinduism and Judaism and then moves on to chapters on God; Jesus and the Gurus; Spiritual Liberation and Salvation; The Scriptures; Worship; Personal Devotion; Ceremonies; Authority; Ethics and finally, Attitudes to Other Religions.

The authors found themselves obliged to deal with what might be described as the normative forms of both the faiths and consequently were not able to delve deeply into issues of theology which question, critique and challenge the faiths mutually. That said, they were able to explore those areas of contact which merit further dialogue. Here the oneness of God and God's grace are prime examples. Equally significant is the exploration of the humanitarian concerns that lie at the centre of the teachings of both Guru Nanak and his successors and Jesus of Nazareth. They deal with the ineffability of God, the One who is 'beyond time', formless and personal, according to Sikh belief. The matter of the incarnation is explored, as is the authority of the scriptures and the nature of that authority. The book is a fine basis for study of the encounter of the two faiths and can pave the way for further and deeper theological reflection.

In 1997 *Meeting Sikhs* was published by a British group known as Christians Aware. The group's aim is to promote understanding of other faith communities and this book, edited by Dr Joy Barrow, aims to fulfil that purpose. It comprises a number of opening chapters describing Sikhism and its practice written by both Sikhs and Christians whose trust and friendship Joy Barrow experienced over years of a mutually beneficial relationship in dialogue. The book well illustrates the nature of Sikh life in Britain with fine descriptions of various ceremonies and meetings. One of the more moving examples of the trust established between the communities is a poem written in the light of taking *amrit* – the initiation ceremony into the Sikh faith. Three short paragraphs reflect the depth of emotion and trust established between the believer and God the Guru:

> The tears flow ceaselessly from the utter relief that comes from surrender to the Guru's guiding light and not from my own agonising cerebral activity. The Guru has made me His as fiercely as I am His.

Today I sacrificed my ego self and donned the garb of a saint-soldier without a backward glance at my soul's achievement hitherto. From today I can see with perfect vision. I can uphold the image of my beloved Guru through the channels of my garb, thought and deed. I mourn not the loss of all that was dark in me, past and present; I only celebrate my new found divine power of protection.

Death is now a stranger hounded out of this temple, now fit for habitation by my Guru. Arm in arm we walk now in the garden of abundance where the green shoots reciprocate my rebirth.[2]

Whilst some of the vocabulary may be unfamiliar, Christian readers will be familiar with not only the nature and depth of relationship with the Divine which comes through surrender to God's will, but will be faced with the challenge that the Sikh faith poses in terms of humankind's ability to establish such a relationship of love and acceptance. Years ago when Sikhs spoke and wrote in this way missionaries were forced to question their exclusivism and rejection of the Sikh faith. Likewise in a new place and generation Christians are forced to reconsider their attitudes to the faiths of others as were those missionaries.

The essays in Barrow's book also indicate the manner in which the Sikh faith is no lightly held channel of social cohesion providing security in an alien environment. Read Harshinder Kaur Malhi's testimony, for that's what it is:

Sikhism means everything to me – it is the air that I breathe; it guides my every action. It helps me set out my own moral standards: how to react to others, how to bring up my family ... It affects how I undertake my role as a teacher. From the moment I wake up I try to make the first words I say under my breath: *'Satnam Waheguru',* which means 'Truth is God's name' ... Before I leave home I bow down to a picture of the Gurus and ask God to be by my side, protecting me through the day.[3]

---

2 Paramjit Kaur Bamrah: *The Wine of Life* in Barrow J. (1997) p. 57.

3. Harshinder Kaur Malhi: *Living the Gursikhi as a Teacher* in Barrow J (1997) p. 93.

The issue of communicating the faith to the coming generation is a major concern of the Sikh community and is considered in one of the essays. Owen Cole in conversation once put this graphically when he said that whereas in the Panjab you imbibe Sikhism with your mother's milk, in the diaspora you have to learn the faith. One way of learning has been the establishment of Sikh camps for young people during the summer holidays. Increasingly such camps are being established in the United Kingdom and the USA using English as the medium of communication since many young Sikhs in the diaspora are doubly alienated from, for instance, the Sikh scriptures. Whilst they have a fair knowledge of spoken Panjabi, many are unable to read the Gurmukhi script and few have knowledge of both script and the sacred language which dates from the sixteenth century. There have also been complaints from young people that the Panjabi trained *Granthis* who often lead worship in the *Gurdwaras* in the U.K. do not understand the nature of life here and fail to respond to their needs. Hence the camps are seen as an important element in maintaining the faith and are reflected on in Barrow's book.

However, with regard to the encounter of Sikhs and Christians, *per se*, two essays were included. One written by myself reflects in brief on some of the theological issues dealt with in this present book. The second, by Charanjit Ajit Singh, reflects on her own understanding of Christianity in the light of both her training as a historian and the considerable experience she has had of interfaith dialogue. Her early experiences of Christians were some time after Indian independence in Shimla where aloof white people made little attempt to make contact with the Indian community. It was not until she worked alongside Christians in the struggle against racism in south-west London and later in attending the Canberra Assembly of the World Council of Churches that she began to experience anything like the warmth of relationship that can be established between people of differing faiths.

For me, and reflecting vested interest, the most interesting part of her essay is that which deals with the consultations of Sikhs and Christians which I organised on behalf of the United Reformed Church. Like me, she was moved by the closeness and trust developed with the mutual acknowledgement of differences and similarities and the willingness to learn from each other. Included in those differences were her finding it difficult to accept that Christ is the only son of God and the only way to God. Original sin she also finds difficult to fathom and accept since according to Sikh faith a human being has the potential for both good and evil inclinations but should cultivate those good inclinations through prayer and service to one's fellow human beings. It was the scripture studies we shared which most moved her, and for that matter, others who so avidly joined in. The end of our allotted time for such studies was always a matter of regret. Let her own words sum up her feelings:

> What I have learnt at a personal level from the experience has been a great revelation to me. Our Christian friends would be the first to say that many wrongs were done by the colonial administrators in the name of Christ, the monarchy and country towards their subjects and opponents. They have shown openness and trust in sharing the goodness of their faith and their spirituality with people from a very different and non-European background [and in] their willingness to learn from others ... [4]

We move to two further publications, both by Pat Hooker, who had spent ten years working under the auspices of the Church Missionary Society in North India with her husband, Roger, followed by several years in Smethwick in the West Midlands. The first is a small booklet in the Grove Books series entitled *His Other Sheep*, published in 1989. She opens the book with a description of life in the 1980s in Smethwick for the Sikh community where the town's heavy industry had been involved in the manufacture of parts for the automobile industry. Such was the work for which Panjabi Sikhs were recruited. With the collapse of British car manufacturing many Sikh men found themselves unemployed. Some had problems with alcohol, most were dependent on their wives for the family's meagre income. For some there was a confusion of life-style with well established rural mores undermined by twentieth century Western freedom of expression. Many wanted to protect their children, to maintain honour within the family. Many of the older men would have been highly regarded village leaders had they remained in the Panjab, now manoeuvring for position in the *Gurdwaras* was all that was left to maintain dignity and respect.

4   Charanjit Ajit Singh: *A Sikh's Understanding of Christianity* in Barrow J. (1997) p. 120.

Having described the context Pat Hooker goes on to write of her pastoral support for neighbours, pointing out, the sad loss of similar loving and respectful support which is offered by Panjabi families to their elderly white neighbours who, regrettably, fail to grasp the richness of the relationship that is being offered to them. 'Those who have made the imaginative leap over this cultural barrier have often been delighted to be taken into the heart of a Sikh family where old age is deeply respected. They have realised that, whereas previously in their isolation they were only partly living, now they are experiencing the truth of Martin Buber's well known words: 'All real living is meeting.' They have to work at this. We all have to. As we do so it becomes increasingly clear that such meeting is at the heart of the gospel. Our faith is founded on relationship between God and man. It is about relationships growing and deepening in the creative love of Christ and it enables relationships of mutual trust and mutual forgiveness among people.'[5] This leads us to the central issue of her dialogue and witness: God's love for humanity expressed in the life and nature of Christ and his followers.

There are dilemmas, however. How does one deal with folk beliefs which have little to do with Sikhism *per* se, but which play a significant part in the daily lives of Panjabis? Rural tales of spirits which dominate human-beings driving them near insane are very real to an older generation. How does one find a tangible symbol of release through the care of God? How does one deal with humiliating helplessness? How does one respond to the knowledge of the twentieth century medical or social worker and the wisdom of rural tradition, and how does one cope with the ignorance of both? Interfaith dialogue takes on a new dimension such as is never spoken of in theological college.

Pat Hooker goes on to write of the need for mutual understanding and includes in this practical advice on visiting *Gurdwaras*. As someone of evangelical background her reverential manner on visiting a *Gurdwara* is model for her peers:

Normally now when I visit the Gurdwara I go to stand for a moment to where the Sikhs bow down before their Scriptures. I put my hands

---

5.   Hooker, Pat, (1989) *His Other Sheep*, Nottingham Grove Books, p. 9.

together, bow my head, and pray that in my meeting with the people in the Gurdwara I may be alert to the promptings of the Holy Spirit and be a faithful witness to Christ. In doing this publicly there I am confessing that I believe that God is one and is to be reverenced and honoured here as in church, but my response makes it clear to all who see me that I am deliberately not conforming to their custom and am rather insisting on the real differences which lie between us. I may perhaps provoke questions as Jesus did by my unconventional behaviour.[6]

Whilst other Christians may be comfortable enough in bowing down, prostration in Christian prayer predates today's more relaxed stance, Mrs Hooker's dignified demonstration of reverence is an important Christian gesture. But, as she indicates, the deep, disturbing, difficult questions still arise, the answers may not be fully understood by Sikh listeners, but the Christian witness is challenged to find new ways of expressing his or her faith. In dialogue one finds theological stimulation and a recognition, Pat Hooker would say, that one finds 'His Other Sheep.'

By 2005 she had also produced a fine five session study course for Christians on Sikhism.[7] The opening paragraph indicated something of a less exclusive line taken by her or maybe a change in house style and stance: 'We take as our own position the fundamental Sikh assumption: namely that all religions are authentic avenues of approach to GOD. It is, however, of the essence of believing that the believer will not compromise his or her faith. These two ideas will be held in tension in the course, as they must in any creative discussion between people of faith.' In this short study she introduces the background and history of the Sikh faith, including a life of Guru Nanak and the founding of the *Khalsa*. In terms of theology she explores Sikh understandings of God and revelation, and later the power of suffering. Central to Sikh thought is the nature of the scripture and its use. She also explores the implications of Sikh faith on life style. These issues having been explored she considers how the Christian faith may be communicated to the Sikh community. What stands out in this work is the non-judgemental manner in which

---

6. Hooker, Pat (1989) p. 17.
7. Hooker, Patricia M (2005) Birmingham, *Faith to Faith*, p. 1.

she writes. Indeed what is most valuable about this course is the challenge Pat Hooker places before her readers to reconsider issues of Christian belief and behaviour that are questioned by members of the Sikh faith. Here is a piece of work by one who is intimate with the Sikh understanding of faith and experienced in winning the trust of her Sikh colleagues in dialogue. It is an important contribution to mutual understanding.

Pat Hooker's work leads us to the one set of essays presented outside India and the U.K. which we shall explore. These are papers presented at a symposium on Sikhism sponsored by the Associated Canadian Theological Schools in Langley, British Columbia in May 1994. The papers vary in both standard and attitudes taken. Some authors attempt to demonstrate the inadequacy of the Sikh faith and the superiority of Christianity whilst others provide an honest summary of those aspects of the Christian faith which may prove to be hindrances to an acceptance by Sikhs of Jesus Christ as their Lord and Saviour.

Among those who presented papers two experts whom we have previously recognised were invited to participate. In one paper John C.B. Webster reflects on the nature and work of Christian missions in the Panjab. In a section on the role of the Institute for Sikh Studies in Batala he shows how there was a development from Clinton Loehlin's emphasis in Christian apologetic which lay first of all in the concept of grace and then secondly with regard to the Kingdom of God, to the new starting point developed which was the concept of Guru. This movement was initiated in two papers by James Massey and Maqbul Caleb and found in the work of the other expert then present, Clarance O. McMullen [(1976): *The Nature of Guruship.*[8]]

It is this concept of Guru that provides a basis for Sukhwant K. Bhatia's development of a Christology for Sikhs.[9] It is an attempt to 'contextual(ise) biblical truths about Jesus Christ so as to communicate effectively to Sikhs.'[10] There is an introduction to the concept of God

8. McMullen, Clarence O. (1976), *The Nature of Guruship*, Delhi, ISPCK. McMullen was the other expert present. He presented a paper on the religious practices of Sikhs in the Panjab.
9. Bhatia, Sukhwant S. (1994) *"Developing a Christology for the Sikhs"* amongst conference papers at the Symposium on Sikhism at Langley, British Columbia, 1994.
10. Bhatia (1994) p. 11/163.

in Sikhism, to the role of Guru and then he makes the claim that a case can be made that the Sikhs' longing for the *Satguru* is fulfilled in the person of Jesus Christ, but that the purity of the Gospel must be safeguarded through recognition of six unique characteristics: his incarnation, his sinlessness, his atoning death, his resurrection and second coming and his claims to being God. It is a tightly argued piece, quoting from both Christian and Sikh scriptures, and will be much appreciated by many Christians as they seek to portray the figure of Christ to Sikh friends. In all it is a fine example of an evangelical apologetic. But it will convince those who want to be convinced. Bhatia, in absolute fairness to him, is not unaware of this ... 'Having the right cognitive input alone, will not ensure evangelistic fruit.'[11] Herein is a major dilemma for the Christian, our contextualisation, however well-done and well-intentioned, may, from a Sikh perspective, simply be the hi-jacking of concepts. Jews would feel much the same with regard to our re-interpretation, as they would see it, of the concept of messiah.

Joel V. David provides a clear and well researched paper entitled *"Evangelising the Sikhs: Philosophical, Cultural and Sociological Hindrances"* and this deserves analysis. After a short introduction dealing with the history of missions in the Panjab, followed by an indication of the variety of sects within Sikhism, he goes on to his major theme, that of hindrances to Sikhs' properly comprehending the message of the Gospel. This is a realistic piece which pulls no punches and recognises that such hindrances are of no insignificant nature. Some are with regard to matters of philosophy/theology and mutual understanding, others with regard to Sikh perceptions of Christianity.

Whilst David claims that Sikh theology is 'underdeveloped' I would argue that it is the systematisation of Sikh theology which is underdeveloped. The claim may arise from the tendency of Bhatia, David and other evangelical colleagues to use Christianity as the norm, a plumb-line against which to measure other faiths which are themselves 'stand-alone' systems. This will become apparent as we consider Joel David's essay.

---

11. Bhatia (1994) p. 27/179.

He considers a variety of philosophical factors as 'conversion barriers'. Some theological terms, he explains, are apparently held in common but actually have different meanings, for instance grace and salvation. He warns against the dangers of superficial similarities. With regard to epistemological considerations he claims that the Sikh mind 'does not naturally think in a logical, linear style... especially on religious or spiritual matters. A Sikh will not – unless he has already in some extraordinary way been prepared by God to receive the message – be persuaded by a logical, systematic presentation of the gospel.'[12] An invitation to a vibrant, personal relationship with Christ within an alive, vigorous community of believers is seen as the requirement.

He considers theological hindrances: the Sikhs' denial of the incarnation and their ability only to understand Jesus as being human as other Gurus; the incompatibility of the Trinity with the Sikh assertion of the unicity of God; the lack of distinction between creation and Creator; the concept of God as *nirvair* – without hatred – in contrast with the biblical understanding of the just and righteous God's wrath against evil and the Sikhs' lack of understanding of the holiness of God are his major themes with regard to the doctrines about God. With regard to humanity, Sikhs are said to fail to grasp the need for atonement because they fail to grasp the significance of sin. Grace as a reward for striving after the knowledge of God is contrasted with the Christian understanding of the provenience and un-merited bestowal of God's grace.

With regard to Guruship, David rejects the title *Satguru* for Jesus because it reduces Christ to the level of humanity only. Similarly he rejects the universalism of Sikhism because it fails to recognise Christ's uniqueness as the only Saviour and Mediator through his unique death.

From a social perspective Sikhs are portrayed as being pre-occupied with mammon and materialism so that the Christian worker must set the example of a simple lifestyle. Other factors mentioned that may hinder Sikh acceptance of the Christian life include the fact that Christians of differing genders sit together in worship, that sometimes

---

12 David, Joel V. (1994), *"Evangelizing the Sikhs: Philosophical, Cultural and Sociological Hindrances."* Langley papers, pp. 52-77.

the Bible is left on the floor, that conversion may undermine the *izzat*, honour, of a family and that in India, Christians tend to be of the lower strata of society.

David acknowledges the significance of these hindrances but nevertheless goes on to state that he believes it appropriate to present the Gospel in a clear, constant and culturally appropriate and loving manner. I have a high regard for the research and scholarship which is reflected in this paper but am uncomfortable with the technique used. Let one example serve our purposes. That God, *akal*, the one beyond time, is referred to as *nirvair* – without hatred, is true, but that this should then be interpreted as God's lack of demand for justice flies in the face of the imperative upon the Sikh to struggle and fight against injustice and righteousness and that this imperative is the *hukum*, the will, of God.

Reading these papers I gain a sense of *déjà-vu*. Some of the early indigenous Indian Christian theologies, most remarkable though they were, give the impression that they were written by people who had become Christian and were now trying to justify their conversion using the terminology and conceptual framework of their previously held faith. The commentator is faced with the tension of the appreciation of carefully constructed contextual theology on the one hand and the need to criticise conceptual hi-jacking on the other. That one finds fine scholarship is without doubt, the essays by John M. Birch,[13] Bhatia and David are good examples. What I find difficult to accept is a misrepresentation of the belief of the other person. Thus Vern J. Middleton claims the Sikhs are polytheists,[14] not the monotheists they would claim to be. Steve Avtar Bains suggests that Christians must awaken the 'second generation Sikhs from their fascination with ego (*hunkar*), materialism (*moh*), and greed (*lob*),[15] as if this were not the case for Christians also, and Jasvir Singh Basi writes that 'ultimately Sikh philosophy is irreparably flawed... [and has] internal contradictions, and contradictions with the pure gospel of Christ.'[16] Were I a Sikh I do not think I would find this conducive to

---

13. Birch, John M. *"Contextualising the Gospel for Sikhs."*
14. Middleton (1994) *"A Theology of the Nations."* p. 11/11.
15. Bains (1994) *"The challenges and opportunites of ministering to second generation Sikhs."*
16. Basi, Jasvir Singh (1994), *"Contextualising the Gospel - a response."*

good relations, let alone an encouragement to convert. As a Christian I want to affirm the right to speak of one's faith, but integrity demands that though I may speak critically of the other's faith it must be with gentleness and reverence as Peter writes in his New Testament letter.

The story in the Indian sub-continent in the last two decades has moved away from the theological debate which was initiated by the Christian Institute for Sikh Studies in Batala to, one the one hand, a more practical mutual concern for personal and social development and on the other hand a breakdown in relationships. We shall first explore these developments and then move to the reasons for these changes.

The 1990s saw the creation of *Manov Manch* - the 'Human Forum'. The initiative came from the Diocese of Amritsar of the Church of North India in an attempt to address the search for justice in the areas of social and personal development. This was seen not so much as a matter of theological dialogue but the practical, day-to-day outworking of both Sikh and Christian faiths be it in terms of medical, educational, environmental or human development. Access to support is given through offices established in various church compounds and expertise is drawn from both communities.

Such mutual support has had a knock-on effect in social terms. For instance, for several years at Christmas time in various villages the Sikh community has organised celebrations, including services of worship with hymns and readings from the Bible, when the Bishop has been invited to address the congregations of both Sikhs and Christians. Greetings have been brought by leaders of several faith communities. Often this has included tributes to Jesus Christ correlating his message with their own faith and, as with any Sikh organised meeting, *langar*, a meal, has been served. The response from the Christian community has been reciprocal in nature. From time to time Sikhs celebrate their *gurpurbs*, usually celebrations of the births of the Gurus. The normal practice is to process through villages and towns stopping at the various *gurdwaras*, and now, at church buildings, where the Christian community provides refreshments. Such mutual hospitality is not untypical of the Indian scene and is not particularly difficult to organise, but makes such a difference to local relationships.

Whereas in the West the International Women's Day of Prayer has been confined in the main to the Christian community, in the Panjab there have been examples of women of both faiths, sometimes with others, coming together for prayer. Often they have started with the Sikh *Ardas* and going on to readings from the Christian scriptures together with prayers. Again there is always a *langar*. As women meet together they have begun to explore issues which make them question assumptions made. The church, through the Christian Institute for Religious Studies at Baring Union College in Batala organised a seminar on women's empowerment at which several Sikh women spoke. The outcome was a small volume of papers presented, mainly by Sikh women, dealing with the situation of Dalit women in the rural Panjab, empowerment at grassroots level, gender parity, runaway grooms, female infanticide and, finally, rape.[17]

A significant development has taken place within the lives of some women in Sikh community with a consequence for Dalit Christian women. It would seem that as more younger Sikh women have been encouraged to take up education to a higher level than was previously the case, they have been able, therefore, to find employment out of the household. Consequently Dalit women, in turn, have been taking up employment in Sikh households previously barred to them as cooks and cleaners. The manner in which they have been treated has changed. Whereas they were 'unseen' now they are recognised and addressed by name. The language used to address them has changed for the better and the consequence has been a new sense of dignity and self-worth together with marginally greater income.

The welfare of humanity has been a major issue in discussions held between the two faith communities. There are common concerns and quests which have been identified in terms of the need to enable people to find their true identity; the search for human dignity; the call for a casteless society; the dignity of labour, and the following of God's will. Such a list demonstrates the concern that both groups have for the Dalit community and regularly one hears during discussions the call to

---

17. Singh, R.B. & Chaudhary, R.M. (2007) *Women Empowerment: Myth or Reality*, Delhi, Independent Publishing Company.

conscientising that community with regard to their voting power. Politicians have begun to recognise this situation with some practical consequence. Slowly the lot of Dalits may be improved, but it is a long process. Their mobilisation is seen by both Church and *Khalsa* as an important incarnation of the egalitarian spirit of both faiths. This has been enhanced by the love of travelling which is so much a part of the Panjabi character, particularly Sikhs. Many have spent time working in western democratic countries and have experienced the egalitarian nature of such societies which fits into the Sikh understanding of the nature of human beings. The consequence is that on return to the Panjab they have sought to create a similar environment more in keeping with the *Gurus'* Word.

Thus far we have seen some of the positive developments regarding relations between Sikhs and Christians. This is but one side of the story. Whereas from the 60s to the 90s relations between the leaders of the two faiths were at their best one has to recognise that on the Christians' part such people were usually expatriates, highly educated and fairly self-confident. They could certainly approach the Sikh leadership on a basis of equality. The agitation for an independent Sikh homeland of Khalistan, retirement and family issues resulted in many such leaders leaving the Panjab. Many Panjabi Christians come from the Dalit community and did not have the confidence or educational background to involve themselves in dialogue, particularly those who were landless labourers whose relationship with their Sikh Jat landlords was only marginally more than feudal.

In recent times the growth of Pentecostal churches in the Panjab has had a profound effect on both Sikh and Christian communities. They have challenged the mainstream churches in terms of witness and have baptised great numbers of people. They have placed considerable emphasis on healing through prayer and on repentance. Many people have been freed from their drug and alcohol dependence. From a Sikh perspective, however, their work has received severe condemnation. In conversations one hears Sikhs speaking of the Pentecostalists' "exaggerated claims to be able to perform healing miracles most of which have no basis in reality and which have duped villagers." All Christians are tarred with the same brush and in some areas the relationship between church and *khalsa* has been strained to the point of breaking. Some newly recruited Pentecostal pastors are said to have continued to wear the 5 Ks, thus blurring religious boundaries from the perspective of those Sikhs caught up in the debate regarding the nature of Sikh identity. This is considered to be deception and with the unfulfilled promise of miracle cures undermines village cohesion. Add to this the aggressive evangelicalism of the Pentecostalists together with their theological exclusivity and one recognises that this would be quite contrary to the Sikh understanding that all paths lead to God. Attempts to bring about the conversion of Sikhs to Christianity are viewed as anathema and vehemently rejected and in conversations were the biggest cause of concern.

Relations with the Sikh community have been further undermined by the response of the Sikh leadership to the analytical method of Prof. Hew McLeod and particularly those Sikhs who have been guided by him in their academic research. The consequence has been a call for research on the Sikh scriptures to be banned, as some Sikhs see it, to preserve the integrity of the Guru Granth Sahib. This has been particularly the case amongst a growing conservatism amongst *granthis* across the Panjab in their response to the growing fundamentalism in many faiths. Although Prof. McLeod has rejected his erstwhile association with the Christian faith, some within the Sikh community have seen his work as part of a Christian onslaught against Sikhism.

We are now at a point at which we may be able to analyse why so little dialogue between Sikhs and Christians takes place.

Perhaps the major sponsor of dialogue between the two faiths from the mid 1960s onwards was the Christian Institute for Sikh Studies of which Clinton Loehlin was one of the founding fathers. For many years it was ably led by a number of successors, but by the mid 1980s two factors came into play. The Sikh community was preoccupied with the struggle for recognition and survival, especially after the period of hostility with the central government. Dialogue was to become almost impossible, particularly during times of tension. From the Christian perspective attention was paid to the plight of the Dalit community whose support now became the central area of concern for the Church's socio-economic action. Indeed the raison d'être of the Christian Institute was altered to reflect this development. That is not to say that dialogue with the Sikh community came to an end, it continued in terms of the dialogue of daily life, but the theological aspects of dialogue were no longer a priority.

This was also a period when the Sikh community was exploring its own identity. The question of 'Who is a Sikh?' was a matter of great significance, especially in the light of the growing fundamentalisms which were the concerns of all the world's major faiths. The Sikhs like the Christians are a minority faith, but are faced with a degree of porosity when it comes to religious faith boundaries, especially with Hinduism. For generations, Sikhs and Hindus would comprise members of single families, one member of the family could be a Sikh, a brother or sister a Hindu. This was, however, a time when distinctiveness and its definition were of prime importance. The time for dialogue was not at this moment.

By this time Hew McLeod was beginning to make significant contributions to the study of Sikhism. These were in the light of his rigorous training as a historian. Three areas of study may be considered here. The first is in terms of his consideration of the historicity of Guru Nanak. Perhaps this is most vividly illustrated by the length of biographies written about Guru Nanak. Often one finds descriptions of what may be termed the Guru Nanak of faith, that is, lives of the Guru written by devout Sikhs and often in the region of 150 to 200 pages in length. McLeod's biography is reduced to some one and a half pages of what he believes reflects historicity. This vast discrepancy caused great furore amongst many in the Sikh community reflecting something of the Jesus of history and Christ of faith debate within the church. A second matter of dispute was the textual analysis of the Sikh Scriptures made by one of McLeod's research students. Again this was a cause of offence and described by some as 'cutting up the body of our Guru'. Thirdly his intervention, as an 'outsider', in the 'Who is a Sikh?' debate was not welcomed by all. Many would see this as an internal matter to be resolved by Sikhs themselves. As we have seen, McLeod was a member of staff at Baring Union College. By this time he had lost faith as a Christian but this did not stop disgruntled Sikhs from accusing Christians as a whole of trying to undermine the Sikh faith as had been the case amongst missionaries of a bygone era. McLeod's contribution to Sikh studies has been enormous and appreciated by many, including some Sikh academics, but his rigorous methodology has equally offended, unfortunately at a time when Sikhs were aware of their minority status and the opprobrium of the majority religious and political community.

In more recent years the evangelistic methodology of the Pentecostal movement in the Panjab has undermined relations, particularly the aggressive enthusiasm and dismissive exclusivism of those newly converted. There were a number of occasions when I was told in no uncertain way by Sikh colleagues of the hypocrisy of the false claims made with regard to miraculous healing. That someone should leave the faith and then clam to be able to perform miracles has left many Sikhs with the sour taste of resentment, a matter of regret since it is not a sound basis for dialogue. That this has been the case in the heartland of Sikhism, the villages of the Panjab, has meant that the mainstream churches have had an uphill struggle.

But visit Baring Union College, Batala, or attend a meeting of the *Manov Manch* today and you will gain a very different impression of relationships between the two communities. It is in the practical outworking of faith on a daily basis that relationships are enhanced and developed, so, for instance, both groups have deplored the inequality of casteism and consequently struggle for an egalitarian environment. By the same token note how both Sikhs and Christians in the United Kingdom struggle to overcome racism. In both places, however, further work is still vital in terms of the enhancement of mutual theological understanding, for instance in exploration of the nature of scripture and its interpretation; the nature of incarnation and the debate over incarnation through a single individual or a group. These issues, together with an exploration into the identity of the people, or peoples, of God will have important implications for God's mission and the establishment of the reign of God.

12

Sketching a presentation of Christianity to Sikhs – a personal view

This chapter started life as an attempt to sketch an apologetic to Sikhs. What follows is essentially personal and an attempt to present on my own efforts to talk about the Christian faith with Sikh colleagues. In doing so I have had to question the nature of my own faith and its means of expression. I may use borrowed language from the work of others, but they should not be blamed for the inadequacy of my belief or its expression. Nor is this an attempt to find ways of presenting Christianity to Sikhs with a view to conversion, but it is about witness. I am reminded of a letter from the Rev'd J.F.Ullman in the Presbyterian *Home and Foreign Record* in which an Indian convert from Islam had studied, in English, the 'evidences of Christianity' as they were called in the Nineteenth Century, but though he understood them, yet he often expressed the remark that evidences are far more for believers than unbelievers.[1]

Before considering the nature of Christian faith, there needs to be a word about the language we use. It seems to me that so much of our understanding of God and of humanity is clouded by the fact that many Christians have attempted to take literally that which was originally expressed as metaphor. If we try to speak about God, we are undermined by three matters. The first is that finite human-beings cannot understand the nature of an infinite God. The second is that our language is inadequate and fails to express our understanding of God and our relationship with 'him'. And that last word leads to the third matter, that is the lack in English of a gender neutral third person singular pronoun. Hence my resorting to the use of inverted commas – but more about this issue later.

---

1. Webster, John C.B. (1976) p. 33.

242 The Word of God is Not Bound

In any presentation of my faith I do not want to start with Jesus or even God, but to take a leaf out of the Buddhists' book and look to an analysis of the human condition. The first issue, I would suggest, is to recognise that many people seem to be alienated, from others, from their environment, from themselves and from God. Their behaviour reflects that in terms of the manner in which they treat others, express dissatisfaction with their lives and are prepared to hurt others and abuse their environment for their own gain. It would seem to me that Guru Nanak was right when he said that people are essentially self-centred. So we come to the second issue, that of the inherent self-centredness of individuals. I recognise that there needs to be an element of self-centredness for the sake of survival. I am also aware as I talk to feminist colleagues (and I hope I do not reduce this argument too simplistically) that women have been put down so often by men that self-affirmation and a recognition of self-worth is vital. But I still believe that we all are in danger of making self-centred demands on others and when those are not fulfilled we resort to untoward practices. In other words, we are prone to what Christians would call 'sin'. I prefer to recognise and name that which is the cause of sin – our self-centredness. This is not to say that we can reduce sin to being a matter for individuals only. There is such a thing as corporate or collective sin, but again this is often a reflection of greed and desire for corporate or national gain, often motivated by the self-centredness of the search and demand for power.

The third issue, then, is the need to overcome self-centredness, be it individual or corporate. This is something that has dominated Sikh theology and has been a considerable influence on my own thinking. Sikhs talk in terms of the need for the elimination of *haumai*. That's a word which translated simply means 'me/I', in other words self-centredness. In a scripture study with Sikh colleagues we looked at the passage in Luke (9.23) where Jesus indicates the need to take up the cross daily and then goes on to point out that whoever loses his or her life or self – the Greek word *psuche* means 'life', 'human individual' and 'self' – will actually find the real 'him/her'-self. I'm inclined to think that Jesus has something like the elimination of self-centredness in mind when he spoke these words. This leads to the fourth issue, that is, for me and for many fellow Christians, the Cross of Jesus of Nazareth is the ultimate example of giving of one's self for others.

But here I have difficulty with those Christians who use the phrase 'Jesus gave himself for our sins' almost as a mantra, as if that having been done and our having said that's what he did then we're fine with God and need do no more. The Cross is simply the start. For the person of faith living out the cross event in one's own life is the vital, and horrendously difficult, challenge to real faith. Yet paradoxically it is through self-giving that one finds self-fulfilment.

A fifth point arises. That is that there is no way in which we can live the life to which we are called other than through the grace of God. Herein lies a major point of debate with my Sikh colleagues. For them life cannot be lived other than *gur prasadi*, through the grace of the Guru – God. Agreed. However, they would argue that humanity has to earn God's grace, has to take the first step. Bhai Gurdas said that if someone takes one step towards God, God takes a thousand steps towards him or her. I've been brought up on the understanding that we live through God's prevenient grace. We cannot earn it. God starts the process – God so loved he world that he sent his only son.... However, lobbing texts of scripture and Bhai Gurdas's works isn't going to get us anywhere, save to recognise that we are dependant on the grace of God which comes by whatever means.

My Sikh colleagues may well then suggest that the person who lives such a life may well be a *jivan mukhat*. That means one who has gained liberation, maybe we could use the word 'salvation', whilst in this life. I warm to this concept and would suggest that it leads us on to the Christian affirmation about being 'in Christ'. It is life lived presently through God's grace as one follows the will of God for one's life. Likewise, my Sikh colleagues would talk of following God's *hukum*, meaning the same thing, God's will. Consequently one is called to the struggle for forgiveness, for justice, for peace, for integrity: in other words for right relations with other people and the world in which we live. I was challenged by a Sikh friend with words of Guru Nanak: What is the use of your spirituality if my stomach is still empty? It's not just a matter of an empty stomach but also an empty, unfulfilled life. For Sikhs *seva*, service, is vital. The tree is tested by its fruit, not by an empty promise of fruit. That's why theology for me is not just a matter of cerebral understanding, but a challenge to action, reflection and further action. It's a pragmatic process, not just a philosophical exercise.

Thus far there has been a fair amount of agreement with my Sikh colleagues. There have been minor issues of difference, but not to the extent of bitter dispute. I'm not sure it would ever come to that.

I have used the word 'God' as if there is a deal of mutual understanding. To an extent there is, but it's an essentially Christian word in the minds of my Sikh friends. Yes, it affirms transcendence, creativity and graciousness, but Sikhs also use other names for God including *Akal Purakh*, the Being Beyond Time, the Timeless One, the Eternal. Notice, however, the word 'One'. That's the first word of the Sikh scriptures and it emphasises the unicity, the very oneness, of God. But we Christians talk of the Trinity, further confusing our Sikh hearers with phrases like 'the Three in One and the One in Three'. I have Christian colleagues who can speak of this more eloquently, but I need to be able to speak of 'the hope that is within me' as best I can and offer an explanation of sorts to my Sikh friends.

Whatever we say about God is but a fraction of what there is to say and an even smaller fraction is our understanding of that infinite being who is beyond our finite comprehension. I would want to affirm, however, that we have in that being one whose creative power undergirds our very being both in terms of ourselves as individuals and the universe in which we live. Quite how that happened and continues to happen I cannot say. The Genesis story I take to be an attempt to explain in primitive terms, again given the limitations of understanding and means of expression. But I affirm what it implies, that behind the universe is a creative and sustaining God. I think my Sikh friends would agree. I'd like to suggest that the metaphor we use for that is 'God the Father'.

We go a step further. This same being is no absentee landlord of 'his' creation. (I'll come to gender epithets later.) This is a being who makes 'him'self and 'his' will known to humankind. Let me borrow the term *anubhava* from the Indian vocabulary. It refers to the experience of God within one's life. Sometimes it comes through the inner voice, but we have to be careful here lest we hear the false voices of our own making. That inner voice can be vivid and persuasive. It may convey the will of God. It may be very real to us. Sometimes our experience of God arises out of our relationships with our fellow human-beings, perhaps collectively, perhaps through an individual. Like the Friends, known as Quakers, Sikhs affirm the presence of God within us all. Occasionally we experience such a presence and I would suggest that this is what the disciples experienced when they talked and lived with Jesus. So I want to talk of that element of God which is found in personal relationships and demonstrated in the nature of the man Jesus of Nazareth in whom one sees the nature of humanity as we can become, a forerunner of the complete person. Now whereas many Christians may talk of the divinity and humanity of Jesus Christ, the God-Man as it were, I find this difficult to affirm, preferring to talk in terms of the description given of Jesus Christ in the New Testament: 'God was in Christ' (2. Cor 5.19) There is that of God within us all. Those within the Hindu and Sikh fold talk of the *Brahman-Atman* synthesis – the 'soul' of God and the 'soul' of human-beings being of the same nature. (Probably I put this a little too simply and crudely but that may open up the debate.) Perhaps this may be considered the nature of 'God the Son': the one through whom God makes himself and his purposes known, the one who more than any other human being lived out the true God-given life.

We cannot leave it there. That same God who was present at the beginning, who makes 'him'self known in the man Jesus, continues to be present with us. This element of God, the Holy Spirit, is the means of communication, the power of God there both at creation and in our lives. This is the enlivening, renewing, powerful force of God which, often unexpectedly, rests within each of us enabling us to do far more than we could anticipate. It enables us to live life to God's glory, not our own.

Here then are the three elements of the one and same God, each is deeply rooted in the other so that there's an element of relationship and community within God. Some Christians talk of a mutual indwelling of the three elements. That is a celebration of relationship within the Godhead which reaches out to humanity as was celebrated in the Passover story, seen in Jesus and continues amongst God's peoples today. The very nature of the community of the Godhead leads us to recognise the potential we have to be liberated, equal people who live again in community. I can cope with the Trinity in those terms. I get nervous when I'm told this is the very essence of God, the very nature of God's being and this is what I must believe. I'm back to that question of how finite human-beings can talk so knowledgeably about that which is actually beyond their ability to comprehend and express.

So I'm left with the need to distinguish between faith and belief, between the relationship of trust in the purposes of God and the cerebral acceptance of a series of theological propositions. My dialogue with the Sikh community has made me question the latter and made me wonder if the theological stance we make is more a response to psychological need, particularly when disaster strikes in one's life, when one needs the reassurance that there is some higher purpose. I regret writing that may seem cruel and unsympathetic to those who may take that particular faith stance, but God is not there simply to protect or to absorb the blame. My theology finds it very hard to hear the question, 'Why did God allow this or that to happen?' I do not believe in a God that controls automatons.

A word about gender and God: in the 1980s the United Reformed Church in the UK organised a series of consultations of Sikhs and Christians. It was a time when women, and a few men, within the church were beginning to use of the term 'Mother' when addressing God. We Christians thought it a little risqué. The Sikhs giggled. "Oh", they said, "we've been doing that for the last three hundred years plus. In fact it's in our scriptures – 'God, you are our Father and our Mother ...'" It behoves us Christians to recognise that we do not always bring fresh understanding of the nature of God to others. We learnt that God is beyond gender epithet. It was an important lesson.

As to the figure of Jesus, I have seen time and again the respect and admiration that Sikhs have given to him. He has been recognised as a great teacher and guide, as one through whom God has made himself known, but that neither makes him divine or unique as far as they are concerned. 'He's like one of our Gurus,' say some of my Sikh friends. What makes his death any different from the martyrdoms of Gurus Arjun and Tegh Bahadur?' they ask ... 'They both died on behalf of others.' That was the case. 'It's easy,' say my Christian friends, 'It's because of who Jesus was – the God-Man.'

Now, if that is part of your faith as a Christian you are in a position to make a claim that is in keeping with traditional doctrines of the atonement, for instance that Jesus Christ paid the ransom for our sins, or for some, that he propitiated an angry God. I'm afraid that is not something that the Sikh will find convincing. I can't say I do either, to be honest, especially the latter claim. The issue of the ransom may be better understood in terms of the effect on the freed prisoner when a ransom has been paid, that sense of freedom and liberation. That's the essence of the metaphor, not the question of to whom the ransom was paid and whether the one who paid was the most suitable person to pay. For my part, I have a feeling that if any of the traditional theories of the atonement are to be used, then Sikhs might be moved by what Aulen calls the classical theory which sees the cross as a battle between good and evil. I have difficulties with this when it comes to its cosmic dimensions, but if presented in terms of the inner struggle which is of the nature of daily cross bearing then here would be a point of contact and potential understanding. Sikhs know what it is to struggle for justice and, indeed, survival. They may be portrayed by some as militaristic, but this should be seen in terms of battling for the sake of justice and not for the sake of the fight. I mentioned above the importance of the continued struggle. Sikh colleagues relate to that concept. Grace is not cheap but requires constant vigilance.

We need to move on to the nature of our faith community. If you have ever visited a Gurdwara you will experience the *khalsa*, that is the Sikhs as a community, united in faith under the will of God. That gives them an insight into the nature of the Church as the Body of Christ. Herein is a point of understanding, but also a point of difference, for Sikhs reject the idea of incarnation in a single individual, such as the Christian understanding of Jesus Christ, but they do recognise the presence of God amongst God's people. Where people care, demonstrate their love, protest against injustice, worship with sincerity, there is the people of God. It sounds familiar, and if you stay around you sense that warmth characteristic of the local congregation at its best and what's more the food served is superb! Conveying the message of the Gospel, or the Gurus for that matter, is not done simply in terms of what is said. It has to be lived.

And if it is to be lived, then we have to be constantly on our guard to make sure that our faith speaks to the context in which we find ourselves. We cannot simply maintain that which worked in the past.

I seek a church prepared to change as circumstances require, not change for change's sake, but a church which responds to the needs of the community and which is able to communicate to its context. Within the Reformed Churches that's part of our heritage. We cannot stand still relying on what was successful in the past bringing equal success in the future.

The Reformed traditions also have at their centre the authority of scripture. Sikhs will understand that. Walk into any *Gurdwara* and the first thing to be noticed as you move to the worship hall is the centrality of the scriptures, the *Guru Granth Sahib*. Sikhs seek their understanding of God and the prompting of the will of God through its pages. They look for the *Shabad* – the Word. There are so many parallels with the term *logos* that for the Christian to speak of the Word of God would find initial understanding on the part of the Sikh and an opportunity to explore further the implications of the Word. Within my own denomination we acknowledge that our understanding of the scripture is given through the guidance of the Holy Spirit of God, that element of God's nature that enables the believer to experience the presence and greater understanding of God within his or her life. Sikhs would talk in terms of the *Shabad* within their scripture having a similar function.

Before the Mission conference which took place in Edinburgh in 1910 a questionnaire was sent out. It was in part a mission audit which elicited considerable information about the context in which participants worked. Among the questions was one which asked about the points of contact with local people and their faith. What we have seen above are just such points of contact. They provide starting points for discussion which may not necessarily be points of agreement. However, sometimes one is surprised by the responses made. A while ago I spoke to a Sikh colleague about some of the central matters of the Reformed traditions: *sola gratia* – by grace alone; *sola fide* – by faith alone; *soli deo Gloria* – to the glory of God alone; *sola scripture* – through the scriptures alone; and *ecclesia reformata semper reformanda* – the Reformed Church must keep on reforming. The response was: 'That's much the same that we Sikhs would affirm.' If you read Sikh theology you'll see that is very much the case.

My own experience as I have spoken about my faith with Sikhs is that I have been challenged to find ways of articulating the faith in a manner that they can understand. They have questioned my assumptions both about them and about my own faith. They have made me realise that I cannot be content with an individualistic concern about the so-called spiritual dimension of my life, but that any religious faith must also have pragmatic social implications for the whole of human life and God's creation. Any presentation of Christianity which does not include these issues will fall on deaf ears, and rightly so!

13

Conclusion

The implications of the encounter of Sikhs and Christians

At the outset it must be recognised that the dialogue between Sikhs and Christians is incomplete. The issues for a continuing debate are still not fully defined. This study betrays its essentially Christian origins by the matters which have been taken up, in particular the exploration of the figure of Jesus Christ as seen by Sikhs and the nature of the Sikh response to mission. A Sikh agenda may be more concerned with concepts of service or grace or the presence of God within the community of faith and would have viewed Christianity in the light of Sikh preoccupations.

Be that as it may, the encounter has taken place and a pattern may be discerned, particularly if viewed from the 1830s onwards with the coming of the American Presbyterians and later the C.M.S.

From a Christian perspective there was a sense of **hope**. The Sikhs appeared to be ideal targets for mission: they were already critical of Hindu practices and much appreciated for their courage. Sikhs were, nevertheless, regarded as having little in common theologically. From a Sikh perspective the essential element was one of **suspicion**. Here was a group of people ostensibly with a spiritual task in mind, yet closely associated with the alien rulers.

Notwithstanding such wariness there were, nevertheless, Sikhs with a **fascination** for the figure of Jesus Christ, but, along with other similarly inclined Hindus, they appreciated not so much the Christ 'bound' by the Church, but the 'unbound' Christ whose teaching and demeanour had enormous appeal.

It was those early Indian Christians who were to open up a new attitude of **rejection of the otherness of Sikhism**, who influenced foreign missionaries into considering the value of the faith as a preparation for the Gospel.

However, this coincided with a new direction in the missionaries' sphere of action. By the 1880s, after 30-50 years of witness among the Sikhs, there was little to show for it in terms of conversions to Christianity. The 'mass-movement' of so-called 'outcastes' in their search for greater dignity and self-esteem led to a period of **competition** between Christians and Sikhs for the hearts and minds of the rural poor. Such competition was not without **admiration** for the techniques employed by the Christians, if not for the people themselves and their message.

From competition the next stage was one of **co-operation**, thanks mainly to the efforts of Clinton Loehlin during the inter-war and post-war years. It was a time of growing **mutual understanding** amongst Sikh and Christian leaders and intellectuals.

Sadly this was not to last as increasing political unrest led to a **breakdown of trust** and **indifference** towards dialogue. Partly this is due to differences of opinion regarding the nature and techniques of the study of religion, and partly it is due to the lack of self-confidence and academic leadership on the part of the majority, but not all, of the Panjab's Christians whose lowly place prevented a dialogue of equals.

If there is to be any development of dialogue between Sikhs and Christians it will take on differing aspects. In India, particularly the Panjab, Sikh-Christian dialogue will probably develop, outside academic circles, in terms of the common struggle for economic and political justice when the Gospel is 'earthed'. Both Dalit Christians and politically aware Sikhs have little time for anything that does not explicitly contribute to the welfare of society. We have seen in recent years the development of the work of *manov manch* as an indication of this trend. It may be that the major encounter with regard to matters of doctrine will be found in dialogue with diaspora Sikhs.

What are the implications of such a pattern of encounter?

The demeanour of the Christian involved in witness and dialogue is of utmost importance. Seen against the humility of Christ, the arrogance of Christians was early observed by Bhai Gurdas. The 'sahib' mentality,[1] reflecting an absolute and triumphant faith during the days of the British 'Raj' was not likely to inspire awe and allure but the very opposite. Sadly, that same sense of superiority was even reflected in the failure of some missionaries to recognise the strengths of their indigenous colleagues in interpreting the Gospel in ways which reflected the philosophical and devotional background of their peers of other faith communities.[2] I confess to a certain concern about the presentation of Christianity as expressed in some of the papers presented at the conference in Langley, BC, in 1994. I appreciate the positive depth of faith and conviction expressed but have concern when this turns to a means of expression that reflects superiority or triumphalism.

The encounter also highlights other issues and implications of missionary activity. As recognized by Lamin Sanneh 'missionary expectations were determined to a large extent by home-bred ideas and personal experiences ... Yet on any balanced view, we would have to agree that field exposure sometimes wrought havoc with predetermined ways.[3] This is best illustrated in the case of the Sikh-Christian encounter by the response of Newton at the 1862/63 conference at which Keene presented his paper on Sikhism. Newton had maintained his exclusive position[4] towards other faiths, whilst the seeds of respect for Sikhism on the part of Keene were peremptorily dismissed. The comment from headquarters staff about the 'strange' prayer meeting for rain conducted by Edward Guilford is another example.

The fascination with the Christ figure on the part of Sikhs has been noted earlier and not only has it led to Gopal Singh's poem but to the

---

1.   See: James Massey: *Dalits in India*, New Delhi, 1995, p. 100. Massey quotes both Lesslie Newbigin and C.F.Andrews on the use of 'Sahib' (Lord) as a means of address. Andrews illustrated this by recounting an occasion when he was walking with an Indian gentleman who saw a Sahib driving past in his trap, his groom seated behind him. 'The crowd scattered before him, and the policeman saluted smartly. "Look", said the Indian gentleman, "there is your Christianity driving along! That Sahib's the missionary of this place, and that is his position, and that is how he goes to his work." (C.F.Andrews: *North India*, Oxford, 1908, p. 164.)

2.   See above regarding the work of Padri Daud Singh.

3.   Lamin Sanneh: *Translating the Message*, Maryknoll, Orbis, 1989, p. 5.

4.   'Princeton Theology played an important role in establishing patterns of interaction between the Presbyterian missionaries and the people of India. Because this theology derived from an infallible scripture which provided the divine standard according to which all truth must be

use of Christ almost as a standard or norm against which other religious practices may be measured.[5] By contrast, rarely, if at all, has one found in recent years Christian reviews[6] of Guru Nanak or his spirituality. This may be partly due to the exclusive views held by some Christians with regard to other faiths. These would be expressed in terms of sheer disbelief that any other saviour figure could exist or have existed. Such people may also simply disregard Guru Nanak as 'another *avatar*.'

In his book, *The Mediators*,[7] John Macquarrie reviews the life and work of ten great religious leaders 'who have set in train movements and communities in which their insights have been further developed and sometimes, it must be said, corrupted.'[8] Regrettably, Professor Macquarrie consciously chose not to include Guru Nanak,[9] preferring to conclude his book with a review of the life of the Prophet Muhammad (p.b.u.h.). A full-scale Christian 'appreciation' of Guru Nanak of the nature of Cragg's *Muhammad and the Christian* has yet to be written.[10]

In a similar vein the encounter of Sikhs and Christians has yet to be reflected in a full-scale apologetic to Sikhs. Clinton Loehlin made a start on this matter with his short study *The Christian Approach to the Sikh*,[11] but it is more an introduction to the Sikh faith than an apologetic. Two reasons may be given for this.

The first is that from an early time in the history of the encounter little attempt was made to differentiate between Hinduism and Sikhism.

---

judged and which was therefore not open to criticism based on any human (i.e. non-Biblical) standard of truth, it allowed only for one-way interaction. The missionaries who came to India as bearers of this truth had everything to teach and nothing of importance to learn; the Indians, as proponents of human systems, were expected only to accept the missionaries' truth with repentance, faith and thanksgiving - or reject it to their eternal peril.' See: John C.B.Webster: *The Christian Community and Change in Nineteenth Century North India.* p. 34.

5. See: Saran Singh's editorial in *The Sikh Review*, Calcutta, April 1994, p. 3f. in which Jesus Christ is described as dying 'on the Cross in full glory of his golden (sic) locks - as Man's "natural covering of the head" (Ps. 68.21)'. This is used as an argument to support the Sikh maintenance of uncut hair.

6. In so stating I differentiate between those Christians who write from a history of religion or comparative religion perspective and those who would review the life of the Guru in terms of his contribution to the world's spiritual resources.

7. John Macquarrie: *The Mediators*, London, S.C.M., 1995.

8. Macquarrie (1995) p. 129f.

9. Letter to the present writer, 11:xi:'95.

10. This is not to say that Christians have not written about Guru Nanak, but the guiding academic discipline has been more in terms of the History of Religions than the field of Spirituality.

11. London, Edinburgh House Press, 1966. See above p. 58.

As was seen earlier[12] so influential a figure as C.F. Andrews was encouraged, and that by a Sikh, to present Sikhism as a sect of Hinduism at the 1910 Edinburgh Conference.

Secondly, it was noted[13] that by the 1880s the attention of the missionary societies in the Panjab had been taken up with work among the Dalit community who were turning to the Church in large enough numbers as to cause consternation in the household of Sikhism. This being the case there were few 'specialists' in Sikhism among the missionaries and Guilford who was thus viewed later found himself as an administrator with a wider brief than activity among the Sikhs. It was not until nearly one hundred years after the arrival of the first American Presbyterians that Loehlin appeared on the scene to address this task.

Loehlin raises a major question for missionaries. For all their claims he asks: 'Where is the Sermon on the Mount fulfilled in the Christian Church?'[14] In this simple question Loehlin challenges the church of his day, and in every generation, with the Sikh critique that Christian spirituality is found wanting if it is not reflected in the practical service in everyday life. Within the Panjab today it will be the Church's involvement in the struggle for justice that will win the trust of Sikhs. This is reflected today in the work of *manav manch*. Is this the pattern of service and witness which the Church must develop?

Throughout this present work it has been noted that two matters have appealed to the Sikh community. One is a selfless Christian lifestyle of service. The other is the figure of Jesus Christ who provides a universal model. One may argue the case for Atonement or Trinity but it will cut no ice. Dogmatics have little or no part in Sikhism. Dogma was said to 'smother religious experience'[15] An experience of the living Christ reflected in the Body of Christ carries far more weight.[16]

Many Western Christians reading Gopal Singh's poem about Jesus Christ will find the portrayal at first sight to be quite foreign to their expectations. That does not preclude the attempt to define a 'Sikh'

---

12. see above p. 49.
13. see above p. 113.
14. *The Christian Approach to the Sikh*, p. 72.
15. See above, p. 63.
16. It is not without significance that the 'Sikh and Christian Theology' project was abandoned by the Christian Institute for Sikh Studies. See above p. 63.

Christ or countermine its validity. Michael Amaladoss points out[17] that 'God is always present and active in creation and in history. That is the meaning of the universal salvific will of God. The presence is articulated in various manifestations that are ordained to a unity. This does not mean that all manifestations are the same or of the same value. It does not mean either that the human response is not conditioned by sin and imperfection, or even by refusal. But it does mean that we must always have a global perspective. God manifests Godself in various ways to various persons and groups in sovereign freedom. Such manifestations are not arbitrary, but ordained to the global plan of God for humankind.'

Gopal Singh's contribution must also be seen in the context of a Christ figure, the fullness of whom is always *to be.* discovered,[18] it is never there already in a conceptual pattern that explains and predicts everything. Once again there are echoes of Guru Nanak's dictum that the more you say about God, there more needs to be said. The same applies to Jesus Christ. It is a matter of the ever continuing search. If, as Amaladoss claims 'God manifests Godself in various ways to various persons and groups in sovereign freedom', then people of other faith may be included in that search. Further, because the first covenant which God made is with Creation (the Noahic Covenant) it should not surprise the Christian if God meets us in people of Other Faiths. From that general covenant one may go on to speak of other particular covenants, e.g. with Abraham, but why should not God use Guru Nanak or Gandhi or Gopal Singh to open up new dimensions in the understanding of God's manifesting Godself in Jesus Christ. Schreiter points out that even Paul held a Christological pluralism.[19] One must, therefore, concede that Gopal Singh's contribution must be seen as one amongst many. Nor should the danger, if that be the case, of syncretism stifle Christological attempts.

The encounter of Sikhs and Christians has provided a basis for a review of the nature of the Church's witness, but far more substantially it has revealed once again that 'the word of God cannot be bound.'[20]

---

17. Michael Amaladoss 'The Pluralism of Religions and the Significance of Christ', in ed. R.S.S ugirtharajah: *Asian Faces of Jesus*, London, S.C.M. 1993, p. 91.
18. See: Rowan Williams: 'Trinity and Pluralism' in d'Costa: *Christian Uniqueness Reconsidered*, New York, Orbis, 1990, p. 8.
19. Schreiter: *Faces of Jesus in Africa*, London, S.C.M., 1992, p. 26.
20. 2 Tim 2.9.

Bibliography

Ahluwalia, Jasbir Singh: *Sikhism Today - The Crisis Within and Without.*

Ahluwalia, Jasbir Singh: *The Sovereignty of the Sikh Doctrine,* New Delhi, Bahri Publications, 1983

Ahmad-Shah, E.: *Sikhism and Christian Faith,* Lucknow, Lucknow Publishing House, n.d

Andrews, C.F.: *North India,* London, 1908

Anderson, Howard E: *Gospel Romance in the Huts of the Punjab,* New York, Revell & Co, 1925.

Archer, J.C.: *The Sikhs in Relation to Hindus, Muslims, Christians and Ahmadiyyas: A Study in Comparative Religion,* Princeton, Princeton U.P., 1946

Bains, Santokh Singh 'Christianity and Sikhism - A Comparative Study of Two Significant World Religions' in *The Sikh Review,* Oct., 1987

Bala, Shashi: *The Concept of Monotheism - A Comparative Study of Major Religious Scriptures,* Delhi, ABS Publications, 1993

Balanyne, Tony: *Between Colonalism and Disapora,* New Delhi, Permanent Black, 2007

Barrier, N.G.: *Banned, Controversial Literature and Political Control in British India, 1907-1947,* Delhi, Manohar, 1976

Barrier, N.G.: *The Sikhs and Their Literature,* Delhi, Manohar, 1970

Barrow, Joy: *Meeting Sikhs,* Christians Aware, 1997

Bevans, Stephan B.: *Models of Contextual Theology,* Maryknoll, Orbis, 1992

Boyd, Robin: *Krishtadvaita,* Madras, Christian Literature Society, 1977

C.M.S.: *Face to Face,* London, The Highway Press, 1971

Chaker, Amar Singh: *Varan Gian Ratnavali Bhai Gurdas Ji,* Amritsar, Sromani Gurdwara Parbandhak Committee, 1981

Chawla, Surjit Singh: *Martyrdom of Guru Tegh Bahadur,* Gurgaon, Harmony Publishing House, 1991

Clark, H.M.: *Robert Clark of the Panjab - Pioneer and Missionary Statesman*, London, Andrew Melrose, 1907

Clark, Robert: *A Brief Account of Thirty Years of Missionary Work of the Church Missionary Society in the Punjab and Sindh, 1852-1882*, Lahore, The Albert Press, 1883

Cole, W.O.: *The Guru in Sikhism*, London, D.L.T., 1982

Cole, W.O.: *Sikhism in its Indian Context 1469-1708*, London, Darton, Longman and Todd, 1984

Cole, W.O., Parry, J.M. & Sambhi, P.S.: *Guidelines for Sikh-Christian Dialogue*, London, United Reformed Church, 1992

Cole, W.O. & Sambhi, P.S.S.: *Sikhism and Christianity: A Comparative Study*, London, Macmillan, 1993

Cole, W.O. & Sambhi, P.S.S.: *The Sikhs: Their Religious Beliefs and Practices*, London, R.K.P., 1978

Cullmann, Oscar: *The Christology of the New Testament*, London, S.C.M., 1963 (2nd)

Cunningham, J.D.: *A History of the Sikhs*, Delhi, Low Price, 1994. (1849)

Dhillon, Gurdarshan Singh: 'The Sikhs and the British - 1849-1920' in *P.P.P.* Vol. XXIV, No.2, Oct. 1990

Fakirbhai, Dhanjibhai: *Khristopanishad*, Bangalore, Christian Institute for the Study of Religion and Society, 1965

Farquhar, J.N.: *The Crown of Hinduism*, London, 1913

Firth, C.B.: *An Introduction to Indian Church History*, Madras, C.L.S, 1961

Forman, C.M. 'Who are the Sikhs?' in *The Foreign Missionary*, Nov. 1882

Fraser, J.G.: *The Golden Bough*,

Ganaliel, J.C: *The Gospel of God to the Sikh*, Delhi, ISPCK, 1997

Ghai, R.K. 'Christian Conversion in the Punjab: A Critical Analysis (1849- 1914 A.D.)' in *P.P.H.C.*,17, 1982

Giani, B.S.: *Planned Attack on Aad Sri Guru Granth Sahib: Academics or Blasphemy*, Chandigarh, International Centre of Sikh Studies, 1994

Gibran, Kahlil: *The Prophet*, London, Mandarin, 1993

Gill, Kirpal Singh 'Unity of Religions - Similarity of True Worship in All Religions' in *The Sikh Review*, Nov., 1987

Gordon, A.: *Our India Mission*, Philadelphia, 1888

Goulder, Michael: *A Tale of Two Missions*, London,S.C.M., 1994

Guleria, J.S.: *Bhai Vir Singh: A Literary Portrait*, Delhi, National Bookshop, 1985

Grewel, J.S.: *The Sikhs of the Punjab*, Cambridge, Cambridge U.P., 1990

Guleria, J.S. 'The Martial Traditions of the Sikhs' in *The Spokesman Weekly*, (Baisakhi Number), 13 Apr.,1992

Griffiths, Paul J.: *An Apology for Apologetics*, Maryknoll, Orbis, 1991

Guilford, E.: *Sikhism*, London, 1915

Hans, Surjit Review of McLeod: *The Sikhs: History, Religion and Society* in *J.S.S.*, Vol. XIV, No. 2, Aug. 1987

Hansrao, Gurdev Singh: *Ideology of the Sikh Gurus*, Dhode Majra (Ropar), Hansrao Publishers, 1990

Hayward, Victor: *Three Studies of North Indian Churches*, London, Lutterworth Press, 1966

Heiler: *The Gospel of Sadhu Sundar Singh*, Delhi, I.S.P.C.K., 1989

Hick, John: *The Metaphor of God Incarnate*, London, S.C.M., 1993

Hira, Bhagat Singh: *Semitic Thought and Sikhism*, Delhi, National Book Shop, 1992

Hooker, Pat: *His Other Sheep*, Nottingham, Grove Books, 1989

Hooker, Pat: *A Study Course for Christians on Sikhism*, Birmingham, Faith to Faith, 2005

Hooker, Roger: *Uncharted Journey*, London, C.M.S., 1973

Hooper, J.S.M.:*Bible Translation in India, Pakistan and Ceylon*, Bombay, O.U.P., 1963

Jones, Kenneth W.: *Arya Dharm*, Delhi, Manohar, 1976

Kaur Madanjit 'A Documentary Evidence of the Sikh Reaction at Trumpp's Translation of the Adi Granth' in *P.P.P.*, Vol. XIV, No. 1, Apr. 1980

Khalsa, Fatha Singh 'Nanak Naam' in *The Sikh Review*, Vol. 43.10, Oct. 1995

Khan, Rev'd Inyat: *SHABAD in Christianity and Sikhism*, Ferozepore Cantt c. 1961

Kitamori, Kazoh: *Theology of the Pain of God*, London, S.C.M., 1966

Klostermaier, K.: *A Survey of Hinduism*, New York, State University of New York Press, 1989

Kohli, Surrinder Singh: *A Conceptual Encyclopaedia of Guru Granth Sahib*, New Delhi, Manohar, 1992

Kohli, Surindar Singh: *Guru Granth Sahib: An Analytical Study*, Amritsar, Singh Brothers, 1992

Kohli, Surindar Singh: *Real Sikhism*, New Delhi, Harman Publishing House, 1995

Kuriakose, K.M.: *History of Christianity in India: Source materials*, Madras, Christian Literature Society, 1982

Lambert, Ruth: *What might Christians learn, theologically and spiritually, from Christian Sikh encounter?*, unpublished M.Phil thesis, University of Nottingham, 2001.

van Lin, J.J.E.: *Protestante Theologie der Godsdiensten van Edinburgh naar Tambaram*, van Gorcum & Comp. B.V., Assen, 1974

Loehlin, C.: *The Christian Approach to the Sikh*, London, Edinburgh House Press, 1966

Loehlin, C.H. 'Christianity and Sikhism' in *Religion and Society*, Vol. XI, No. 1, March, 1964

Loehlin, C.: *The Granth of Guru Gobind Singh and the Khalsa Brotherhood*, Lucknow, Lucknow Publishing House, 1971

Loehlin, C.H. 'Guru Nanak's Religion with Special Reference to Christianity' in *S.S.C.R.*, Vol. 1, No. 1, Oct. 1982

Loehlin, C.H. 'The History of Christianity in the Panjab' in *P.P.P.*, Vol. VII, Pt. 1, April 1973

Loehlin, C.H. 'The History of the Gurmukhi Panjabi Bible' in *P.P.H.C.*, Vol. III, March 1968

Loehlin, C.H. 'The Riddle of Sikhism' in *I. R. M.*, Vol. 27, 1938.

Loehlin, C.: *The Sikhs and Their Scriptures*, Delhi, I.S.P.C.K./LPH, 1958

Lowrie: *Historical Sketches of the Indian Missions*, Allahabad, 1886

Macauliffe, M.A.: "The Holy Scriptures of the Sikhs' in *Asiatic Quarterly Review*, Oct., 1919

Macauliffe, M.A.: *The Sikh Religion* *(3 vols)*, New Delhi, S. Chand & Co., 1983

Macquarrie, John: *Jesus Christ in Modern Thought*, London, S.C.M., 1990

Macquarrie, John: *The Mediators*, London, S.C.M., 1995

Macquarrie, John: *Principles of Christian Theology*, London, S.C.M., 1966

Mann, J.S. & Singh, Kharak: *Recent Researches in Sikhism*, Patiala, Punjabi University, 1992

Mansukhani, G.S.: *Hymns from Bhai Gurdas's Compositions*, Southall, Sikh Missionary Society, 1988

Mansukhani, G.S.: *The Quintessence of Sikhism*, Amritsar, S.G.P.C., 1985

Mansukhani, G.S. 'Studies and Language of Dialogue in World Religions' in *S.S.C.R.*, Vol. VI, No. 1

Massey, James 'Christianity and Culture: Their Relationship in the 19th and 20th Centuries Punjab' in *B.C.I.S.S.*, Vol. 17, No.1, Jan. 1988

Massey, James: *Dalits In India*, New Delhi, Manohar, 1995

Massey, James 'Literary Heritage of Panjabi Christians: An Analysis' in *B.C.I.S.S.*, Vol. 21, No. 1, Jan, 1992

Massey, James: *Masihat ik Parichay*, Amritsar, Faqir Singh & Sons, 1976

Massey, James: *The Ultimate Reality in Sikh Religion*,

McLeod, W.H.: *The Evolution of the Sikh Community*, Oxford, O.U.P., 1976

McLeod, W.H.: *Exploring Sikhism*, New Delhi, O.U.P., 2003

McLeod, W.H.: *Guru Nanak and the Sikh Religion*, Oxford, O.U.P., 1968

McLeod, W.H.: *Sikhism*, Harmondsworth, Penguin, 1997

McLeod, W.H.: *Sikhs of the Khalsa*, New Delhi, O.U.P., 2005

McLeod, W.H.: *The Sikhs: History, Religion and Society*, New York, Columbia U.P., 1989

McLeod, W.H.: *Textual Sources for the Study of Sikhism*, Manchester, Manchester U.P., 1984

McLeod, W.H.: *Who is a Sikh?*, Oxford, OUP, 1989

McMullen, C.O.: 'The Impact of Christianity on the Punjab' in *Indian Missiological Review*, Vol. 9, No. 3, Jul., 1987

McMullen, C.O.: *Religious Beliefs and Practices of the Sikhs in Rural Punjab*, London, Jaya Books, 1989

McMullen, C.O.: 'The Self Image of the Christians in the Punjab' in *B.C.I.S.S.*, Vol. 6, No. 1, Jan. 1977

Mueller, Max: *Introduction to the Science of Religion*, 1909

Newton, John: *History of American Presbyterian Missions in India*, Allahabad, 1886

O'Connell, Israel & Oxtoby: *Sikh History and Religion in the Twentieth Century*, Toronto, University of Toronto, 1988

Oberoi, Harjot: *The Construction of Religious Boundaries*, Delhi, Oxford University Press, 1994

Packer, J. I.: *Knowing God*, London, Hodder and Stoughton, 1973

Pannenberg, Wolfhart: *Jesus: God and Man*, London, S.C.M., 1968

Parananda: *An Eastern Exposition of the Gospel of Jesus according to St. John*, London, Hutchinson, 1902

Parry, John: *Dialogue with Sikhs in the U.K.* in *The Indo-British Historical Review*, Madras, October 1993

Parry, John: *Exploring the Ways of God with People of Faith* in *International Review of Mission*, Vol. LXXIV, No. 296, October 1985

Parry, John: *Interfaith Dialogue with Diaspora Sikhs* in *Current Dialogue*, 17, December 1989, WCC, Geneva

Parry, John: *Sikhism* in Markham and Ruparell: *Encountering Religion*, Oxford, Blackwell, 2001

Parry, John: *"Sikhism: From Competition to Co-operation,"* in Race & Hedges: *Christian Approaches to Other Faiths*, London, SCM, 2008

Parry, John: *Sikhs and Christians Study Scripture Together – Some Reflections* in Price, Sepulveda and Smith: *Mission Matters*, Frankfurt am Main, Peter Lang Verlag, 1997

Parry, John; *Southall – a Crossroads of Faith* in Charles Brock: *Sightings of Hope*, London, URC, 1994

Parry, John: *So you think you have all the answers – Other Faiths' views of the Decade of Evangelism*, pamphlet URC

Parry, John: *"Truth is Highest, but Higher Still is Truthful Living" – The Nature of Sikh Theological Method* in ed. Israel Selvanayagam: *Moving Forms of Theology – Faith Talk's Changing Contexts*, Delhi, ISPCK, 2002

Parry, John: *"Worship in Sikhism"* in *The New SCM Press Dictionary of Liturgy and Worship*, London, SCM Press, 2002

Pathak, Sushil Madhura: *American Missionaries and Hinduism*, Delhi, Munshiram Manoharlal, 1967

Peris, Aloysius: 'Mission of the local Church in relation to Other major Religious Traditions' in *Sedos Bulletin*, 82, 5, Mar. 1982

Pillai, K.V. Paul: *India's Search for the Unknown Christ*, New Delhi, Fazl Publishers, 1978

Randhawa, G.S.: *Guru Nanak's Japji*, Amritsar, Guru Nanak Dev U.P., 1990 (2nd)

Samartha, S.J., *The Hindu Response to the Unbound Christ*, Madras, Christian Literature Society, 1974

Samartha, S.J.: *One Christ - Many Religions*, Bangalore, Wordmakers, 1992

Sambhi, Piara Singh 'A Sikh looks at the Christian Church' in *The Expository Times*, Vol. LXXXVIII, No. 10, Jul. 1977/*S.S.C.R.*, Vol. III, No. 2, Oct.1984

Sanneh, Lamin: *Translating the Message*, Maryknoll, Orbis, 1989

Shackle, C.: *A Guru Nanak Glossary*, London, S.O.A.S., 1981

Shan, Harnam Singh 'Macauliffe and his Contributions to Sikh Studies' in *S.S.C.R.*, Vol. IX, No. 2, Oct. 1990

Sharma, Raj Bahadur: *Christian Missions in North India*, Delhi, Mittal Publications, 1988

Sharpe, E.J.: *Not to Destroy But to Fulfil*, Uppsala, Gleerup, 1965

Sharpe, E.J.: *The Riddle of Sadhu Sundar Singh*, New Delhi, Intercultural Publications, 2004

Sherring, M.A.: *The History of Protestant Missions in India 1706-1821*, London, Truebner & Co., 1875

Singh, Attar: 'Liberation Theology and Sikhism' in *S.S.C.R.*, Vol. IX, No. 2, Oct. 1990

Singh, Daljeet Review of McLeod: *The Sikhs: History, Religion and Society* in *J.S.S.*, Vol. XIV, No. 2, Aug. 1987

Singh, Daljeet Review of McLeod: *Who is A Sikh?* in *S.S.C.R.*, Vol. IX, No. 2, Oct. 1990

Singh, Daljeet: *Sikhism: A Comparative Study of its Theology and Mysticism*, New Delhi, Sterling, 1979

Singh, Darshan: *Western Perspectives on the Sikh Religion*, New Delhi, Sehgal, 1991

Singh Dharam: *Sikh Theology of Liberation*, New Delhi, Harman, 1991

Singh, Fauja: *Historians and the Historiography of the Sikhs*, New Delhi, Oriental Publishers and Distributers, 1978

Singh, Fauja et al: *Sikhism*, Patiala, Punjabi University, 1969

Singh Fauja & Talib, G.S.: *Guru Tegh Bahadur: Martyr and Teacher*, Patiala, Punjabi University, 1975

Singh, Ganda "The Singh Sabha and other Socio-Religious Movements in the Punjab 1850-1925' in *P.P.P.*, Vol. VII, Pt. 1, Apr. 1973

Singh, Ganda: *A History of the Khalsa College, Amritsar*, Amritsar, n/a, 1949

Singh, Ganda; Verma, Devinder Kumar & Singh, Parm Bakshish: *Seditious Literature in the Panjab*, Patiala, Punjabi University, 1988

Singh, Godwin Rajinder: *Gur Prasad: Sikh Doctrine of Divine Grace: An Interfaith Perspective*, Hong Kong, Christian Conference of Asia, 1992

Singh, Gopal 'A Sikh Scholar Speaks to the World Church' in *The North India Churchman*, Vol. XII, No.II, Nov.,1983

Singh, Gopal: *The Man Who Never Died*, New Delhi, World Book Centre, 1987(2nd)

Singh, Gopal: *The Religion of the Sikhs*, New Delhi, Allied Publishers, 1971

Singh, Gopal: *Thus Spake the Tenth Master*, Patiala, Punjabi University, 1978

Singh, Gopal: *The Unstruck Melody*, New Delhi, World Book Centre, 1989 (2nd)

Singh, Gurmukh Nihal: *Guru Nanak: His Life, Time and Teachings*, Delhi, Guru Nanak Foundation / National Publishing House, 1969

Singh, Harbans (ed): *The Encyclopaedia of Sikhism* (Vol. 1), Patiala, Punjabi University, 1992

Singh, Harbans, *The Heritage of the Sikhs*, New Delhi, Manohar, 1985

Singh, Harbans & Barrier, N.G.: *Essays in Honour of Dr Ganda Singh*, Patiala, Punjabi University, 1976

Singh, Herbert Jai: 'The Christian Approach to the Sikhs' in *Religion and Society*, Vol. XI, No. 1, Mar. 1964

Singh, Herbert Jai: Editorial re 1963 bilateral conference in Batala in *Religion and Society*, Vol. XI, No. 1, Mar. 1964

Singh, Ishar: *The Philosophy of Guru Nanak: A Comparative Study*, New Delhi, Ranjit Publishing House, 1969

Singh, Jitinder Jeet: *The Concept of Guru in Sikhism and its fulfilment in Jesus Christ 'the SatGuru'*, (unpublished research paper), Bangalore, Southern Asia Bible College, n.d.

Singh, Joginder: 'The Founding of the Singh Sabha' in *B.C.I.S.S.*, Vol. 10, No. 1, Jan. 1981

Singh, Joginder: 'The Khalsa Samachar: Some if its Major Concerns and Approach, 1899-1920' in *P.P.H.C.*, Mar., 1982

Singh, Kapur: *Parasaraprasna*, Amritsar, Guru Nanak Dev University, 2001[3]

Singh, Kartar: *Life of Guru Nanak*, Ludhiana, Lahore Bookshop, 1958

Singh, Khushwant: *A History the Sikhs* (Vols. I & II), Delhi, Oxford University Press, 1977

Singh, Mohinder: *Prof. Harbans Singh - Commemoration Volume*, New Delhi, Prof. Harbans Singh Commemoration Committee, 1988

Singh, Padri Daud: *Mangalsamachar*, Ludhiana, Mission Press, 1873

Singh, Pritam: *Sikh Concept of the Divine*, Amritsar, Guru Nanak Dev University Press, 1985

Singh, R.B. & Chaudhary, R.M.: *Women Empowerment, Myth or Reality*, Delhi, Indepenmdent Publishing Co. 2007

Singh, Ranbir: *Guru Tegh Bahadur, Divine Poet, Saviour and Martyr*, Amritsar, Chief Khalsa Diwan, 1975

Singh, Santokh: *Philosophical Foundations of the Sikh Value System*, New Delhi, Munshiram Manoharlal, 1982

Singh, Saran: Editorial in *The Sikh Review*, Apr. 1994

Singh, Sher: *Philosophy of Sikhism*, New Delhi, Sterling Publications, n.d.

Singh, Tahil: *Sat Swami Nihalank Autar Prabhu Jisu Masih*, Lahore, Punjab Religious Book Society, 1900

Singh, Teja: *Essays in Sikhism*, Lahore, Sikh University Press, 1944

Singh, Teja: *Sikhism*, Amritsar, Khalsa Brothers, 1938

Singh, Trilochan: *Ernest Trumpp and W.H.McLeod As Scholars of Sikh History, Religion and Culture*, Chandigarh, International Centre of Sikh Studies, 1994.

Singh, Trilochan: *Guru Nanak's Religion: A Comparative Study of Religions*, Delhi, Guru Nanak Foundation, 1968

Singh, Trilochan: *Hymns of Guru Tegh Bahadur*, Delhi, Delhi Sikh Gurdwara Management Committee, 1975

Singh, Wazir: *Philosophy of Sikh Religion*, Delhi, EssEss Publications, 1981

Singh, Wazir 'The Sikh Pespective on Death and Suffering' in *J.S.S.*, Vol. IX, No. II, Aug., 1982

Singh, Wazir: *The Sikh Vision*, Delhi, EssEss Publications, 1992

Singh, Wazir: *Sikhism and Punjab's Heritage*, Patiala, Punjabi University, 1990

de Smet & Neuner: *Religious Hinduism*, Allahabad, St Paul Publications, 1968 (3rd)

Spencer, Anand: 'Church History of the Panjab: Some Overlooked Facts - A Case for re-Study' in *P.P.H.C.*, May, 1992

Spencer, Anand: *The Concept of Word in Christianity and Sikhism*, unpublished PhD thesis, Patiala, Punjabi University, Sugust, 1979.

Stewart, William: *India's Religious Frontier*, London, S.C.M.,1964

Sugirtharajah, R.S.: *Asian Faces of Jesus*, London, S.C.M., 1993

Sugirtharajah, R.S.: *Frontiers in Asian Christian Theology - Emerging Trends*, Maryknoll, Orbis, 1994

Symposium on Sikhs Conference Reports, Langley, B.C., Associated Canadian Theological Schools, 1994

Talbot, Ian: *Punjab and the Raj, 1841-1947*, New Delhi, Manohar, 1988

Talib, G.S. & Singh, Attar: *Bhai Vir Singh - Life, Times and Works*, Chandigarh, Punjab University, 1973

Talib, Gurbachan Singh: 'Ernest Trumpp's translation of the Adi Granth' in *S.S.C.R.*, Vol. III, No. 2, Oct. 1984.

Thomas, M.M.: *The Acknowledged Christ of the Indian Renaissance*, London, S.C.M., 1969

Thomas, M.M.: *Risking Christ for Christ's Sake*, Geneva, W.C.C., 19**

Thomas, P.: *Christians and Christianity in India and Pakistan*, London, 1954

Thornton, Douglas M: *Parsi, Jain and Sikh*, Religious Tract Society, 1898

Trumpp, E.: *The Adi Granth*, London, W.H.Allen, 1877

W.C.C.: *Dialogue Between Men of Living Faiths*, Geneva, W.C.C., 1971

Walji, Pandit: *The Dawn of Nanak Saheb's Religion*, Bombay, Andra Vernacular Press, 1895

Walji, Pandit: *Hari Charitra*, Lodiana, Lodiana Mission Press, 1893

Ward, William: *A View of the History, Literature and Mythology of the Hindus*, 3 vols, London, Kingsbury, Parbury and Allen, 1822.

Webster, J.C.B.: 'Christians and Sikhs in the Punjab: The Village Encounter' in *B.C.I.S.S.*, Vol. 6. Special Number

Webster, J.C.B.:*The Christian Community & Change in Nineteenth Century North India*, New Delhi, Macmillan, 1976

Webster, J.C.B.: 'Welcome Address' to 'Popular Religion in the Punjab Today' conference in *B.C.I.S.S.*, Vol. 3, No. 1, Jan. 1974

Weitbrecht, H.U.: *A Descriptive Catalogue of Urdu Christian Literature*, London, Religious Tract Society, 1886

Wessels, Anton: *Images of Jesus*, London , S.C.M., 1990

Whale, J.S.: *The Protestant Tradition*, Cambridge, Cambridge U.P. 1955

Wherry: *Our Missions in India, 1834-1924*, Boston, Stratford, 1926

Wherry, E.M.: 'Was Nanak a Christian?' in *The Indian Standard*, Mar. 1903

Woodruff, P.: *The Men Who Ruled India* (Vols I & II), London, 1971

Young, Frances: *The Art of Performance*, London, Darton, Longman and Todd, 1990

Youngson, F.W.: *Forty Years of the Panjab Missionof the Church of Scotland*, Edinburgh, R. & R. Clark Ltd.

Index